PIRATE WOMEN

LAURA SOOK DUNCOMBE

PIRATE WOMEN

THE PRINCESSES, PROSTITUTES, AND PRIVATEERS WHO RULED THE SEVEN SEAS

CHICAGO
REVIEW
PRESS

First edition
Published by Chicago Review Press Incorporated
814 North Franklin Street
Chicago, Illinois 60610
ISBN 978-1-61373-601-2

Library of Congress Cataloging-in-Publication Data
Names: Duncombe, Laura Sook, author.
Title: Pirate women : the princesses, prostitutes, and privateers who ruled
    the Seven Seas / Laura Sook Duncombe.
Description: Chicago, Illinois : Chicago Review Press, Incorporated, [2017] |
    Includes bibliographical references and index.
Identifiers: LCCN 2016031175 (print) | LCCN 2016049773 (ebook) | ISBN
    9781613736012 (cloth) | ISBN 9781613736036 (adobe pdf) | ISBN
    9781613736043 (epub) | ISBN 9781613736029 (kindle)
Subjects: LCSH: Women pirates—Biography. | Women pirates—History. |
    Piracy—History.
Classification: LCC G535 .D848 2017 (print) | LCC G535 (ebook) | DDC
    910.4/5—dc23
LC record available at https://lccn.loc.gov/2016031175

Typesetting: Nord Compo

Printed in the United States of America
5 4 3 2 1

To my mother, whose admonition
that I never stop writing has gotten me
through many a rough day and night
And to my father, the president
of the Singapore Sue fan club

With never-ending love and gratitude

Contents

Introduction

OR AS LONG AS there has been a sea to sail upon, there have been pirates. Modern scholarship claims they have played an enormously important role in shaping world history. They have been called raiders, sea dogs, buccaneers, freebooters, corsairs, bandits, and many other names in many languages. They have sailed throughout every millennium. They hail from every inhabited continent, in every age, color, and creed imaginable. What unites these vastly diverse people across time and space? Is it the peg legs and eye patches? The rum and the parrots?

These common tropes pervade modern depictions of piracy, but true piracy is so much more than these cartoonish trappings. The heart of piracy is freedom—freedom from society, freedom from law, and freedom from conscience. Pirates capture people's hearts as easily as they capture their prey because they actually do what many people only dream of doing—they cast off home and comfort for a chance at life outside society's confines. A person who does not condone a pirate's criminal actions can still be inspired by her courageous and adventurous spirit.

No, that was not a typo: pirates have always answered to "she" as well as "he." (During the periods covered in this book, the gender binary was still firmly in place. As far as I am aware, all the pirates in this book identified as female. My use of "she" reflects the available research on these pirates and is in no way meant to invalidate other expressions of gender.) Female pirates have fought alongside and, in some cases, in command of their male counterparts since ancient times, despite the widespread belief that women at sea were bad luck. For a woman to cast off her petticoats—and often her identity—and take up arms seems impossible, but many persevered. Yet history largely ignores them, and most people are ignorant of their existence.

So who were these women pirates? From royalty such as Queen Teuta to the penniless orphan Gunpowder Gertie, they ran the gamut from princess to pauper. Some were barely out of their teens, such as Sadie the Goat, while others such as Sister Ping were older when they started their careers. Grace O'Malley pirated for many years, and Margaret Jordan participated in only a single piratical venture. Sayyida al-Hurra took to the sea to revitalize her community, while Jacquotte Delahaye sought revenge for her parents' deaths. Pirate women existed essentially everywhere male pirates did, in nearly every major period of pirate history. They had little in common with each other, except for their gender and their desire to escape the traditional role that their gender dictated.

If pirate women are so prevalent in history, why are they so seldom known? They had to fight at least twice as hard as male pirates to make it to sea and prove their worth, so surely they are doubly worthy of study. Yet all too often, they are left out of the piratical discussion. With the exception of Anne Bonny and Mary Read, and more recently Grace O'Malley, they are given short shrift by history, identified only by nicknames or titles if they are mentioned at all. Of the numerous pirate books on the market, precious few discuss women, and almost none hold women pirates as their focus. David Cordingly, a leading pirate scholar, devoted an entire book to women (originally titled *Women Sailors and Sailor's Women* before being renamed the less-patronizing *Seafaring Women*). He expressed disbelief that Mary Read and Anne Bonny actually lived aboard a pirate ship and questioned how a woman could tolerate the rough working conditions at sea. When even a historian covering women sailors refuses to acknowledge that women pirates existed, there is a problem in the field.

Women pirates are often absent in historical discussion because their very existence is threatening to traditional male and female gender roles. Pirates live outside the laws of man, but women pirates live outside the laws of nature. Women pirates are left out because they don't fit nicely into the categories of "normal" women or traditional women's virtues. As historian Jo Stanley puts it, female pirates "like to be on top . . . and maraud fiercely where maidens should step sweetly." They are "social outrages—and the embodiment of women's terrifying power." They upset the balance of power in a patriarchal society and for that reason are not to be discussed, let alone celebrated, by traditional historians.

Pirate women also interfere with man's storied and complex relationship with the sea itself. Water is primal; life cannot exist without it. Many creation myths feature water, and it's no wonder—humans are surrounded in water-like amniotic fluid in the womb before birth. The sea, which was here before man and cradles man, is like a mother to sailors—a woman. It is connected to the moon and tides, which have also been associated with women all the way back to the Greek goddess Artemis. Ernest Hemingway opines in his famous novel *The Old Man and the Sea* that "[the main character] always thought of the sea as 'la mar' which is what people call her in Spanish when they love her. Sometimes those who love her say bad things of her but they are always said as though she were a woman. . . . The old man always thought of her as feminine and as something that gave or withheld great favors, and if she did wild or wicked things it was because she could not help them." Mermaids and sirens, legendary creatures who lure men to their deaths on the sea, are traditionally female as well. Ships are often named for women, and women are frequently featured on the bows of boats as buxom figureheads. Undiscovered islands on the sea are "virgin" and are "conquered" by colonizing men. For man, the sea and things associated with it are feminine, ripe for male subjugation or, at the very least, male adventure. The feminine sea is an exclusively male domain, where men can prove their bravery or seek their fortune. Adding women to this equation dilutes the established gender binary and threatens the near-sacred relationship between sailor and the sea.

For these and countless other reasons both conscious and unconscious, male historians often exclude women pirates from their work. Unfortunately for women pirates, the vast majority of history has been recorded by—and from the perspective of—men. Scholar Dale Spender explains that "women have been kept 'off the record' in most, if not all, branches of knowledge by the simple process of men naming the world as it appears to them. . . . They have assumed their experience is universal, that it is representative of humanity. . . . Whenever the experience of women is different from men, therefore, it stays 'off the record,' for there is no way of entering it into the record when the experience is not shared by men, and men are the ones who write the record." Deidre Beddoe echoes that sentiment, saying that recorded history "is the history of the men and male affairs . . . wars, diplomacy, politics, and commerce." Indeed, without the efforts of women historians such as Anne Chambers, Dian Murray, and Joan Druett, much of the existing knowledge of women pirates would not have come to light. As long as men control the narrative, women pirates will be mostly left out.

Even if male historians today were inclined to write about pirate women, they would have a difficult time doing so because of the dearth of primary sources about them. Since women have been considered unworthy subjects of historical documentation in the past, it is now difficult to study them—a vicious cycle that persists in keeping women "off the record." To date, no one has discovered a journal or first-person account of pirating written by a female pirate. Newspaper articles are few, court documents are even rarer, and books written around the time the pirate was active are virtually nonexistent. It is not particularly surprising, given all this, that pirate women have not achieved the celebrity status of their male peers.

But despite all the challenges, these stories deserve to be told. The tendency to exclude women from the narrative ignores a vital part of the history of the sea. As mythologist Suzanne Cloutier explains, "Women's souls cannot be known without stories—their stories must be told." This book is an attempt to collect in one volume the stories of female pirates through the ages. Feminist theologian Carol P. Christ claims that "without stories a woman is lost when she comes to make the important decisions in her life. She does not learn to value her struggles, to celebrate her strength, to comprehend her pain. Without stories, she cannot understand herself." The existing mere paragraphs and footnotes scattered across the vast expanse of pirate lore do not do justice to the breadth and depth of pirate women's involvement in the trade. Presenting these women together demonstrates how long women have been part of piracy and how much they have achieved. Telling their stories adds them back into the historical record and gives a clearer picture of what life at sea was actually like. After reading the accounts of their lives, it will be impossible to dismiss lone pirate women as anomalous phenomena. Each pirate woman is part of a grand tradition that has been around since the dawn of piracy itself.

Beyond simply retelling these women's stories, this book examines the storytellers and their motives—the "why" as well as the "who." Since so many of these stories, particularly the earliest ones, were recorded by men, taking a look at the man's reason for writing the story is informative in understanding why the events and portrayals in the story are shaped as they are. A medieval monk, for example, would describe a woman differently than a nineteenth-century penny-dreadful author. Questioning who is responsible for spreading these legends and what agenda might have prompted him or her to do it will help to extricate the stories from the grasp of authorial intent and allow them to unfold more organically as they might have actually happened.

A very important caveat: most if not all of these stories are a combination of myth and fact. The nature of piracy is such that it is difficult to separate fact and fiction because pirates were, by necessity, not frequently a part of historical record. Robert C. Ritchie explains that "parish registers, censuses, and tax lists are of no use in studying a population that existed in the fringes of, or even beyond, settled societies." Even Capt. Johnson's *Pyrates*, which is called by Jo Stanley "as central an early [pirate] text as the Bible is to Christians," is known to be both embellished and frequently anecdotal. The gold standard of historical fact might be said to be multiple high-quality primary sources—documents written at the time, speaking directly about the subject. Many pirate stories, especially female pirate stories, fail to meet this standard. However, since many of these stories come from the time of the pirates, these mytho-historical (and sometimes just mythic) pirates are still vital to the larger tapestry of piracy. Author Gabriel Kuhn claims when it comes to pirates, "The legend and the reality [of pirate life] are woven into a fabric impossible to unravel. However, the *way* this fabric is woven can be examined. . . . We are exploring the pirate myth rather than trying to expose a pirate truth." Wherever possible, the historical backing of the stories here is explained.

Thus, this book is not a pure history book. I am not a historian. Although many historical events are described to give context to these women's stories, nothing should be taken as comprehensive on those subjects. Those seeking to learn about, say, the American Civil War or the Great Leap Forward should seek other works on the subject. Resources are listed in the back of the book to aid readers in their quest. I am a storyteller and a lover of pirates, and so while every effort has been made to present a clear and accurate historical account, this is a book primarily about pirate stories. And besides, as historiographer Keith Jenkin says, "The past and history are two separate things."

Though fashions, weapons, and even treasure changed over time, all pirate women have at least one thing in common: the desire to be masters of their own fates, whatever the cost. Perhaps an exploration of what that desire meant to these women and how much they endured for it will inspire the next great adventurer—or the next great storyteller. In any case, Audre Lorde reminds us that, in terms of writing by and about women, "we must each of us recognize our responsibility to seek those words out, to read them and share them and examine them in their pertinence to our lives." May this book be a worthy addition to the ever-growing pantheon of women's words about women.

Laura Sook Duncombe
Alexandria, Virginia
May 17, 2016

1

Dawn of the Pirates

"**S**TRANGERS, WHO ARE YOU? Where do you sail from? Are you traders, or do you sail the sea as pirates, with your hands against every man, and every man's hand against you?"

These lines come from Homer's *Odyssey*, one of the earliest existing texts. Piracy—one of the world's oldest professions—has been around even longer than the blind poet and also shares a birthplace with him: the Mediterranean. Since the late Bronze Age, this area has been a hotbed for piratical activity. In fact, the word *pirate* comes from the ancient Greek word *piero*, which means "to make an attempt." According to an Egyptian clay tablet from the period, the people of the eastern Mediterranean were attacking ships as early as the fourteenth century BCE, and it is not a big surprise given the geography of the area.

Greece is one of the most mountainous countries in Europe, with a rugged terrain unsuitable for farming. Hence, civilizations sprang up only in flat pockets near the shore, where the mountain ranges tapered off, but even in these flatter areas, the rocky soil was of too poor quality to be hospitable to crops. Villages by necessity had to be small and humble—they could not grow large and prosperous because there was not enough arable land to grow food to feed a large village.

Since the ancients could not grow enough food to be profitable, they were forced to take up fishing as a way to make a living. In the water beyond their shores, food such as fish, squid, octopus, and shellfish flourished. An average able-bodied man would have had access to a boat for fishing. For him to be successful, he also needed navigation and sailing skills. Sailing in the ancient world bore little relation to the sailboats and speedboats enjoyed by sailors today. Without the modern inventions of GPS, sonar, power engines, and the National Weather Service, sailors had to be conscious every moment of the water depth, the weather conditions, and their position in the sea in order to avoid running aground, capsizing, or becoming lost. These skills, learned by necessity for fishing purposes, came in handy for the men and women who eventually turned to piracy.

The scarcity of good soil and natural resources naturally led to trade. Since it was virtually impossible to cross over any of the Greek mountains in those days (and moving stuff by sea is always easier anyway), the sea turned into the Greek "highway" system as the best and most efficient way to get around and conduct trade. One city-state would specialize in a particular good or crop and ship it to other city-states, selling their product and purchasing the products of other city-states. Over time, the best routes to navigate from city-state to city-state became well known and well used—and irresistible to pirates.

In fact, the very geography of the sea itself helped to foster piracy. The Mediterranean basin is essentially an obstacle course of small islands. Large trade ships were forced to sail in very narrow lanes between the islands and the shore in order to avoid shipwrecks. Before the advent of the steam engine, sailors were at the mercy of the currents and tides and unable to deviate from the courses nature charted. Ships could not sail in the winter or during rough weather. All these factors combined meant that large trade ships were likely to pass through only certain small areas and only under certain weather conditions. They were sitting ducks for the pirates, who had only to lie in wait among the many islands along the coast for a big ship to pass by.

Beyond the physical geography, political reasons helped piracy take off. The small, isolated villages that grew out of the landscape created independent settlements that were not easily governed by a single body. Greece was not one unified country as it is today but rather a collection of loosely connected groups who had their own governments, identities, and ways of life. These city-states were allied in name but were often rivals in practice; hostilities between city-states were not uncommon. Piracy easily sprang up between the city-states because it did not seem like stealing from one's own country. Capturing a merchant ship from another city-state was fair game in an area of scarce resources.

With all these factors in its favor, piracy was considered part of the rhythm of life during the late Bronze Age. Despite its happening all the time, everywhere, people did their best to thwart it whenever they could. The opening quote of this chapter demonstrates how Odysseus the sailor was greeted by the Cyclops after landing in his port. Outside of the *Odyssey*, newly arrived sailors to any port in the eastern Mediterranean could expect a similar greeting that tried to suss out whether the sailors had come for lawful or unlawful purposes. The fact that sailors were routinely asked whether or not they were pirates is a testament to just how ubiquitous piracy was in the region.

The Taurians, a group of early settlers of the Crimean Peninsula, used an even more extreme method to combat piracy. They had a custom of sacrificing all shipwrecked sailors who landed on their shores to their Virgin Goddess (similar to the Greek goddess Artemis). They would beat the unlucky shipwreck survivors in the head with a club and either throw the bodies off a cliff or bury them. Some scholars use this example to demonstrate how much the Taurians feared pirates and their wicked ways, but given Herodotus's account of the Taurians as "living by plundering and war," it seems possible that the Taurians were just eliminating the piratical competition.

A pirate ship needed the ability to sail into the maze of islands and shallow water where the larger ships could not follow. Merchant ships sailed on very specific routes and could not deviate from those paths, even when under attack, without risking shipwreck. The pirates knew this and used it to their advantage. They lay in wait for the larger ships among the natural coves and harbors along the coastline or in the hidden waters between the smaller islands—wherever they had a good view of the merchant ships' paths. When a large, slow ship sailed by, the pirates would spring into action and sail right up to it, attacking it and stripping it of its valuable cargo. The merchant ship was helpless as the pirates laid claim to whatever they liked. After the raid, the pirates reboarded their small ships and sailed quickly away, back to their hiding spots, where merchant ships could not reach them due to the shallow waters. For a long time, it was the perfect crime.

Historians agree that many pirates took advantage of this system and routinely attacked merchants. But while there is much evidence of piracy, there is very little historical documentation concerning specific pirates. The names of the ordinary men and women who took to the seas to raid and plunder are, for the most part, lost to history. There may have been scores of pirate women of low birth, but history has neglected to remember them. The pirates from this era who *are* known are generally either military commanders or rulers. This makes sense, given how history is usually recorded. Literate historians write most often about people in their own class—other wealthy people of high station. The legends from this era feature the larger-than-life characters of gods, demigods, monsters, and kings. Everyday citizens did not get starring roles in the epic poems of this era, unless they were victims of kidnapping by Zeus. The women pirates known from this era are no exception to the rule. All of them were queens as well as pirates.

⚓⚓⚓

The earliest known female pirate from the Mediterranean, and perhaps of all time, was Queen Artemisia I of Halicarnassus. Most of what is known about her comes from Herodotus's *Histories* and Polyaenus's *Stratagems of War*. Sometime in the fifth century BCE, she was born to a Carian father and a Cretan mother. Her childhood was spent in her father's gubernatorial land: Halicarnassus, a large coastal city-state in the region of Caria (modern-day Turkey). As the daughter of a government official, she was destined to marry well, and in 500 BCE, she married the king of Halicarnassus. (In a strange twist of fate, it is *his* name that is lost to history.) Before the king died, he and Artemisia had one son. The newly widowed Artemisia ascended to the throne of Caria and ruled in her dead husband's place. Herodotus notes that she had a grown son, and thus had no reason to go into battle herself, but she did so anyway. Whether he said this with pride or disgust is not certain.

At this point, it is vital to note that ancient Mediterranean piracy was not identical to the modern conception of piracy. These ancient pirates were not bands of outlaws who swore allegiance to no one; they were more like enemy powers who raided other city-states on both land and sea. Their methods, however, would be copied by more modern pirates—methods such as lying in wait for their prey, plundering large merchant ships, and using the geography of the area to their advantage. More important, these ancient pirates set the tone for more modern pirates, who would likewise follow their desire for riches to the sea and take them by any means necessary.

Piracy was more accepted in ancient times than it is today because it was more like intertribal warfare than nationless piracy. Acts of warfare, unlike acts of piracy, are generally accepted as legitimate in most times and countries. St. Augustine offers a provocative story in *City of God* that speaks to the delicate line between legitimate warfare and illegitimate piracy. As the story goes, Alexander the Great once captured a pirate and questioned him, asking, "How dare you molest the seas?" The pirate answered, "How dare you molest the whole world? Because I do it with a small boat, I am called a pirate and a thief. You, with a great navy, molest the world and are called an emperor."

Part of Artemisia's queenly duties involved waging war against rival city-states. She took to this task with relish, not just commanding her fleet but actually taking the helm of her own ship. Caria had fallen under Persian control, so technically Artemisia sailed with the Persians. Some sources state that she secretly was in sympathy with the Greeks and hated Persia. Whatever her feelings were, Artemisia is known to have plundered both Greek and Persian ships, so it appears that she felt no particular loyalty to anyone save herself.

Her status as queen afforded Artemisia many freedoms not available to the lower-class women of Greece. In ancient Greece, women's rights varied from city-state to city-state, but in general women were considered less valuable than men. Most of the existing historical accounts come from Athens, but it is important to remember that Athens does not stand for all of Greece. Athens was one of the more severe city-states, where women were not allowed to vote or own property beyond minor gifts—which her guardian could dispose of without her consent. Legally, a woman did not have an existence independent from men. She was guarded by her father, then by her husband, and if her husband died before she did, she was either absorbed back into her father's guardianship or put under the care of her adult sons. All but the poorest Athenian women had slaves to take care of the domestic tasks such as cooking and cleaning, so their only tasks were to bear children and be attractive. Pericles said, "The best reputation a woman can have is not to be spoken of among men for good or evil."

Only one type of woman besides royalty was afforded similar freedom, and that was the hetaera—the courtesan. These women were oddities in almost every way. They were educated, renowned for their achievements in dance and music, and they paid taxes. They were allowed to participate in the symposia, the drinking parties where philosophy was discussed and debated. They were single women who occasionally had sex with the men they spent time with, but they were not prostitutes. Their lives were a far cry from those of ordinary married female citizens in the stricter city-states. As Apollodorus explains in the case against Neaera, a legal case brought against a hetaera who tried to pass her children off as Athenian citizens, "We have courtesans for pleasure, concubines to take care of our day to day bodily needs, and wives to bear us legitimate children and to be the loyal guardians of our households."

Some city-states, such as Sparta, were more relaxed in their attitudes about average women citizens. (However, not everything written about Sparta was written by Spartans, so that should be taken into account.)

Like Athenian ladies, Spartan women had slaves to take care of their domestic tasks such as housework, but the similarities end there. Spartans were concerned chiefly with physical fitness above all else, so young girls as well as boys were athletically trained. Women were even able to race chariots during festivals. According to Pausanias, a woman named Cynisca won at four-horse chariot racing at the Panathenaic games, and a statue at the Temple of Zeus at Olympia commemorated her achievement.

Spartan women were not confined to the home as much as their Athenian sisters. Chastity was not held as sacred to a Spartan woman as it was to an Athenian, and so women were not forced to stay indoors in the women's quarters of the house. Their short tunics led other city-states to derisively call them "thigh-showers." Spartan women had to be the head of the household when the men were in training and away at war. Military duties kept men away full-time until their late thirties and part-time after that. In return for their management skills, Spartan women were allowed to inherit wealth from their families and were permitted to seek a divorce as well. Plutarch said in his *Life of Agis* that "the men of Sparta always obeyed their wives, and allowed them to intervene in public affairs more than they themselves were allowed to intervene in private ones."

Most ancient city-states fell somewhere between these two extremes. Even in Sparta, however, women were relegated to duties that were second best. The tasks left to them were considerably more interesting than what Athenian women were called on to perform, but they were still tasks that the men deemed unimportant. No city-state placed women first or elevated their status as equal to men.

Little information exists on exactly what day-to-day life would have looked like for the women of Artemisia's home city-state, Halicarnassus. After Artemisia's time, Queen Artemisia II of Halicarnassus (often confused with her piratical predecessor) ruled side by side with her husband, and the pair issued joint decrees, which indicates a relatively elevated status of women—or at least of queens. A Halicarnassian marble relief sculpture from the first to second century CE, currently on display at the British Museum, offers a compelling peek into Artemisia's society. This sculpture portrays two female gladiators locked in combat, demonstrating a notion of feminine power outside the domestic sphere. Rather than depicting women washing dishes or lying around in perfumed robes, the Halicarnassian artist presented women as warriors. We can extrapolate, based on this tableau, that Halicarnassian women were not confined solely to the home and that they enjoyed rights more similar to Spartan women than Athenian ones.

Artemisia's pirating career before the Battle of Salamis is not well documented. Her first pirating adventure is unknown, as is exactly when she started pirating. Polyaenus's *Stratagems* describes an early exploit of hers, when she sacked the city of Latmus using a cunning trick. She and her men camped right outside the city walls and staged a full-blown festival, complete with dancers and music. When the curious people of Latmus came outside to see what all the fuss was about, Artemisia and her crew stormed through the open gates and took the city.

Whatever else her early career consisted of, it is clear that Artemisia had been sailing for Xerxes for some time before the Battle of Salamis. Xerxes I, also known as Xerxes the Great, was a Persian king whose goal was to conquer all of Greece. He may be most familiar to the general public due to the graphic novel and film *300*, which very loosely depicts the Battle of Thermopylae between the Greeks and Persians. A sequel to this film features a character based on Artemisia, portrayed by actress Eva Green.

In reality, Xerxes invaded in 480 BCE, taking many large cities, including Thermopylae, Artemisium, and even Athens. While Xerxes held all of Attica and Boeotia—a large chunk of present-day central Greece—the allied Greek forces held the key location the Isthmus of Corinth, which kept the Persians out of the Peloponnese Peninsula. If Corinth fell, Xerxes could march right into western Greece and keep expanding his holdings.

Xerxes believed the powerful Athenian navy had to be defeated for him to continue his Grecian domination. A decisive naval victory for either side could swing momentum the victor's way. Both the allied Greeks and the Persians knew this, so each side began looking for the ideal opportunity for a naval battle. Xerxes was very concerned about his chances in a naval battle. His Persians were not particularly skilled sailors. Their capital city, Sula, was nearly a thousand miles from the sea, and they had not even had a navy of their own before the war. The Persian navy in the autumn of 480 BCE was cobbled together from privately owned ships and crews, a mismatched band of barely trained sailors.

Just as the pirating in antiquity was very different from the popular idea of pirating, the pirate ships of ancient times bore little resemblance to the tall-masted ships with billowing sails depicted in movies and television. The most common ships of the period were biremes and triremes, both a type of galley ship. Probably invented by the Phoenicians, these wooden ships were about 80 to 130 feet long and had either two (bi) or three (tri) banks of oars. The ships were built for speed and were comparatively easy to maneuver. They might have had a single sail for use when the conditions were favorable, but their main power came from rowers. A ship required anywhere from one hundred to two hundred rowers, often slaves. Biremes and triremes had sharp, pointed bows, sometimes covered in metal, for ramming other ships. Frequently the bows had large eyes painted on them so that they could "see" their prey. Many depictions of ships from this era still survive today on pottery held at the British Museum, among other places.

Ships chosen for use by the pirates were for the most part smaller, faster versions of the biremes and triremes. They were small, so as to be easy to hide and maneuver, and light enough to travel in shallow waters. A pirate ship could not win a head-to-head battle with a ramming bireme, so it had to be able to outrun the larger ships. Illyrian pirates were said to have invented their own special brand of pirate ships called *lembi*, which were small and very fast, with a single bank of oars and no sails. This allowed them to sneak up on larger ships, sack them, then zip away to shallower and safer waters. Less sophisticated pirates sailed in dugout canoes and raft-like craft. The Persian ships were the larger and less maneuverable kind, while the allied Greek ships were much swifter and lighter, similar to pirate ships, which would be a major factor in the coming battle.

Because Xerxes was not convinced that his ragtag navy could beat the allied Greeks in a fair fight, his plan was to continue waging war on land until the perfect opportunity to take Greece by surprise at sea came his way. Xerxes believed that opportunity finally came in September of 480 BCE, in what is now known as the Battle of Salamis.

According to Herodotus, the Greek general Themistocles laid a trap for the Persians. He sent a messenger, disguised as an escaped slave, into the Persian camp to tell the Persians that the Greek navy was anchored in the straits of Salamis. Salamis was a small island one nautical mile off the mainland coast, and the straits of Salamis were the narrow waters between the island and the coast. Themistocles hoped that the Persians would accept the bait and come to battle, where the Greeks—who would not be caught unawares after all—would surprise them with their organized and ready forces.

The narrow body of water seemed to Xerxes an ideal place to finish the Greeks off once and for all. He thought if he could block their exit from the straits on both sides he would effectively trap the Greeks inside the bay, where he could slaughter them. As he prepared for this battle, he asked his council of advisors, including Artemisia, what he should do.

The entire council voted unanimously to go into battle, except Artemisia. She advised him not to go, telling him to save his ships and avoid the battle. She reminded him that they had already taken Athens, which had been his goal, and there was no need to risk a naval battle against superior seamen. Besides that, their land force was still doing a fine job, and if they kept up the assault they would soon take all of Greece anyway without having to fight at sea at all.

Needless to say, her prudent advice did not go over well among the battle-hungry Persian men. They were power drunk after their recent victory against Athens, and they wanted to win the whole war sooner rather than later. Herodotus says that after Artemisia gave her advice those "who disliked and envied her, favored as she was by the king above all the rest of the allies, rejoiced at her declaration, expecting that her life would be the forfeit." Unfortunately for them, Xerxes praised her advice, saying he valued her now more than ever. But nevertheless, he readied the fleet for battle.

Themistocles's trap worked just as he had planned. The smaller, more maneuverable Greek fleet clustered along the shore near the Straits of Salamis, mimicking a cowering position. The larger Persian fleet, around twelve hundred ships, sailed into the narrow bay as *they* had planned, with lines of ships three deep.

When the Persian lines packed into the bay, the Greeks made their move. They surged forward, closing the gap between the two navies and effectively pinning the Persians against the mainland Greece shoreline. The front line of Persians was able to turn around to retreat, but they ran into their own second and third lines, unable to escape the press of their own forces. The confused and immobile Persians were fish in a barrel to the superior sailors of the Greek navy, who sailed their lighter ships around the edges of the Persian lines and rammed the Persian ships. Greek reinforcements sailed in from the north, blocking the exit into the Bay of Eleusis. The Persian ships were too bulky and too numerous to be able to make a hasty retreat.

What had started out as an easy win for the Persians was shaping up to be a devastating loss. The Carian ships, including Artemisia's— identified as the *Lykos* by Klausmann, Meinzerin, and Kuhn, authors of *Women Pirates and the Politics of the Jolly Roger*—were most likely in the second Persian line toward the southern side of the battle, near the Gulf of Aegina. Right in the middle of the fray, Artemisia realized her prediction had come true: the Greeks were going to defeat the Persians at sea. Persian ships were floating in pieces all around her, and her comrades were dead and dying in the water both in front of her and behind her, fallen from sinking ships or shot down by the Greek archers. The cracks of splintering wood echoed like gunshots while the screams of dying men filled the air.

Artemisia was not interested in joining the ranks of the Persian dead. It was time to make her escape. There was only one problem—she was in the middle of the battle, with allied Calyndian ships blocking her escape route toward Piraeus and the sea. The Greeks were gaining on her with every minute. What could she do?

The *Lykos* slammed into an ally ship at full speed. Some sources claim that before Artemisia rammed the ship, she lowered her Persian flag and raised a Greek one to confuse the Greek fleet. In fact, Polyaenus reports that Artemisia routinely sailed with two flags, one Greek and one "barbarian," and she chose which one she flew based on where she was.

Xerxes had been watching the battle from a hill high above the bay with some of his advisors, one of whom saw Artemisia's well-known ship sink another ship. The man wrongly assumed that she had taken down an enemy ship, not an ally, which would have raised Xerxes's ire, so he informed the king of her victory. In response to her attack, Xerxes is reported to have said, "My men have become women and my women have become men."

According to Herodotus, Xerxes never discovered that Artemisia had actually sunk a Persian ship because nobody from the Calyndian vessel lived to tell the tale of her treachery. But the Greeks knew—the Greek captain who witnessed it figured she was either herself a Greek or she had deserted the Persians.

The Greeks, thanks to Themistocles's cunning trap and Xerxes's refusal to take Artemisia's advice, won the Battle of Salamis. Afterward, Artemisia almost completely disappears from historical records. Some accounts suggest that Xerxes sent her to the Greek city of Ephesus to raise his illegitimate sons and that she lived out her days as a surrogate mother and teacher to the boys. This idea fits in with the "bad girl goes good" archetypal plot, in which a wild woman is tamed and surrenders to her destined gender role. This type of story is perennially popular with male historians as a way of diminishing the power of a warrior woman's legend. It is meant to teach the reader that although a woman can have her fun and possibly even do something great, in the end, she will go home and raise babies like she is supposed to. It is possible that Artemisia did retire after the battle or chose to lay low, surmising that her treachery against Xerxes might be discovered if she remained in the public eye and that she would pay for it with her life.

The claim that she gave up seafaring life to care for Xerxes's sons seems like a stretch.

Even more doubtfully, a scandalous story recounted by Photios, the ecumenical patriarch of Constantinople in the first century CE, claims that once Artemisia arrived in Ephesus, she fell in love with a man who rejected her and she killed herself. This story has not been readily accepted, and not just because Photios was writing about a thousand years after Artemisia's death. Photios, a religious man, had an explicit motive for writing this story: to warn clergymen against forming romantic attachments. His agenda to spin a compelling cautionary tale may have led him to fabricate a ridiculously undignified end to a legendary pirate's story.

⚓⚓⚓

This example of a historian changing, faking, or editing a woman pirate's story to make his own point crops up again and again. For example, some scholarship suggests that Queen Dido of *Aeneid* fame was a warrior and perhaps even a pirate herself. Klausmann, Meinzerin, and Kuhn explain that Elissa of Tyre, a warrior and leader, is the person on whom Virgil based his portrayal of Dido in the *Aeneid*. However, Virgil played fast and loose with dates and locations, twisting Elissa's life story for his own purposes and making "Dido" into an ideal Roman woman, then using her to justify the Punic-Roman vendetta.

According to Klausmann, Meinzerin, and Kuhn, the real Elissa/ Dido was not only a founder of Carthage but also a pirate. She was the firstborn child of the king of Tyre, a city in Phoenicia, which was a group of several allied ports in the eastern Mediterranean and home to a vibrant community of sailors and traders. She was heir to the throne, but her brother Pygmalion ousted her and claimed it for himself. She fled the city in search of a place to found a new Phoenician homeland. Over her eleven-year odyssey, she endured many hardships and visited many strange places before finally landing in present-day Tunisia, where she would found the city of Carthage. Other scholars disagree with this assessment, stating that numerous historical and biblical accounts establish Elissa's identity and place her much too late in time to have been alive—never mind romantically involved—with Aeneas during his flight from Troy. However, it is an intriguing theory that Virgil co-opted heroic Elissa and made her into the lovelorn Dido, and it is certainly not impossible that a heroine could be slandered by historians in such a way.

No matter what really happened at the end of Artemisia's life, the stories that exist about her paint a fascinating picture of an early pirate queen who was not afraid to stand up to a king or to turn her back on her allies to save her own skin. This act of self-preservation will serve as a prototype for later female pirates' nationless ways. Two hundred fifty years later, another female pirate would follow in Artemisia's footsteps—Queen Teuta of Illyria.

⚓⚓⚓

Much of what is known about Queen Teuta comes from hostage-turned-tutor-turned-author Polybius, who wrote *The Histories*, a forty-volume work of ancient history of which only five volumes survive today. As a Greek, he would have grown up exposed to Hellenic attitudes about women. This antiwomen bias that claimed women were hyperemotional and not valued in the social sphere outside domestic tasks, along with some of the sources he drew on to write his books, might have colored his treatment of Teuta. Nevertheless, he is the largest source there is on Queen Teuta and therefore cannot be avoided in recounting her life. The reader must, however, remember his bias and weigh his statements accordingly.

Queen Teuta's rise to power began when her husband, King Agron, died as a result of a drinking binge. Illyria was a city-state along the coast of the Adriatic Sea, located in the present-day Balkan Peninsula. In 231 BCE Agron's military forces defeated the Greek city-state of Aetolia, and the king threw a banquet in celebration. He partied a little too hard and died a week later. His death gave Teuta a chance to rule through her stepson Pinnes, for whom she served as regent during his infancy.

Upon taking the throne, Teuta decided to expand Illyria's riches. She granted every ship in her navy a license that gave them permission to attack ships from other city-states—even city-states with which Illyria was currently at peace. Essentially, Queen Teuta turned her whole fleet into pirates and encouraged them to plunder as much as they liked, on land or sea—provided they brought the riches home to Illyria, of course.

Teuta's pirates were wildly successful. They preferred land pillaging to sea pillaging and plundered villages up and down the Illyrian and Italian coast. Twin cities, meant to curb piracy, instead worked very much to the Illyrians' advantage as they looted without fear of reprisals.

The development of twin cities—one close to shore for commercial purposes and one farther inland to house the military forces and other resources—was a solution that kept the riches and resources of the city safe from attackers, including pirates. Piracy had weighed heavily on the minds of city planners as they developed their communities. People were so afraid of attacks that they didn't dare build their cities along the coastline, even though that was the most logical thing to do for trade purposes.

A famous example of this twin cities construction was Athens and Piraeus. Athens, located twelve miles inland, was the center of the arts, culture, and philosophy for all of Greece. The city was built around the Acropolis, a high peak in the middle of the city crowned with temples and monuments to the gods. Athens featured the senate building, the agora (outdoor marketplace), the Panathenaic stadium where the precursor to the Olympic Games was held, and numerous theaters and temples.

Piraeus was the port of Athens and its twin. Everything that Athens needed from elsewhere came in through Piraeus. It consisted of three separate ports—one for commercial work and two for the navy. Piraeus was a thriving city in its own right. It hosted shipyards where navy ships were constructed, offices, warehouses, and brothels. It was not the hub of culture and sophistication that Athens was, but without it, Athens could not exist.

Two long walls connected Athens to Piraeus. These walls were four and a half miles long, with a space between them where people and animals could travel. Athens was also surrounded by high walls, which protected the city from invaders and ensured that supplies could be transported from the port of Piraeus during a siege or warfare. As long as Athens was not cut off from Piraeus, it would be able to survive.

This twin cities idea, intended in part to help curb piracy, instead served to further its influence. When the pirates such as Teuta and her band discovered that the coastal cities had to wait for the local military force to make the journey from the inland city in order to mount a defense, they knew they could sack a town and be long gone before the guard made its way to them.

Teuta herself occasionally accompanied her pirates on the raids and enthusiastically participated in the mayhem. Polybius tells a story of Teuta and her crew landing outside a city and approaching the wall with water jugs. The crew cried out that they were dying of thirst and begged for water. When the citizens opened the gate, Teuta and her crew ditched the jugs, grabbed the swords that were hidden inside them, and proceeded to attack the town.

Teuta became known as the Terror of the Adriatic. Once she tired of winning every battle she started close to home, she turned her eyes to the Romans and the riches they had to offer. Her ships attacked a number of Roman merchant vessels, meting out various horrors that ranged from plundering the ship's goods to enslaving the crew. Polybius claims these actions got the attention of the Roman government, which decided to send two emissaries to Queen Teuta to put this woman in her place and make sure she understood that Rome was not to be treated rudely.

When Roman brothers Gaius and Lucius Coruncanius arrived in Illyria, they attempted to engage in civil discourse with the queen. The brothers requested that she issue a ban on attacking Rome, an idea she listened to with an "insolent and disdainful air," according to Polybius. She then replied that Illyria's policy was not to interfere with private citizens' right to attack whom they chose, even if that happened to be Rome. Lucius, the younger brother, would not take this insult to Rome lying down and told her either she would issue the ban or they would make her issue it. Teuta received this threat with "womanish passion" and "unreasoning anger."

The Roman negotiators, doubtless shocked to their very core that anyone, let alone a woman, had the audacity to disobey them, started off toward home. Unluckily for Lucius, Teuta's men were obedient to her, and a group of them carried out her orders to "kill the one who had used his plainness" in speaking so rudely to the queen. (Another historian, Appian, tells the story a little differently, attributing the murder of Lucius to Teuta's husband, King Agron, who does not die as early on in his version of the story.)

According to Polybius, Rome was very upset by Teuta's assassination of Lucius. Lucius's death alone, however, was not enough to goad Rome into war with Illyria. Teuta might have escaped Rome's notice altogether if she had refrained from picking up her late husband's land campaign. The queen, along with her royal governor Demetrius, had begun capturing cities along the western coast of present-day Greece. That move expanded Illyria's territory southward and brought them dangerously close to interfering with Roman land interests. Now Teuta was no longer just the leader of an annoying pirate band; she was a legitimate threat. When she came knocking on Rome's back door, they had to act.

In 229 BCE Rome declared war against Illyria and readied sea and land campaigns of its own against her. Unfortunately for Teuta, her reign of terror over the entire region had left many Greek provinces petrified, and they were willing to turn to any major power who promised to oppose her—including their enemies the Romans. Under the guise of protection from the big bad Illyrians, the Romans gobbled up territories all around Illyria, assuring the people that Rome would aid them in their fight against Queen Teuta—all for the small price of complete surrender to the Romans.

Rome's naval campaign was as successful as its land campaign, particularly because Teuta's own governor Demetrius sold her out to the Romans; he remained in power and with a large part of her land after her surrender. With the Illyrian forces on the run, Teuta was forced to flee from her capital city to her fortress at Rhizon, where she and the subjects who remained loyal to her endured a yearlong siege.

Finally, in 228 BCE, Teuta's supplies and fortifications against the siege gave out, and she was forced to surrender. She sent messengers to Rome to negotiate a treaty. According to Polybius, she agreed "to pay a fixed tribute, and to abandon all Illyricum, with the exception of some few districts: and what affected Greece more than anything, she agreed not to sail beyond Lissus with more than two galleys, and those unarmed." In contrast, Appian claims she begged forgiveness from the Romans for the dirty deeds done not by her but by her husband.

Regardless of the specifics, Rome graciously forgave her and accepted her surrender. After that, Teuta virtually disappears from historical records. When Teuta's stepson Pinnes came of age, he took the throne.

Polybius had many motives for portraying Queen Teuta as a power-hungry villain. First, many of his primary sources were Roman authors, who would naturally paint Teuta as the instigator of war and color themselves blameless. Also, he probably held with the antiwoman bias of his time and wanted to ensure that future generations of Hellenes knew the consequences of putting a woman on the throne. This type of historical revisionism runs rampant on the journey through pirate history.

⚓⚓⚓

Fast forward about a thousand years, and historical revisionism has not been left behind. In fact, the Viking chroniclers take it to a whole new level, weaving bare historical records with outlandish fictions to spin their stories of dangerous feminine power. The wild Viking women pirates were—according to sources from the time—in the end conquered by men and returned safely to the home, where they became housewives and mothers. Did the Viking women pirates even exist, or were they just the product of men's imaginations used to warn women to stay in line?

2

Gatekeepers of Valhalla

E VEN IN A HISTORY chock-full of myths and legends, few civilizations stand taller than the Vikings. Even a child can point to a
horned helmet and identify it as Viking gear (despite the fact that
the Vikings never wore these; they were added to the Vikings legend
in the 1800s, but that's another story). These famously ferocious sea
raiders ruled much of Europe and even parts of Asia in their prime,
and many parts of the modern world still bear their mark. But what is
really known about these Scandinavian scoundrels?

The short answer: not much. Virtually all the information that
exists about the Vikings comes from secondary sources. The Vikings
did not have a written culture as the term is understood today, using
runes only for very short messages and labeling rather than writing
down a story. They preferred to pass down their histories and traditions
orally through songs and sagas, a practice that continued even past the
introduction of Christianity and the Latin alphabet to the Vikings. So
the only documents that exist from the Viking era that give accounts of
their civilization come from the people whom the Vikings conquered—
hardly a neutral source. The Christian monks who had just lost much
of their treasure and many of their brethren to these attackers would
not be kindly disposed to the Viking people when they recounted the
story of the attack. Thus, much of what is written about the Vikings,

in books such as the *Anglo-Saxon Chronicles* and *The Annals of Ulster*, has to be taken with at least a grain if not a sea full of salt.

Centuries later, the Viking sagas were eventually written down, and many of those accounts survive. So stories composed by the Scandinavians for the Vikings do exist, and their study has been instrumental in understanding more about how these ancient peoples lived. For example, one saga led archaeologists to find a Viking settlement site in Newfoundland, L'Anse Aux Meadows, which is believed to have been settled hundreds of years before Columbus arrived in America. However, these sagas cannot be accepted at face value as absolute truth. Viking sagas were told for entertainment purposes, often after meals at mead halls. These stories were crafted to glorify and inspire, not to educate. The deeds that are recounted in these sagas likely did not happen exactly as they are described.

Recent archaeological findings have given historians unparalleled new insight into Viking life. Bones and household objects cannot lie the way that stories can. The past thirty years have yielded some remarkable findings that offer a new glimpse into the Viking world. Archaeologists have discovered Viking artifacts such as coins, combs, and other household items all over Europe—evidence that the Vikings were involved in extensive and far-flung trade as well as in plunder. In fact, their trading predated their raiding. The Vikings were far from a peaceful people—they did pillage and murder, and their religious concept of an afterlife was based on glory for warriors—but they were more than just battle-hungry men and women. They left their homeland and went to sea in search of more hospitable places to live and people with whom to do business. Polygamous practices at home meant more heirs to divide inheritances and land between, and so they had to sail away to find other spots to build homes and farms. They spread their products and ideas across the world, opening up new routes for trade and commerce. When the Vikings intermarried and joined non-Viking societies, they did so peacefully and easily. Not interested in spreading any sort of ideological agenda, they instead became part of their new, adopted culture. These businesslike, necessity-driven people were a far cry from the bloodstained, vicious men of legend.

Archaeology has also unearthed more information about the role women played in Viking society. A 2011 study published in the journal *Early Medieval Europe* set the Internet ablaze with the headline that half of all Viking warriors were women. A more careful reading of the study does not back up this claim but instead reveals that, at a burial site, out of thirteen "Norse migrants," six were female and seven were male. Previous studies relied on grave goods (objects buried alongside bodies) to determine the gender of the deceased, but this was an inexact science. This new study proclaimed gender with more certainty by using bone analysis rather than grave goods. This study proved two things: one, that women traveled along with men on voyages to new lands, most likely to immediately be part of a settlement after an area had been conquered; and two, that modern people are absolutely desperate for proof of women Vikings, as evidenced by the enthusiastic online reaction following the study. People want to believe that women were there beside the men, slashing with iron swords and uttering harsh battle cries. People yearn to know if Valhalla is populated with the souls of women warriors as well as male ones.

Saxo Grammaticus, author of the seminal twelfth-century Danish text *Gesta Danorum*, certainly thought so, or at least wanted his readers to think so. He writes, "There were once women among the Danes who dressed themselves to look like men, and devoted almost every instant of their lives to the pursuit of war." He states this in a digression, almost as if he knows that modern audiences will have trouble accepting his statements and, understanding that, wants to emphasize that he is not making this stuff up. His work, not surprisingly, is a primary source for many of the stories that exist about Viking pirate women.

Despite Saxo's claims, many scholars insist that, while women were indisputably a part of Norse society, they were never warriors. Danish historian Nanna Damsholt calls Saxo's stories "pure fiction." Professor and Viking scholar Judith Jesch also disagrees with Saxo and other sources, claiming that she has never uncovered any credible evidence that women were a part of the Viking raiding parties. Although archaeologists have uncovered women buried in ships, they have not been able to prove that these women were anything more than members of a seafaring society. Nevertheless, the stories of women Vikings, whether they are based on fact or fiction, have powerfully persisted over the centuries. Besides the Viking women profiled in this chapter from the Viking age, there are legends stretching through the centuries of Scandinavian women, possibly Viking descendants, who took to seafaring piracy, such as Christina Anna Skytte, Elise Eskilsdotter, Ingela Gathenhielm, and Johanna Hård. Clearly something about these peoples and this land breeds stories of women pirates, if not pirate women themselves.

A vital question to ask about Viking women pirates is whether Vikings really ought to be called pirates at all. They did most of their raiding on land and did very little actual fighting at sea. They traveled to the places that they pillaged by boat, and they were undoubtedly a seafaring culture, going so far as to bury many of their dead in their boats. They did pioneer methods that were copied by later pirate groups, such as Queen Elizabeth's sea dogs and the buccaneers. But were the Vikings pirates? If one accepts Queen Teuta and her ilk as pirates, then the Vikings can probably be lumped into the category as well. Jo Stanley addresses this, explaining that piracy is based in theft and that for the Vikings "to conquer enemies, to defeat others, could be seen as theft: of their lives, their ships, and their right to fight for a cause." She goes on to say that almost any time a woman is a sea-based warrior, there is a tendency to call her a pirate anyway, so it makes sense to include Viking women in female pirate history. As the centuries advance, the definition of piracy evolves constantly, and to make too narrow a definition leaves out a great number of women who made their mark on the seafaring world and could have served as role models and inspiration for the more traditional pirate women who came after them.

The earliest documented Viking raid was at the monastery at Lindisfarne, a small island off England's northeast coast, in the summer of 793 CE. Lindisfarne was a renowned monastery, producer of the Lindisfarne gospels, and a place of learning where many Christians had donated treasures and riches for the glory of God—and in hopes of saving their souls. Although the inhabitants of Northumberland had been shoring themselves up for some sort of disaster all year due to a number of ill omens, such as lightning storms and whirlwinds and even reports of "fiery dragons" in the air, according to the *Anglo-Saxon Chronicle*, this attack was beyond their worst expectations. The carnage and extent of the damage was more than they ever feared possible. According to Simeon of Durham, a twelfth-century church historian, the monastery was looted for valuables; even the altars were dug up. Many of the monks were killed, either by sword or by drowning in the sea. Other monks were carried off by the Vikings to become slaves. A contemporary historian explains that the attack would have been felt as an incident that affected not only Lindisfarne but also England's very soul.

Lindisfarne was far from an isolated incident. The hits kept coming as the Vikings worked their way from England to Ireland, increasing their reach as they snapped up new camps and islands. No coastal area felt safe, although the monasteries were by far the most frequent targets of the Vikings. Christians across Europe felt that the attacks were a punishment from God. A quote from Jeremiah 1:14 reinforced their suspicions: "Out of the North an evil shall break forth upon all the inhabitants of the land." Nobody had the resources or fighting skills to resist these northern marauders. From 793 until the beginning of the eleventh century, they roamed wherever they wanted and took whatever riches they liked.

The Vikings did not confine themselves to the British Isles, either. The Frankish king Charles the Bald, after losing cities such as Paris, Bordeaux, Limoges, Rouen, and Toulouse to the Vikings, finally decided to pay protection money to the Vikings to stop the carnage. By the beginning of the tenth century, the French had forked over twelve tons of wine, livestock, silver, and grain in a Mafia-style arrangement.

Farther afield in eastern Europe, the Vikings were so intertwined with the founding of Russia that even the country's name comes from a Viking term. The Swedish Vikings were called the Rus, Swedish for "boatman," which makes sense since the Vikings came downriver by boat. Legend has it that the Viking king Rurik unified the warring Slavic tribes and established the foundation of the Russian nation.

The recently discovered Newfoundland settlement demonstrates that the Vikings' settlements stretched all the way to North America. There were very few parts of the globe that did not feel the Vikings' presence.

Despite all their success, Vikings did not enjoy a particularly comfortable life. According to Joan Druett, author of *She Captains*, longships, while excellent sailing vessels, did not offer a lot of living space, so while on voyages the Vikings had to sleep onshore in leather sleeping bags with their weapons at arm's reach. They ate raw meat, kept watch around the clock, and used dogs as first aid: their loyal hounds licked their wounds clean. On top of this primitive lifestyle, the actual raids brought more hardship and suffering, to say nothing of the frigid winters back home. Perhaps the rough life they lived is what made the Vikings such consummate warriors.

⚓⚓⚓

A number of women warriors show up during the Viking age. There is not a wealth of information available about each one, but the very fact that the literature is peppered with so many of them sends a message. Unfortunately, the tales have been taken from their Norse roots and rewritten through a Christian lens, which spins many of them as cautionary tales to be heeded by good Christian women. Jo Stanley, in an essay about Viking women in her book *Bold in Her Breeches*, claims that "society was being persuaded that lethal, wild, vengeful, and free-roving ways of living should be given up and that women should accept a meek and home-based role, and a Christian one at that."

The Norse and Icelandic sagas, passed down orally but eventually written down, offer another option to explore the Nordic view of women, although the stories were almost certainly meddled with by Christian scholars, whose work reflected contemporary worldviews rather than true accounts of the Viking age. They do not for the most part cover *pirate* women, instead relating the tales of Aud the Deep-Minded, who was known as a settler; Freydis, the sister of Leif Erikson; and other women. Viking women wove tapestries, which have newly been the subject of research: textile as text. Stories told in cloth, although they do not always feature women, are presented from a woman's perspective and are a compelling window into the mind of the storyteller. The stories that exist about these women may have been put down with a clear agenda in mind, but the reader is free to imagine what the authors left out and to attempt to construct another version of these tales, one free of religious or political motive.

In book 3 of the *Gesta Danorum*, the reader is presented with Sela, who we are told is a "skilled warrior with experience in roving." Her brother, Koll (sometimes called Koller or Kolles), king of Norway, is jealous of the pirate Horwendil's (or Orvendil) success and wants to eclipse him in popularity. (It is telling that a king could feel envy for the life of a pirate.) Koll sets off with his fleet to find Horwendil, and eventually the two run into each other. Rather than decimate their fleets in battle, the two men decide to settle their difference in single hand-to-hand combat. They promise to fight with honor and bury the loser as befits his station. When Horwendil bests Koll, he decides (for reasons not given in the narrative) to chop off another limb of their family tree and fight Sela, too, who is called in some translations "a warring Amazon and an accomplished pirate."

Why was Sela in close proximity to the fight? Was she sailing in Koll's fleet at the time? Did Koll choose her as a sort of second in the duel with Horwendil? Saxo's account leaves out all these details. Some versions of the story claim that Sela and Koll were bitter rivals, one on each side of the law. Whether or not they disliked each other, it is generally agreed that both siblings were slain by the pirate Horwendil, although the lavish funeral rites bestowed on Koll are not mentioned in Sela's case.

Book 8 offers another case of sibling rivalry—this time between Tesondus (also known as Thrond) and his sister Rusla. In some translations, Rusla is called Rusila, although Rusila appears to be a different maiden who, along with her sister Stikla, fought King Olaf for his kingdom. Rusla is also sometimes linked to the mythological figure Ingean Ruadh (the Red Maiden). Tesondus had lost the crown of Norway to the Danish king Omund, which galled Rusla to no end. She could not bear to see her beloved country taken over by Danish rule, and she was annoyed that her brother seemed content to let it happen. So she decided that if her brother was not going to take any action, she would have to do it herself. Rusla declared war on her people who had declared allegiance to the Danes. Omund was not pleased with this dissension and sent a unit of his best soldiers to put an end to her rebellion. Rusla destroyed the Danish contingent, and that gave her a brilliant idea. Why not aim a bit higher than independence from the Danish? Why not take over Denmark and rule both nations herself instead?

Fortune turned her back on Rusla, whose invasion of Denmark did not go well, forcing her to turn tail and run to save herself and her troops. As she retreated from the Danes, she ran into her brother, whom she overpowered in short order, stripping him of all his ships and troops but refusing to kill Tesondus himself; that decision would prove to be her fatal mistake. King Omund sent his fleet to Norway to attack Rusla's fleet, and again she was defeated by the Danish forces. As she retreated for a second time, her brother Tesondus attacked and killed her. Some stories claim that he beat her to death with oars. For taking care of Rusla for him, Omund gave former rival Tesondus a governorship.

This story has more meat to it than Sela's story, but there are not enough details to satisfy the reader's curiosity. What was Rusla's life like before she took to the sea? Did she regard the repulsion of Danish forces as her patriotic duty or a splendid adventure? When Omund's forces followed her back home to Norway for a second battle, did she realize that she would not beat them? Did surrender ever cross her mind? And why did she spare Tesondus's life? Could she have believed that, when their places were reversed, he would do the same for her?

Book 8 also tells of three women longship captains, who, although they had the bodies of women, had been blessed with "the souls of men." Wisna, Webiorg, and Hetha were all fighters by land as well as sea. Each woman receives only a few lines of text devoted to her. Wisna is said to have been made a standard-bearer in battle and then to have lost her right hand in combat. Webiorg felled a champion before being killed in battle, and Hetha was appointed the ruler of Zealand (part of modern-day Denmark). Although there is almost no information about these women, the scanty tidbits are juicy enough to pique the reader's interest.

While it may be initially surprising that this warrior culture, packed to the hilt with testosterone-laden images and heroes, had so many women warriors, a look at the religious structure at the time reveals that women were always, at least symbolically, part of battle. Yggdrasil, the tree of life, was the center of the Norse world. At the tree's roots lived the Norns, mythical women who shaped the destinies of humans and even gods. These women were similar to the Fates of ancient Greek mythology. The powerful male gods, such as Thor and Odin, were subject to the whims of the Norns. In their hands they held life, death, and everything in between. It seems that, in Norse mythology, women ran the world.

Besides the Norns, Norse mythology also includes the Valkyries. These attendants of Odin moved among the Viking battlefields, selecting who would live to fight another day and whose battle was permanently ended. Among the slain, they also chose who would go on to glorious Valhalla, the big dining hall in the sky where warriors prepared to help Odin during Ragnarök, which is the Viking end of the world. The unselected dead were escorted to Fólkvangr, a field of the afterlife ruled over by goddess Freyja. The Valkyries are portrayed as beautiful and noble, helping weary warriors to their final destination, but they are also sinister—some early tales show them gleefully cackling while weaving a tapestry of fate made of human entrails and severed heads. They exist in various permutations across many pre-Christian traditions but have remained in Western popular culture almost exclusively as Viking Valkyries. These women, existing alongside men and performing a vital part of the battle rituals, demonstrate an acceptance by the Old Norse that women did have a part to play in war.

Modern research suggests that Valkyries were neither male or female but a third unnamed gender, which had masculine attributes while being physically female. Original depictions of Valkyries support this assertion and are a far cry from the sexy, undeniably female bodies shown in art today. Mortal Viking women seem to share this mix of masculine traits and feminine bodies, much more so than originally thought. Marianne Moen's study of grave sites suggests that the positioning of grave sites and grave goods suggests a smaller difference between men and women than originally believed. She cites Cedrenus, an author from 970 BCE, who witnessed a battle between the Rus and the Byzantines and claimed that the Byzantines were surprised by the number of women they found among the dead on the battlefield. Even the traditional roles held by women, keeper of the keys or lady of the house, may have been more public (male) than private (female) than previously thought due to the role of houses in trade; a Viking woman would have been more like a store or factory manager than a housekeeper, since houses were used as trade centers by the Vikings. Moen's research presents some new possibilities for understanding Viking life that are worthy of continued study.

⚓⚓⚓

A major pirate woman from this era was Ladgerda (also called Lagertha). Book 9 of the *Gesta Danorum* tells her story, which starts inauspiciously. According to Saxo Grammaticus, Swedish king Frey kills a Norwegian king and, in an especially cruel move, puts the dead king's womenfolk into a brothel so that they might be publicly humiliated. Ragnar of Denmark is moved by the women's plight and goes to Norway to break them out—and cause some havoc for the Swedish king Frey. When the news of Ragnar's coming reaches the brothel, many of the women dress as men, sneak out, and join his army. One of them is Ladgerda, who "fought in front among the bravest with her hair loose over her shoulders."

Ragnar must have been shocked upon arriving at the brothel. He expects to be hailed as a strong and handsome hero by the bound and nearly nude women, who would weep in gratitude for his selfless rescue plan. Instead, he finds an armed team of warriors already in place, ready to aid him. Even if he weathered that change of plans, he would have been really surprised to discover that his fierce new comrades were actually the very women he was meant to be saving. It was enough to knock any man down a few pegs, but it appears Ragnar did not worry too much about it; he was too busy engaging in a furious battle—with the women's help, of course.

Ragnar and the women win the skirmish. Afterward, taking a leaf from the fairy-tale playbook, he goes on a hunt, asking everyone he can find who the mystery woman was: the one who had caused him to "gain the victory by the might of just one woman." When he discovers that she is Ladgerda, who is not only brave and gorgeous but also of noble birth, he resolves to woo her. She is unimpressed with him but seems to know that rejecting him outright is not particularly safe, so she allows him to woo her as she installs a vicious dog and a bear in front of her dwelling to protect herself from any unwanted visitors (namely, suitors). Ragnar, apparently unable to take a hint, goes to her, kills the bear, chokes the dog, and grabs Ladgerda in his arms. The two marry and have three children.

Lest the reader worry that Ladgerda suffered an ignoble fate, be assured that the story is not over. Her husband leaves her for another woman, apparently realizing at last that a wife who puts out wild beasts to keep men away might not be that into him. However, when Ragnar gets embroiled in a civil war back home in Denmark, he sends to Norway for help. Guess who rides in and saves the day? Ragnar's ex-wife, Ladgerda, who turns the tide of the battle with her 120 ships, ensuring a victory for Ragnar. However, the reunion of the old lovers is not a sweet one—after the battle, Ladgerda stabs her former husband with a spearhead she has concealed in her dress. She then wipes the blood off herself and claims the Danish throne, for, as Saxo Grammaticus tells us, "this most presumptuous dame thought it pleasanter to rule without her husband than to share the throne with him."

Ladgerda's story includes many more details than do the accounts of most of the other women who are featured in the *Gesta Danorum*, but it still does not feel like enough. Her actions demonstrate clearly just how she felt about being forcibly married, abandoned, and then summoned to help her ex-husband. But what happened in between all these episodes? What became of this remarkably gutsy woman? Some scholars have pointed out the similarity of her tale with the story of the goddess Thorgerd, the subject of several myths. If Ladgerda is in fact a goddess and not a mortal woman, her story makes a bit more sense. She alone among the warrior maidens is able to get the better of a man who desires her and rule a kingdom. She is the only one who gets a happy ending. A little pagan divine intervention might have been the only way for a Viking woman to come out on top in this collection of stories about bringing wild women in line with Christian values. Goddess or mortal, Ladgerda's pluck, skill, and ambition make her an irresistible heroine and a model early pirate.

⚓⚓⚓

Besides the numerous shield maidens and other Viking warrior women who appear in the *Gesta Danorum* and other sources, there is at least one woman who is explicitly labeled "pirate" from this period. Princess Alfhild, also called Awilda, is often listed alongside other famous female pirates, such as Anne Bonny and Grace O'Malley. She comes to the reader originally from the *Gesta Danorum*, followed by a sixteenth-century text, *History of the Northern Peoples*, written by Olaus Magnus. According to Joan Druett, Alfhild entered the modern era through Charles Ellms's 1837 work, *The Pirates Own Book*, which is in essence a summary of Magnus's description of her with a lot of embellishments aimed at selling copies. Ellms's account is responsible for an oft-cited but totally inaccurate fact. He places Alfhild's story in the fifth century during a Viking-Saxon skirmish. However, all previous accounts of the princess's life place her much later, during the Viking age, circa 790 to 1000 CE. Presumably, Ellms picked the first Viking conflict he found as his setting and did not feel the need to do anymore research. The popularity of Ellms's book ensured that Alfhild's tale is more often than not attributed to the wrong century.

Dating concerns aside, Alfhild's story is fascinating. She was, Saxo Grammaticus tells us, a princess, daughter of Siward, King of the Goths.

Her beauty was legendary. She was so striking that she went to great pains to conceal her face in her robe, in order to keep her attractiveness from "provoking the passion of another"—frustrating but perhaps unsurprising early evidence of the deeply rooted idea that women are responsible for men's reactions to them.

Alfhild's beauty and wealth, despite her best efforts, managed to attract plenty of suitors. Her father in his wisdom offered her two snakes as guardians. Some versions of the story also claim that he locked her up in a high tower, Rapunzel-style. Anyone who wanted to marry Alfhild had to defeat the snakes before he could have the princess. Anyone who made an attempt but failed would be taken away and beheaded. His severed head would be impaled on a stake, presumably to warn other would-be suitors of the peril of the quest.

King Siward's protection of his daughter might seem extreme, but it was actually pretty common in Viking times (minus the trained snakes). According to Druett, women, and princesses in particular, were property—valuable commodities to be bestowed or bargained. If a woman's virtue was damaged, she was less valuable. Fathers and brothers took great pains to keep a woman pure in order to make sure she was in mint condition for maximum returns on their investment when it was time to marry her off.

Despite the hefty cost should one be unsuccessful, many suitors did accept the challenge for Alfhild's hand. There was no shortage of heads on spikes when Prince Alf decided to give it a go. He employed a clever trick to get past the dreaded snakes: he covered his outfit in blood to drive the snakes into a frenzy. He got rid of the first snake with a piece of red-hot steel, which he shoved down the snake's throat. The second snake met its maker by a spear to the mouth. Saxo's explanation makes it sound like Alf was particularly clever in his dispatch of the snakes, but the idea of stabbing them could have occurred to any number of previous potential husbands. Perhaps earlier suitors were not as skilled in spear craft as the handsome Prince Alf.

Having killed the princess's snakes, Prince Alf demanded her hand. What he did not know was that there was a twist—King Siward declared that, for the match to be made official, Princess Alfhild had to approve of the man. No doubt the king thought that his daughter would look on the handsome prince with kindness and the marriage plans would be under way in no time. However, Alfhild had other ideas.

There are a few different versions of what happened next. In some accounts, Alfhild says she does like the look of Prince Alf, but she decides to ask her mother for advice. For some reason, her mom is against the marriage and scolds Alfhild, basically accusing her of giving up her chastity for the first handsome hunk who came along. The conscientious maiden is horrified and immediately rejects Prince Alf. In other versions of the story, she is not at all interested in the prince and disappears before he can attempt to woo her. Magnus, the fifteenth-century author, explains that "a woman's madness" causes her to give up the prince. Her determination to "stay chaste" is to blame for her spurning the handsome suitor.

The idea that her mother talked her out of the marriage is a fascinating one. What motivation could the queen have had? Did she perceive some character flaw in the prince that the story leaves out? Or did she want to spare her daughter the life she herself lived, wedded to a warlord? Perhaps she wanted her daughter to hold out for a better offer that would be more valuable to the family. Whatever reasons she had, it is rare to see not only a woman deciding whether or not she should marry someone but also another woman having sway in that decision.

Regardless of why Alfhild decided to reject Prince Alf, all stories agree that she did. She ditched her maiden's garb, presumably including her chaste face-hiding robe, and donned men's clothes. She gathered together some like-minded women who were apparently also hankering for a new way of life, and together they stole a boat. Before long, this crew of ladies had become pirates.

How could this have happened? Presumably, the princess and her friends did not have any prior sailing experience. She would not have had knowledge of how to find her way by the stars, how to read the tides, and how to take cues from nature, such as understanding the path of migrating birds. Her life in the tower would have done little to prepare her for the hardship and privation that awaited her at sea. She was young, sheltered, and up until recently exceedingly concerned with remaining chaste and avoiding arousing men's passions. Whatever possessed her to run away and become a pirate? Did she mourn the loss of her home and family but view it as a necessary by-product of her struggle to remain unsullied by man? The reader can only wonder what was running through the princess's mind as she watched her home fade into darkness while her ship sailed farther and farther away from everything she had ever known.

Never mind Alfhild's feelings—how did she and her friends manage to sail a longship on their own? Longships were not, as a rule, ideal for novice sailors. These powerful ships are as much a part of the Viking legacy as the (inaccurate) horned helmet. Typically, they were around one hundred feet long. They had long, lean hulls that were made of overlapping planks with waterproofing material in between, all secured together by iron nails. This style of hull construction is called clinker-built. The masts were often gilded, and the rigging was traditionally dyed red. Warriors' shields were hung off the ship's sides during sailing; this provided additional protection as well as more decoration.

Although these ships were remarkably beautiful, they were constructed primarily for speed as well as durability. They were used for commerce as well as for war. The longships specifically built for exploration and pillaging were especially light, in order to be easily run aground during land raids. Some were so light they could even be carried by their crew. They could navigate in only a few feet of water. About fifty oars were used to move the boat forward. Some of the longships had a mast and a square sail, which was painstakingly constructed and decorated by the women with bright and luxurious colors and fabrics. The ships did not have a front or a back, per se, and thus could be reversed quickly, a lifesaving technique in treacherous conditions. Because of the Viking custom of burying men in their ships, many have been unearthed over the years and, as a result, much is known about these vessels. The largest mostly intact ship recovered to date is the *Skuldelev 2*, which is nearly one hundred feet long and is currently on display at the Viking Ship Museum in Roskilde, Norway.

So how did Princess Alfhild and her friends manage to keep their longship afloat? Saxo Grammaticus does not offer any details on how they accomplished this feat, but he does not leave them unaccompanied for long. By miraculous good fortune, the women happen upon a group of men who have just lost their captain. They are either impressed with Alfhild's beauty or press-ganged into service, depending on which account is to be believed. The men end up on Alfhild's ship under her command. Both versions of the story have preposterous elements. No self-respecting band of sailors would accept an outsider captain, especially a woman, simply based on her looks. Men have been known to do foolish things for a pretty face, but this would put their very lives and livelihoods at risk. And if the men were captured, what would cause Alfhild and her crew to commit this act of kidnapping? Did they need extra help on the ship, or were they simply hungry for some male companionship? The reason for their voyage in the first place was to escape marriage, so it seems improbable that they would experience a change of heart and decide they did want men on their boat after all. In any case, Alfhild's crew expanded, and they continued pillaging as before.

Although we have accounts of what Viking raids were like, told from the perspective of those who survived them, we do not have any information on Alfhild's particular style of pirating or on any of her raids. Saxo does reveal that Prince Alf made many trips to find her, so it can be inferred that she was hard to locate for some time. She was said to have done deeds "beyond the valor of a woman," so it is implied that some of her pirating voyages were successful. She at least manages to elude capture for a while.

Eventually, after an escapade that involves walking over some frozen sea to engage in battle, Alf and his men catch up with Alfhild and her pirate women. (By this point in the story, the men she conscripted earlier have mysteriously disappeared.) Alf and his men start to fight with her crew, and they are struck by how graceful and supple limbed their foes are. Borgar, Alf's comrade, knocks off Alfhild's helmet and reveals to

Alf that his opponent is actually his beloved whom he has been seeking all this time. (This part of the story doesn't add up, as Viking helmets did not obscure the whole face and would not have been effective in concealing Alfhild's identity.) As soon as he recognizes her, he realizes that he must "fight with kisses and not with arms." In what is most likely supposed to be a romantic passage, he holds her close, forces her to swap out her manly attire for a more ladylike costume, and impregnates her with a daughter, who is called Gurid. Alfhild's second in command, Groa, suffers a similar fate with Borgar, one of Alf's crewmates.

At the end of the story, the women are returned home, the men are back in charge, and the order of the universe is restored. Nobody bothers to ask Alfhild how she felt about being forcibly captured by the man she had already refused once. But modern readers cannot help but worry about poor Alfhild's state of mind as she sailed back toward home, virtually a captive. Offered a fate she wanted no part of, she had cast off her identity and become someone new. She succeeded at sailing and pillaging, two difficult tasks, but in the end her success was completely disregarded. Despite all she accomplished, she is still a woman, and a when a woman is wanted by a man, her own wishes and desires do not matter. No matter how high she rises, she cannot overcome her own biology. Why is there not more outrage on Alfhild's behalf? Why does the story not end with the couple returning home, only to have King Siward, or better yet, his wife, chopping off Alf's head for disrespecting their daughter's wishes and placing it on a spike next to all the other suitors? Alfhild does not get justice in Saxo Grammaticus's version—someone else will have to pen that story.

Saxo Grammaticus crafted Alfhild's story as a moral-laden fable. This, combined with the plot hole of how Alfhild managed to sail a longship, makes her legend hard to swallow as is. However, that does not mean there is no truth to her story. Enough characters in her saga have been confirmed to lend some credibility to her existence. It might be that she did in fact live, but her life could have unfolded very differently from the story that Saxo laid down in his book. Perhaps it was his effort to contort her life story into a cautionary tale that necessitated the narrative leaps in logic that are so galling to readers. Regardless of whether Alfhild actually lived, her story is a beloved one, ending notwithstanding. Since the twelfth century, she has been a part of the Norse folklore, enduring long past the stories of people who definitely existed.

The Viking age was in decline by the dawn of the eleventh century. By then, they had run out of people and places to conquer and had for the most part settled down across mainland Europe. It would be nearly three centuries before female pirates would become headliners again. It would take a century-long war—the Hundred Years' War in Europe—to give a number of women the opportunity to step out of their traditional roles and become warriors and leaders. Some of them would become not just warriors but also pirates.

3

Medieval Maiden Warriors

HE MIDDLE AGES STRETCHED for ten centuries in Europe, from the collapse of the Roman Empire to the Renaissance. It was a turbulent period full of fighting over lands, titles, religions, and even women's rights. In fact, one of the biggest and bloodiest conflicts of the Middle Ages—the Hundred Years' War—was sparked over a question of whether women could inherit the French crown. If Isabella of France had been allowed to claim the throne for herself in 1328, or even allowed to claim it for her son, as she attempted to do, perhaps the conflict could have been avoided or would have at least looked very different.

Salic law, which prohibited Isabella from inheriting the French crown even though she was the next in line by blood, is a code of laws that governs many aspects of civil and criminal life. Its best-known tenet is probably the part that pertains to women: "No portion of the inheritance shall come to a woman: but the whole inheritance of the land shall come to the male sex." Its roots stretch back to around 500 CE, when the laws were written down by the Franks. Their most famous ruler was Charlemagne, but he was not responsible for the codification of Salic law. From 500 CE on, various incarnations of the law existed and it was enforced to different degrees by different groups. A Merovingian king, for example, specifically divided his estate equally between his daughter and sons, despite the law. In France, it had been the law of the land since 1316, which meant Isabella could not inherit the crown, nor could she pass the inheritance to her male offspring, since one cannot bequeath a right one does not have.

Over the centuries, many arguments were employed to enforce the practice of male-only inheritance, from the merely misogynistic to the ridiculously illogical. Pierce Butler in *Women of Medieval France* attempts to parse an argument used by a French lawyer. The argument claims that (a) the Gospel of Matthew proclaims that lilies of the field are gloriously arrayed *but do not spin* (emphasis Butler's), (b) France is the Kingdom of the Lily due to the proliferation of the fleur-de-lis symbol on royal arms, so (c) the kingdom cannot be passed from a gloriously arrayed man, symbolized by a sword, to a less glorious woman, symbolized by a distaff, which is a tool used for spinning wool or flax. It seems that there is no limit to some men's creativity when coming up with reasons why women are not equal to men.

While Salic law was used to justify keeping women off the throne, noblewomen in the Middle Ages generally had more rights than did women of low birth. In some ways, class was the predominant divider of the period much more than gender was. A wealthy woman could wield some influence through her powerful husband, and sometimes she had more control over her household if her husband was absent. Besides access to money and material goods, wealthy women also typically had servants to assist them in domestic tasks such as cooking, sewing, and laundry. Power belonged only to the wealthy, so even if a poor woman had access to everything her husband had, she would not have expected to exert any social power since the husband had none to begin with. A peasant woman could expect to help her husband in his business, whether he was a farmer in the country or an artisan in town. Whatever his craft, his wife assisted him in his labors in addition to doing her own work of cooking, cleaning, child rearing, and other domestic tasks.

⚓⚓⚓

With all the disorder of this era, piracy naturally experienced an upswing in popularity. Highly opportunistic sailors knew that kingdoms would be too busy fighting one another to devote much effort to curbing piracy. Seafaring piracy during this era was greatly assisted by the fact that kingdoms did not have official navies. With political alliances shifting constantly and countries changing hands over and over, there were no unified forces that could band together to resist the pirate threat. Eventually, as the Middle Ages went on, groups such as the Hanseatic League—a group of guilds and cities based in present-day Germany—were able to come together to combat piracy. One of the Hanseatic League's contributions to maritime life was its overhaul of the design of a round-hulled, one-masted ship called a cog. These Hanseatic cogs had many practical features, such as a square-rigged sail and high sides, that would heavily influence the design of nearly all European sailing ships and warships in the centuries to come.

Besides the general piracy of the period, early forms of privateering occurred during this time as well. Privateering is the practice of pirating for someone else as an "official pirate" of that entity, usually a government. It required a license, or a letter of marque, bestowed by the entity (such as a king) onto the pirate. This made the illegal pirate into a legal privateer. With the letter of marque, the ship could attack merchant vessels that were enemies of the kingdom without suffering criminal punishment, as long as the raiders brought back a share of the treasure to the kingdom. Many rulers, notably Queen Elizabeth I, were fond of privateering because it allowed private citizens to do the bidding of the state without the state having to get its hands dirty. It was a decent way to earn a living, and it was extremely beneficial to the home nation, which was able to gain vast amounts of wealth for little effort. It's easy to see why privateering endured for so many centuries, although the term *privateer* was not used regularly until the eighteenth century.

Despite the monumental hardships that medieval women had to endure, some women pirates became famous during this period. Although they were women of noble birth and therefore suffered less than their poorer contemporaries, they still survived childbirth and medieval notions of health care to battle their way into history.

⚓⚓⚓

The War of Breton Succession, which took place at the beginning of the Hundred Years' War, is referred to by Klausmann, Meinzerin, and Kuhn as the "War of the Three Jeannes" due to the women at the center of the action: Jeanne de Montfort, Jeanne de Clisson, and Jeanne de Penthièvre. In particular, two of these Jeannes fought for their family's right to the throne—by land and by sea. These women proved themselves to be extraordinary fighters who fiercely defended what they felt was theirs. Their lives and legends serve as a bridge, connecting the Viking women who came before them with the Barbary corsairs who followed them.

To fully understand these women, a brief history of the conflict is necessary. Brittany, a province on the west coast of present-day France, was its own state during the Middle Ages, ruled by a duke. Parts of Brittany were loyal to the English while other parts swore allegiance to the French, but the majority of Bretons considered themselves Bretons first and foremost. Their culture, unlike English and French culture, was uniquely and healthily dosed with Celtic and pagan traditions as well as the more modern Christian ones. They were loyal to the Duke of Brittany over the kings of England and France; they would not be united with France until 1532. In short, the duchy was important to the Bretons, and the fight to figure out who had a rightful claim was something over which they were willing to wage a war. Both England and France were invested in the outcome, given that the Breton duke usually made alliances with one country or the other. As the Hundred Years' War started, both sides knew that Brittany could be a powerful ally in their struggle.

John III was Duke of Brittany in 1341 and died childless. Originally, he had named as his successor Jeanne (or Joan) de Penthièvre, his niece. Joan was married to a powerful nobleman, Charles de Blois, who was related to the French king, Philip VI. Unsurprisingly, the French backed Joan's (and Charles's) claim to the duchy. However, before John III died, he reconciled with his long-estranged stepfamily and named a new heir, his half brother John de Montfort. John was the English choice for the duchy. These two houses—House of Blois and House of Montfort—both felt that they had the right to the throne, and both were prepared to fight for it.

John de Montfort's biggest asset in this fight was his wife, Jeanne de Montfort. She is also known as Joanna of Flanders, due to her Flemish parentage (her brother was the Count of Flanders). She married John de Montfort in 1329, and the couple had two children together. Much of what is known about her originates from medieval French author Jean Froissart, whose *Chronicles* are important texts in medieval history. He had only good things to say about Jeanne, claiming that she had "the courage of a man and the heart of a lion." Other sources have said that her story may have inspired another famous Jeanne: Jeanne d'Arc.

Despite all of Froissart's coverage, there are still gaps in history's knowledge of Jeanne de Montfort. Froissart is happy to educate the reader on Montfort the soldier and warrior but is mum on the details of Montfort the woman. It is not certain, for example, what her relationship with her husband was like. Did she pursue the duchy so fervently out of love, or out of a desire for power? Although there is more historical documentation around de Montfort than there is for many of the other women pirates, there are still many things a reader might want to know. Froissart's records, although sympathetic to de Montfort, do leave out many things that would enrich the story.

When the duchy came up for grabs in 1341, de Montfort and his wife knew that the French would most likely side with the House of Blois, given that the French king was a cousin of Charles de Blois. They therefore decided to get a jump on the competition and start ruling right away as if John were already the duke. The de Montforts went to Nantes, the Breton capital, and gained a fair amount of fans among the people of Brittany. It seems that if there had been a popular vote, the de Montforts would have had the duchy sewn up. However, it was a matter to be decided not by the people but by the Court of Peers in Paris.

John de Montfort was summoned to Paris to appear before King Philip. On his way, he traveled to England to pay homage to the English king, Edward III. Once de Montfort arrived in Paris, Philip was unimpressed with the argument that he was nearest of kin to the late

Duke of Brittany and thus had the stronger claim. The French king called for the Peers to hear and judge both claims, and he forbade de Montfort from leaving Paris until after the hearing. John was no fool. He knew that there was little chance the Peers would vote for him and that if he stuck around, imprisonment or worse was likely, so he took off in the night and returned to Nantes and his wife.

And who was his rival, this Charles de Blois? Reports of his character are conflicting, with some of them declaring him a saint, while others paint him as a sadist and extremist. He was said to hear Mass several times a day, put pebbles in his shoes, and beat himself black and blue while praying. He was actually canonized as a saint, but his sainthood was revoked in the late 1300s and not restored until 1904. Despite his piety, he was known for his cruelty and brutality in battle. No matter his personal inclinations, his wife's connection to the late duke and his own connections to the French throne made him a powerful contender for the duchy.

In September 1341 the Peers declared the House of Blois as the rightful heirs to the duchy, as John de Montfort had predicted they would. De Blois marched to Nantes and captured Montfort, imprisoning him in a tower at the Louvre in Paris. De Blois probably thought that with his rival in prison, his claim to the throne was secure and his troubles were over. What he had not counted on was his rival's wife, who was not about to be put out of the fight just because her husband was in jail. No, Jeanne de Montfort would not back down from her family's claim, even if she had to do all the fighting by herself.

One can imagine the scene when Jeanne received the report that her husband had been captured. How would she have received the news? Perhaps she felt shocked at first and needed a moment to let the information sink in. This was not a scenario the couple had planned for. What was going to happen now? Would de Blois come for her and her children? Jeanne would have been aware of de Blois's reputation and could only imagine what awful fates he had planned for her and her young daughter and son.

Someone, either a friend and advisor or Jeanne herself, came up with the plan to claim the duchy in her son's name. As long as her male child was alive, the House of Montfort still had a chance. Jeanne had to finish the fight her husband had started if she had any hope of seeing him again.

According to Pierce Butler, Jeanne gathered her remaining loyal friends and soldiers and showed them her little boy, named John after his father. She exhorted the crowd, "Ah! sirs, be not cast down because of my lord, whom we have lost: he was but one man. See here my little child, who shall be, by the grace of God, his restorer." She promised them riches aplenty if they would remain with her. Jeanne took this show on the road, traveling from garrison to garrison and giving out cash and weapons wherever she went to ensure that everyone was happy, well paid, and above all, loyal to her family. After she had secured her troops, she took her family to the fortress of Hennebont. She would await de Blois's attack from there.

It is Jeanne's conduct during the siege of Hennebont, more than any other episode in her history, that endears her to readers. When de Blois and his men arrived, Jeanne herself donned protective gear and rode on horseback all over town, exhorting people to fight bravely with everything they had. She had a special command just for women—to tear up their skirts, pull up cobblestones from the streets, and chuck them at the attackers . . . and if they happened to have some spare pots of quicklime, pour that on them too. From a tall tower, she watched the enemy's camp. When de Blois's men had all ridden out into the fields to ready for the assault, leaving the camp empty except for a few young boys, she made her move. She herself rode out, along with about three hundred of her men, and set the whole camp on fire. Her attack destroyed much of the enemy's provisions, as well as their living quarters. As de Blois's men ran back from the fields, furious, Jeanne and her men snuck away to a nearby castle and sought shelter there until they could return home safely. This daring and effective plan by Jeanne earned her the nickname "La Flamme"—French for "the flame."

Being taken by surprise by this upstart woman enraged de Blois, and he redoubled his efforts to take Hennebont, but his band of men continued to suffer heavy losses every time they engaged with de Montfort's forces. It seems that, army for army, he was not going to capture this prospective duchess at Hennebont. He took a large portion of his men and set his sights on taking nearby Auray instead. The forces he left behind to torment Hennebont did a much better job than de Blois himself had done, and many of Jeanne's advisors urged her to surrender. She refused, insisting that the English forces she had sent for long ago would finally arrive and rescue them. Some accounts claim she prayed to the lords of Brittany that they stand by her and send English help within three days. Once she declared that England was coming, she would not budge despite constant pressure, and she remained posted at the window looking out to sea. On the second day, she spotted the English ships and cried out, "I see the succors of England coming." English forces had indeed come to offer backup, although they had been long delayed due to bad weather.

Despite Sir Walter Manny's arrival and assistance, Jeanne and her troops were losing ground against de Blois and his men. They held onto Hennebont but lost Auray, Dinan, and other cities. She knew that she would not last much longer at this rate and she had to appeal to a higher power—the king of England, Edward III. She sailed to England to make her plea in person.

Eventually, Edward granted her request, and she sailed back toward home with a fleet of ships commanded by Robert d'Artois. Before they could make it back to Brittany, they were attacked by Sir Louis of Spain, who had joined forces with de Blois. Off the English coast, the two fleets fought a fierce naval battle. Reports claim that Jeanne had a small sword that she bravely wielded and fought the Spanish forces hand to hand. After an intense day of fighting, a massive storm came up and blew all the ships in various directions, effectively ending the battle. The French and Spanish ships wound up near the English Channel while Jeanne and her forces landed near Vannes, a once-friendly city that they were able to take back with a small effort. Whether fate, God, or Jeanne's own superior sailing skills led the English ships to a safe harbor the world will never know. Somehow, Jeanne escaped a mighty naval battle after just one day of fighting and found herself not too far from home, which allowed her to safely return to Hennebont.

In 1345 Jeanne's husband, John, escaped from the Louvre and obtained a fighting force of his own from Edward III. He returned to Brittany but was killed in battle. It is unknown whether husband and wife ever saw each other again before his death. Now, Jeanne was truly on her own in the fight for the duchy. She continued to fight for nearly twenty years until 1364, when Charles de Blois was killed in the Battle of Auray. Jeanne de Penthièvre was forced to sign away her claim to the duchy and content herself with being Countess of Penthièvre. With the House of Blois out of the way, young John of Montfort was finally awarded the duchy and named the rightful Duke of Brittany, a title that he held until his death and then passed on to his son.

Some accounts say that Jeanne did not get to enjoy her son's reign, for which she had fought so long and hard. Several stories claim that Jeanne was mentally ill and confined in England to a castle with a caretaker, never to return to Brittany. She probably died in England around 1374. Some suggest that she was not in fact ill but simply a political prisoner of Edward III, who wanted to ensure that Brittany remained an English ally. Although mental illness can afflict anyone at any time of life, it does seem suspicious that a woman who led a successful military campaign for over twenty years and showed no previous signs of illness would suddenly succumb so dramatically that she would require constant care and confinement. It seems more likely that Edward, knowing what the woman was capable of, did not want to leave her (and Brittany's) loyalty to England to chance. If that is true, Jeanne de Montfort's story had a remarkably unhappy ending—betrayed by a man who used her for his own political ends under the guise of helping her. Hopefully she took comfort in the knowledge that at least her battle was not in vain. Even though she might not have returned to Brittany herself to see her son on the throne, she could die secure in the knowledge that the man she considered the rightful heir to the duchy, her son John, was ruling Brittany. Against impossible odds, this woman waged a war and came out on top. The Montforts remained in control of the duchy of Brittany until it ceased to exist when Brittany unified with France in 1547.

Despite her possibly ignominious end, Jeanne is fondly remembered in history. Philosopher David Hume called her "the most extraordinary woman of her age." She is considered the poster child for the fighting woman of France—despite the fact that she fought *against* the French— and is, as previously mentioned, said to have been an inspiration to Joan of Arc. But was she a pirate? Well, she was definitely a warrior, which is a good start. She also fought battles at sea, including her infamous battle against Sir Louis of Spain, even going so far as to engage in sword combat during the battle. Her true piratical pedigree, however, comes from her "theft" of the duchy from the House of Blois, the official pick of Paris. With her cunning maneuver at Hennebont (which recalls the cleverness of Artemisia's sacking of Latmus), she managed to steal the duchy from de Blois's grasp, and that makes her a pirate—not a textbook example of a perfect pirate, to be sure, but clearly worthy to stand up among her sisters in the pirate pantheon.

⚓⚓⚓

Another pirate woman from this era was also named Jeanne—Jeanne de Clisson. She is not as well documented in history as Jeanne de Montfort, although she does merit a brief mention in Gosse's *The History of Piracy*, which de Montfort does not. Her story is still very popular as a French folk legend, despite the fact that in the War of Breton Succession she, like Jeanne de Montfort, fought against the French crown. French historians apparently do not let trifles like allegiance get in the way of a good woman pirate hero story, and their history is all the richer for it.

Jeanne de Clisson was born Jeanne de Belleville in Belleville-sur-Vie, a castle and fortress on the western coast of France. Her parents were wealthy nobles, and she most likely enjoyed a bucolic childhood on the grounds of the castle, which she would eventually inherit. She was called "one of the most beautiful women of her day" by historian Richard Bentley. Her childhood did not last long, however, as she was married off at age twelve to a Breton nobleman. The couple had two children together before he died in 1326.

Jeanne remained a widow for four years before she took her second husband, Olivier de Clisson, a very wealthy nobleman with whom she had five children. By many accounts, the match was, if not exactly a love match, at least a successful mutual partnership. By age thirty, Jeanne had two husbands and seven children under her belt. What would she accomplish next?

When the War of Breton Succession came, Olivier chose to back his friend Charles de Blois in his claim to the duchy. It seems that he fought loyally for the House of Blois, but Charles de Blois became convinced that de Clisson was a traitor and had defected to the English side. Exactly why he believed this to be true is unclear. Some legends claim that when de Clisson was captured by the English at Vannes in 1342, the ransom demanded for his return was, to de Blois, suspiciously low. This led him to conclude that de Clisson had not fought as valiantly as he could have and was perhaps not as loyal to the House of Blois as he claimed to be. Other versions of the story say that de Clisson actually did switch sides, although these accounts are much rarer. In any case, de Blois was no longer certain that his old friend had his best interests at heart. This would not do. During a truce in the fighting in 1343, de Blois hatched a plan with the French king, Philip VI, to have him killed. Olivier and some other Breton lords were invited to France under the guise of a friendly tournament. When they arrived on French soil, however, de Clisson was arrested, carried off to Paris, and tried as a traitor to France. He was convicted and sentenced to death. After he was killed, his head was put on a pike and sent back to Brittany's capital, Nantes, to be displayed as a warning to other would-be defectors from the French cause.

King Philip's actions shocked the public. Olivier's trial did not present any public evidence of his guilt; it only claimed that he had confessed to being a traitor. Furthermore, displaying of a corpse was usually done only when the criminal was common or lower class. People felt that King Philip had gone too far and possibly murdered an innocent man. And nobody was madder than de Clisson's widow, Jeanne de Clisson.

When she found out that her husband had been tricked into going to France and then killed without cause, she sprang into action. If the French were no longer allies to her husband, then she would not support the French any longer. She severed all ties with the House of Blois and devoted her life to making the French pay for what they had done to her family. But first, some sources say, she took her sons to Nantes to see their father's head.

To a modern reader it seems a bit puzzling, to say the least, that Jeanne would choose to expose her young sons to such violence. No doubt the boys were already devastated by the news of their father's death; it seems redundant at best and cruel at worst to traumatize them further with the actual evidence of his murder. But Jeanne was not looking to shield her boys from pain. She knew now how hard and pitiless the world could be— even innocent men could be killed by kings. Jeanne chose to educate her boys on the harshness of life in order to light a fire of hate in them, twin fires to the one that now burned in her breast. In her world, there was no time for sorrow, only revenge.

After her trip to Nantes, Jeanne set about raising the money she would need to mount an army to terrorize the French. Much of her lands had been confiscated by King Philip due to her husband's "crime." She sold what she had left, including her jewels and furniture (and some accounts claim she sold her body as well) in order to outfit an army. Her goal was to kick the French out of Brittany completely. Stories of places she attacked are varied and lack detail, but nearly all accounts agree that whatever locations she did take, she took bloodily. She would massacre every occupant of a place save one or two, leaving them alive to report to France exactly who had committed the deed.

The path Jeanne chose after her husband's murder seems almost unthinkable, but it may have been preferable to the alternatives before her. Whether they were rich or poor, most medieval women could not be said to have pleasant lives. They had two role models: Eve, the fallen woman, and the Virgin Mary (the original manifestation of the Madonna/whore dichotomy). Doubtless many women felt themselves somewhere in between the two icons. They did not have access to education. Life expectancy was not long. Ironically, many scholars claim that after the Black Death of the mid-fourteenth century, the status of medieval women briefly went up due to the dearth of people left alive. Surviving women could receive better wages due to better-paying jobs being available and thus delay marriage, increasing their chances of survival. Childbirth was a specter that haunted all married women. An estimated 20 percent of all women in the Middle Ages died in childbirth, 5 percent during the birth itself and another 15 percent due to complications after labor. Things that today are minor issues were often fatal during this era. The presence of midwives—one of the only trades open only to women—helped to make birth safer, but a dizzying variety of complications could kill an expectant mother. Jeanne had survived childbirth numerous times; she might have felt that she had cheated death and could therefore slay Frenchmen at will, sending them to death in her place.

With her husband gone, Jeanne would have had the option to enter a convent. Nuns' lives were marginally easier than that of the average married woman. For one thing, there was some access to basic education in the convent. Nuns did not have to fear death in childbirth. They still participated in domestic labors, cooking and producing things for the convent in addition to the many hours spent studying and in prayer. Nuns *could* advance up the religious ranks—the only position with any upward mobility for women during the Middle Ages. The leader of a convent, an abbess, sometimes advised not just the nuns in her care but also the monks in an adjoining monastery. Other than being a queen, an abbess was probably the highest office a woman could obtain during the Middle Ages. But Jeanne was not interested in a sequestered religious lifestyle; she sought vengeance. And so to the sea she went, forging a new path.

Jeanne decided that she preferred naval fighting to land fighting. She was still going to make the French pay, but she would do so at sea. With her remaining cash, she sailed to England with two of her sons in order to assemble a small fleet of three ships. Where her other children were during this time is unknown. Some accounts say that on this journey, one of her sons died of exposure. She then allegedly sent the other surviving son to live in the English court with young John de Montfort, who would eventually become the new Duke of Brittany. These details about her sons are only occasionally present in Jeanne's legend. Whether she had her sons with her or not, and regardless of how many of them survived the journey, Jeanne soon had her fleet of ships, which was called the Black Fleet. These ships Jeanne painted black, and she dyed the sails blood red. She was not interested in subtlety or subterfuge. She wanted the people who saw her coming to know what fate awaited them. Her victims would not be taken by surprise, as her husband had been.

Jeanne and her Black Fleet sailed up and down the English Channel, preying on any French ship she could get her hands on. Her plan was the same as it was on land: murder everyone except a messenger or two. Soon, legends of her brutality spread all over Europe, and the "Lioness of Brittany" became a feared pirate. Some accounts claim that she was officially a privateer for England, but the English would have had to overlook her personal penchant for beheading every French nobleman she captured, since that was not exactly privateer protocol. Nevertheless, she may have kept the English forces stocked with supplies during various battles with the French. Her service to the English seems to have been an afterthought, though—much less important to her than the destruction of the French forces. It's unclear if she had any particular love for the House of Montfort, but her hatred of the House of Blois ran deep and was clearly to the de Montforts' benefit.

King Philip VI's death in 1350 did not put a dent in the Lioness's pirating. She continued to wreak havoc on French ships in the English Channel for another six years. Sources estimate that Jeanne's piratical career lasted for a total of thirteen years. Instead of seeing the war through and ensuring that her candidate won the duchy in the War of Breton Succession, she retired eight years before the conflict's conclusion and married an English deputy of King Edward III.

This action of hers, and the historical coverage of this action, leaves many questions unanswered. Why did she choose to marry a third time?

If she was so useful to the English forces, why didn't she help them finish the war? How did she meet Sir Walter Bentley, her new husband? Perhaps this action proves that she was not truly in the fight to back de Montfort but instead simply to cause damage to de Blois and King Philip. But then why not retire at Philip's death? Maybe she ran out of money to maintain her Black Fleet. Maybe the lonely widow fell passionately in love with the English lord. Maybe she just got tired of sailing. Maybe, after so many captures and beheadings, her lust for revenge was one day finally slaked. All that is certain is that she married Sir Walter and left her pirating days behind her. King Edward had bestowed on Sir Walter several castles and lands for his services to England. Some accounts claim that Sir Walter was given control of English territories and interests in Brittany. Stories differ on what properties were given to the Bentleys and when, but most legends agree that the couple eventually settled down back in France in Hennebont Castle, the very same castle that was such a pivotal part of Jeanne de Montfort's story. Jeanne de Clisson died a few years later, sometime around 1359.

⚓⚓⚓

While the Lioness of Brittany does not get as many pages in the history books as the other Jeannes, there are a few historical documents that authenticate her existence. A French court document from 1343 confirms the confiscation of Jeanne's lands due to her betrayal of France. That same year, an English document granted Jeanne an income. She is also mentioned as an English ally in documents relating to the 1347 truce between England and France. So while the legends of her Black Fleet may have grown more exaggerated with time, there is at least some proof that this woman once lived and changed sides in the War of Breton Succession.

Why is there less information on Jeanne de Clisson than there is on Jeanne de Montfort? Surely de Clisson's exploits are more interesting from a purely piratical perspective, but historically, sea conflicts are chronicled less faithfully than fighting that takes place on land, especially if there is a question of succession involved. It's true that de

Clisson was not a direct part of the succession claim, so maybe that is why she has been left out. French folklore has kept her legend alive all these centuries; otherwise she might have been only a footnote in history instead of the main attraction that she actually was.

Why did both of these women escape the moralizing revisionism that their pirate foremothers received? It is difficult to say with certainty, but national pride likely played a part. In a time of constantly shifting alliances, fledgling nations required heroes to rally behind, and they may have been desperate enough to accept a female as their standard-bearer. It is worth noting that while the stories are well known and can be verified in official documents, most of the details of these women's lives are confined to folklore. Official historians passed over these women, which has left their legends free to flourish in retelling by nonofficial people, many of them women. Whatever the reason, it is enjoyable to see such strong women celebrated instead of castigated.

It is worth mentioning Jeanne de Penthièvre, the third Jeanne in the War of Three Jeannes. Although she did not fight on the battlefield as the other two Jeannes did, she was a smart woman whose shrewd tactics kept her husband, Charles de Blois, in play for so long. After her husband's death, she protected the Bretons' right to keep the duchy out of French control, even allying with the de Montforts to ensure that Brittany remained free.

Once the Breton succession question was settled, the Hundred Years' War continued to rage on for nearly a century. Brittany's duchy was secure, but the question of to whom the French and English crowns belonged would cost many more lives and battles before it was answered, embroiling much of western Europe in the fight. Meanwhile, in the Mediterranean, another epic battle was already under way that would give rise to some of the most feared pirates. Pirates are always wrapped in legends, but these particular pirates were subject to some of the most outlandish yarns ever spun. Despite the fact that many of the stories were not true, ironically these tales told by their enemies actually increased the pirates' power and worked in their favor. These pirates were the Barbary corsairs.

4

A Cinderella Story Among the Corsairs

As the Hundred Years' War came to a close in Europe, the Ottoman sultanate rose from a kingdom into a massive empire. The Ottoman Empire was an Islamic state that at its height stretched from southeastern Europe to northern Africa. The Mediterranean basin and surrounding area was, during the sixteenth century, the center for a bitter religious conflict between Christians and Muslims as they battled for control of the area. For about 150 years, from 1500 to 1650, a group of pirates were a vital part of that conflict. These pirates terrorized the area, causing significant damage to the European and Christian powers. Their cruelty was legendary, and stories of their exploits spread across the world. They were known as the Barbary corsairs, some of the most feared pirates of all time. They ruled the Mediterranean Sea until the French acquisition of Algiers in 1830.

Barbary pirates had been around since the collapse of the Roman Empire, but they really picked up steam as a serious threat in the late fifteenth century. Corsair, a term used interchangeably with the word *pirate* but meant to designate the North African pirates, was a household name during this period. Children were told stories of the Barbary corsairs to frighten them into good behavior. If they weren't good, the

Barbary pirates would steal them away and they would never see home again.

While many parts of the Barbary legend are demonstrably false, this one—the kidnapping of people—is absolutely true. The Barbary pirates kidnapped and enslaved Christians regularly during their heyday. Estimates claim that somewhere between one hundred thousand and over a million Christians were captured and sold into slavery by the Barbary corsairs. People disappeared, and very few were ever ransomed and returned to their homes and families. This practice carried into the early period of the British Empire, although it was not often mentioned in the press or literature at that time. Corsairs captured new slaves not only at sea but also from coastal towns in Portugal, England, Spain, and France. The enslavement of Christians by Barbary pirates would soon be echoed by the enslavement of Africans by Christians, which would cause tension for the large numbers of people who protested the horrors of Barbary white slavery while still supporting black slavery.

In 1631 all the people of the Irish town of Baltimore were whisked away from their homes and into a life of slavery in North Africa. In the dead of night, a band of pirates led by the renegade Murat Reis sailed into the harbor with sackcloth-wrapped oars, silent as the grave. He and his men slipped through the streets, positioning themselves in front of every door in town. When the signal came, the pirates sprang into action, bellowing fiercely and smashing down doors. They dragged men, women, and children out of their beds and into the streets, killing those who resisted. In the end, over one hundred prisoners were taken by the pirates. These luckless souls were carried off to Algiers, where they were sold at auction. Only a few of the villagers lived to see Ireland again.

The Barbary pirates' reputation for cruelty could very well have been exaggerated. Given that Christian states were engaged in a holy war against Islamic ones, anti-Muslim bias would have been running high among Christian historians during this time. It was in the Christians' best interest to demonize their foes with extensive propaganda—such as conveniently forgetting that a large number of these Barbary corsairs were actually European-born Christians who switched sides in order to be able to take part in more lucrative pirating. However, the corsairs did not make an effort to counteract their reputation; on the contrary, they relished it. When they swarmed an enemy ship, the crew was often so terrified of the Barbary threat that they surrendered immediately. The legends of the Barbary menace made the corsair's work much easier— they did much of the corsair's work for him or her. Although most of the famous corsairs were men, there was a famous woman corsair who was also a queen: Sayyida al-Hurra, the last woman to legitimately claim the Islamic "al-Hurra" title.

Much of what is recorded about the Barbary corsairs is a tangled web of myth, legend, and fact. For example, the corsairs are often cited as the original source of the word *barbarian* due to their cruel ways. However, the real story is a bit more complicated. The Greek word *barbaros* simply meant "outsider" or "not a citizen." As time went on, it was applied to many different civilizations that were not Greek- or Roman-based, and the term ultimately came to be used for any alien culture. The term *Barbary Coast* is most often linked to the Berber ethnicity of the peoples of North Africa, but it is also said that the Romans called the people of North Africa barbarians due to their non-Roman heritage, regardless of whether or not they were actually Berber. The word *barbarian* is often used to mean simply "people of Barbary," so technically, the word does share a common root with Barbary pirates, but it predates the corsairs' existence. Many other stories involving the Barbary corsairs are similarly tantalizing mixes of fact and fiction.

So what did they actually do? What made them so effective? They are often compared to a later group of outlaws, the buccaneers, due to the many similarities between the two groups. Like the buccaneers, the corsairs were located in a relatively small area. The Barbary corsairs were based mainly out of three ports: Algiers, Tunis, and Tripoli, plus scores of smaller ones along the North African coasts. Both groups were also largely composed of privateers rather than true pirates. Corsairs were technically privateers because they attacked only enemies of the state. The local rulers, called beys, offered privateering licenses to the corsairs in exchange for 10 percent of their profits plus port fees. Buccaneers enjoyed a similar, although often less regimented, arrangement with the local government of their area. Their organizations were not identical, however. Buccaneers and corsairs differed in their methods, attire, and length of time they were active. Corsairs also had a larger hold of the public's imagination while they were in their prime, likely due to a combination of how successful they were and how feared they were.

Under their arrangement with the beys, the corsairs could attack any non-Muslim ships, particularly ships from countries with which the empire was at war, although this rule was not always strictly observed. This system was beneficial to both the beys and the corsairs; the corsairs were able to use the beys' bustling ports to sell and trade their stolen wares, from goods to slaves, as well as to repair their ships and weaponry and to obtain supplies and crew for their next trip. In return, the beys or the sultans of the empire could call on the corsairs to fight against the Christians in naval battles. Indeed, corsairs took part in all the major battles of the sixteenth century, beefing up the sultan's fleet and lending their sailing expertise, to the detriment of the Christian (mostly Spanish) adversaries.

The rulers of the area valued and encouraged the corsairs' privateering, and not just because of their fighting prowess. As Angus Konstam explains in *Piracy: The Complete History*, the geography of the area also played a role in the corsairs' popularity. The coast of North Africa sits right along the edge of the vast Sahara Desert, which makes farming and other land-based pursuits nearly impossible. Riches, if they were to come at all, would have to come from the sea. The corsairs were the backbone of port city economies and brought vast riches into the Ottoman Empire. The empire itself was headquartered in Istanbul, which was far enough away from the North African coast to allow the local rulers and corsairs enough latitude to conduct their business without interference. Except when the corsairs were needed in war, they were mostly left alone by the empire to do as they pleased.

Despite the corsairs' reputation among Europeans as aliens and foreigners, a surprisingly large number of them looked just like their European victims. Estimates claim that several thousand Barbary corsairs were from Europe. Many of those corsairs, including some of the most famous ones, were of Dutch descent. They learned sailing in Europe but made their way to the North African coast to take advantage of the ample privateering licenses that were being issued by the beys and sultans of the area. Converting to Islam seemed a small price to pay to become rich beyond one's wildest dreams. These converts were known as *renegados*, from which the word *renegade* developed. They were said to be among the most ruthless and despised of all the Barbary pirates. The fact that the Western world conveniently forgot to mention that some of the scariest "barbarians" were actually of their own stock is another instance of historical revisionism.

⚓⚓⚓

The corsairs' influence in the Mediterranean basin waned around 1650, yet they deserve a footnote in American history for their role in the development of the United States. Before the Declaration of Independence, the American colonies were protected from Barbary pirates under Britain's peace treaty with the corsairs. Countries that were not at peace with the corsairs either had to risk attack or pay tribute: an exorbitant protection fee. The fees were not regulated and could be changed at any time according to the whims of the rulers (as with the peace treaties). A Barbary ruler could declare a peace treaty over by chopping down the flag outside of a rival nation's embassy.

The United States, no longer under Britain's protection and thus forced to make their own deal with the corsairs, had paid two million dollars in tribute by the time President Thomas Jefferson took office. Jefferson decided that the fledgling nation needed to make a stand to prove that it was to be taken seriously and was capable of defending itself against foreign powers. In 1801 Jefferson declared war on Tripoli. This war spanned over a decade and two presidencies before America was finally safe from the Barbary corsair menace. It also led to the creation of the US Navy, which was built expressly to combat the corsairs. The battle with the corsairs, although often forgotten in modern US history classes and lectures, is nonetheless forever immortalized in American culture through the unlikely vehicle of the Marines' hymn: "From the halls of Montezuma to the shores of Tripoli."

The Barbary corsairs produced a series of notable pirates, none more famous than the brothers Barbarossa. These men are the subject of innumerable legends and stories due to their dominance of much of the Barbary Coast and the war they waged against Spain. Much is said about these men, but very little can be verified—right down to their names. Some sources claim they were called Barbarossa due to their red beards; the words for *red* and *beard* in Spanish and French sound similar to *barba* and *rosa*. However, some say that due to his kindness, brother Aruj was known as Baba Aruj, Baba being an honorific for "father." This term was then westernized to Barbarossa. No matter how they got their name, these men made a huge mark on the history of the region. Allegedly, they aided Sayyida al-Hurra as she was starting out.

From the mighty Barbarossa brothers to the lowliest corsairs, Barbary pirates used roughly the same technique to attack. They sailed up behind an enemy ship and boarded it from the rear. They used grappling hooks and other tools to climb aboard and engage the crew in hand-to-hand combat. They primarily attacked merchant ships, which were not staffed with trained combatants, so the battles were often short. Also, the corsairs' fearsome reputation generally prompted the crews to surrender right away to save their own lives. Those taken would be ransomed or sold into slavery back at port. Many of the people captured by the corsairs were slaves already: galley slaves who rowed the ships. This was another reason corsair ships were often victorious in battle—they had the advantage of being crewed entirely by free pirates, who were more motivated to defend their own ships.

The corsairs' favorite mode of attack was designed around the strengths and weaknesses of their ship. The corsair galley was a sharp departure from the warships of the period and most resembled the pirate ships of antiquity—bearing more than a passing resemblance to the monoreme ships used by the ancient Greeks. The new galleys had one or more masts but also had twenty to thirty oars, which required three to six rowers each. In the Mediterranean basin, the lack of a breeze meant a ship was often dead in the water without another means of propulsion. The return to galley ships allowed the corsairs to practically dance around their prey when the wind was down due to the power of the oarsmen.

Most of the Barbary corsairs used a modified galley design called a galliot. It was smaller and faster than a traditional galley, and this gave the pirates an even bigger advantage on their targets. A galliot had only one mast. Instead of twenty or thirty oars, galliots had twelve to twenty-four oars, which could be rowed by just two oarsmen each. Remember that in pirate galliots, the oarsmen would be freemen instead of slaves, who were the rowers of choice on nonpirate galleys. This was not an entirely altruistic decision—besides the increased fighting motivation, the small size of the ship demanded that everyone onboard was part of the boarding party for maximum impact. The corsairs did have a few larger galleys, but they were used for raiding, backup vessels, and as command ships. Sometimes, a tartan was used in corsair attacks, which was very similar to the galliot except it had two masts instead of one.

The galleys also had a specially built forecastle equipped both with forward-facing artillery and swivel guns. Weaponry was not the most desirable trait of the design, however, because for the corsairs, a firefight was to be avoided at all costs. A gun battle would damage both ships and lower the resale value of the captured ship, and therefore was financially unwise. The galley's lightness, which gave it maneuverability, also meant that it was weaker and more vulnerable in a head-to-head battle. Therefore, the boarding method was popular since it allowed the corsairs to use speed to their advantage without exposing their weaknesses to the enemy ships. The galley's design remained popular throughout the next few centuries and was used by pirates around the world, including, most likely, the pirate queen of the Mediterranean, Sayyida al-Hurra.

⚓⚓⚓

In 1492 Ferdinand and Isabella, Catholic monarchs of Spain, wrapped up a nearly eight-hundred-year conflict between Christians and Muslims over control of the Iberian Peninsula. This bloody battle, known as the

Reconquista, ended with Spain capturing Granada. Many thousands of Muslims found life under Christian rule intolerable and fled Spain, emigrating to northern Africa, which was more hospitable to Muslims. One of the innumerable families who made the trek south was the Banu Rashid, a powerful tribe of some wealth. One of the daughters of a Banu Rashid family, born around 1485, would never forget what exile felt like and the pain it caused her family. She would dedicate her life to making the Spanish pay for what they had done. Her real name has been lost, but she grew up to be called Sayyida al-Hurra, a name that means "the woman sovereign [who exercises] power."

Her childhood was spent in Chaouen, a city in present-day Morocco that housed a large refugee community at that time. Sayyida must have spent countless nights as a child listening to the adults discuss how much they hated the Spanish Christians and how they would do anything to get revenge. Plans to return to Spain were frequently made and sorties against the Spanish were carried out almost constantly. Many exiles were obsessed with the idea of, if not getting back home, at least hurting the Spanish. It makes sense that this group of angry refugees eventually made contact with the corsairs due to their shared agenda. As Sayyida grew up, she bided her time and waited for the opportunity to join the Barbary corsairs herself, which would not come for over twenty years.

As a child, Sayyida was promised to a man named Abu al-Hasan al-Mandri. Sources are not totally clear whether she married al-Mandri the father, who was some thirty years her senior, or al-Mandri II, the son. Regardless of which one she married, he encouraged or at least allowed her to get involved in his political affairs. Her husband was the ruler of nearby Tétouan, also a town in present-day Morocco a little over forty miles from Chaouen.

Even if her marriage was not a love match, it seems clear that Sayyida's husband at least respected her. She was allowed to rule with him and took part in his efforts to rebuild the city of Tétouan, which had been destroyed by the Castilians around 1400. The al-Mandris sent a delegation to the sultan of Morocco, Abu al-Abbas-Amhad ibn Muhammad of the Wattasid dynasty, and asked for his permission to resettle the town and defend it against attackers. This was possibly the first time Sayyida came in contact with the sultan, who would play a huge role in her life after her husband's death. Once the king agreed, the al-Mandris painstakingly restored Tétouan to its former glory and made it into a bustling metropolis, featuring a Great Mosque and narrow, mazelike streets to ward off invaders. Today, old town Tétouan is a UNESCO World Heritage Site.

Sayyida's husband died in 1515. Upon his death, she took his title for herself and proclaimed that she was now the sole ruler of Tétouan. This action set a precedent for many women pirates who would come after her, Cheng I Sao among them. A woman could rise to power by taking over for her husband after his death. Sayyida was officially confirmed as a prefect in Tétouan, but she was soon promoted to governor of the area, legitimately obtaining the title of al-Hurra, meaning "free and independent woman."

During the Ottoman Empire, all Islamic women's lives were ruled by sharia law, a moral and religious legal system considered the infallible law of God. It comes from religious prophecy instead of human lawmakers and governs all manner of topics, from conventional ones such as crime and trade to more personal ones such as diet, sexual congress, and bodily hygiene. Under sharia law, women must be veiled around men who are not their husbands or close relatives. However, during Sayyida's time, women under sharia law had more freedom than women under many Western legal systems. For example, traditional interpretations of sharia law said that Islamic women could divorce, keep their surnames after marriage, and handle their own financial affairs.

Political success was not enough for Sayyida. Now that she had a large amount of power, she decided to use it to make her enemies pay for what they had done to her family and her people. Nearly five hundred miles separated her from the Barbary corsair Khair-ed-din's headquarters in Algiers, but somehow the prefect of Tétouan made contact with the last and most famous Barbarossa brother and obtained some tips on the business of privateering. There are no details on how, when, and where the two met, but one imagines that the fearsome pirate was at first amused, then impressed with the woman from Tétouan. Sayyida began privateering and soon became the "undisputed leader of the pirates in the western Mediterranean," according to Fatima Mernissi in her book *The Forgotten Queens of Islam.*

Sayyida enters the historical record through the transaction logs of the Spanish and Portuguese authorities who dealt with her. She was the person who could get a hostage released or negotiate terms for trade. In Spanish and Portuguese documents, Sayyida is portrayed as a predominant power in the area. Spain and Portugal considered her not a nuisance but a legitimate naval power—a true rival. She is always listed only as "Sayyida al-Hurra"; her real name is never mentioned.

Sayyida ruled the western Mediterranean for twenty years. Although nobody knows for sure whether or not she ever actually sailed with the pirates whom she commanded, she was most definitely in charge and everybody knew it. Her corsair crews raided on land, took prisoners, and enslaved Christians. Corsair crews on the water plundered European ships. The money she obtained from her labors was poured back into Tétouan, which was now prosperous due to her work. Not just Sayyida but also many of the exiled families of Tétouan could feel that they had been paid back for the injustice they had suffered. Sayyida ensured that the Spanish knew the Moors of Granada had not forgotten how they had been treated.

Just before the end of Sayyida's reign, she decided to marry once again. In 1541 the widow of nearly thirty years set her sights high. She chose no less of a suitor than the sultan of Morocco himself: Abu al-Abbas Ahmad ibn Muhammad, ruler of the kingdom of Fez. Many years ago as a newlywed, she had appealed to him for help in rebuilding her city. Now the city he had helped her raise from the ashes was flourishing, and she was the ruler of not just the city but also half the Mediterranean Sea. The young woman seems to have made quite an impression on the sultan, and sources claim he was very fond of Sayyida.

He was so in love with (or under the sway of) his new bride-to-be that he consented to leave his capital city of Fez and travel all the way to Tétouan at her request so that their marriage could take place in her home. The approximately 170-mile journey was not particularly long, but it was a giant distance for a ruler to travel. According to *The Historical Dictionary of Morocco*, it was unprecedented for a sultan to leave his capital city to get married, and this was the only time in Moroccan history that it happened. After the marriage, Sayyida refused to leave Tétouan and continued ruling as before. One wonders why she deigned to remarry at all. Clearly she felt there was some value in it, otherwise she would not have done it, but it does not appear that she was interested in keeping house or even living in the same city as her new husband. Perhaps she felt that an alliance with the sultan would increase her own power.

What thoughts ran through her mind on her wedding day? Did she picture the frightened child she had been, forced to leave her home behind? She had traveled a long way, both literally and figuratively, from her childhood status as powerless refugee to the queen of an empire. When she began her journey, did she ever imagine she would end up here?

Sayyida's story does not mention whether her new husband had other wives or concubines, or who made up his harem—a concept misunderstood by the West since the first Western translation of *A Thousand and One Nights*. Completed in 1717, Antoine Galland's French translation of the stories popularized the titillating images of the captive slave girls of the harem, passive vessels that exist solely for male pleasure. The odalisque of Western art, lounging indolently in semi-undress and making eyes at the viewer, is a part of this same concept. Harems were viewed for many years as a prison for the sultan's women, where men could seek any pleasure.

This view was perpetuated by Western male travelers to the Ottoman Empire. Historian Patricia Ebrey says that "travelers' accounts invariably reveal as much about themselves as about those they describe," and it holds true in this case: men were never even allowed to enter the harems. They invented and extrapolated these sexual playgrounds from fantasy and gossip, and in the process created a myth that would endure for generations. It was not until Western women travelers gained access that a clear picture of life inside the harem began to emerge. The eyewitness accounts from women begin in the Victorian era, so they postdate Sayyida by quite a bit. However, it is the best information available. This knowledge turned the old ideas on their head, but the erotic image of dancing girls endures to this day.

Professor Leslie Peirce says that the term *harem* is "redolent of religious purity and honor," claiming the harem was more akin to a sacred space than a prison, a place where women could escape the coarse world of men. They existed in ordinary homes as well as palaces, and were essentially large rooms where women and the men of their immediate family were allowed to go. These multipurpose rooms were where women ate, entertained company, and sometimes slept, depending on the family. Victorian visitors describe them as sumptuously appointed, comfortable, and extremely pleasant.

Inside royal palaces, including the imperial harem, where the sultan of the Ottoman Empire lived, the same essential function remained, but all the elements were magnified to befit a sultan. According to the Koran, men could have up to four wives. Sultans often had four wives—but it was not common to officially marry these women until after the fifteenth century. When Süleyman the Magnificent actually married his companion Roxelana, it was a shocking break with tradition—but more on that in a bit. Besides the wives, in the legendary Topkapi Palace in present-day Istanbul, the sultan kept wives as well as concubines of various ranks in the harem. Inside the imperial harem were also the children of the sultan and their wet nurses; slave servants, who had no sexual contact with the sultan and served as domestic servants to the women; and the *valide* sultan, the sultan's mother. Every person in the harem had a specific place in the social order, and everyone knew exactly what her role was.

At the top of the harem was the valide sultan. She wielded absolute power inside the harem and often outside it as well. The valide sultan could rule as regent if her son was unable to rule, and many of them continued to rule even once their sons reached adulthood (albeit indirectly through influencing their sons). Her rooms were between the servant quarters and family quarters in order to keep an eye on everyone. She got the largest daily stipend of all of the women of the harem and managed large amounts of money. The valide sultan was in charge of some land grants and tax income, which she used to pay for her public works. History is full of schools, hospitals, mosques, and many other buildings that were constructed under the auspices of the valide sultan. These women could not rule directly, but they did their best within the existing system to exert power on the sultan and control the fate of their kingdom. In the harem, they lived "at the very heart of political life," according to Peirce.

Underneath the valide sultan were the wives, known as *kadin*. The sultan was bound by etiquette to visit his women in a strict order. The only reason a woman would lose her turn in line was if she was for some reason indisposed. Each woman, when she was brought into the palace, would be taken under the wing of a senior palace official. She would be given new clothes, sent to a "charm school" to learn social graces, and taught to read, so she could read the Koran. Girls who showed musical aptitude would be instructed in musical instruments to be able to perform for the sultan. Top performers would be selected as concubines for the sultan. Women of lesser talent might still be retained as an *ikbal*, a lower type of courtesan. If a girl was not chosen to be either, she would become a serving girl, but she could ask to be discharged after nine years of service, when she was usually married off to an upper-level official, complete with a dowry. One imagines a scaled-down version of this system in the Moroccan palace at Fez, but of course Sayyida was never a resident of that palace's harem. She preferred to stay in her own household, under nobody's authority but her own.

Sadly, her marriage did not protect her from what was to come just one year later; in fact, it may have accelerated her fate. In 1542, fifty years after her family fled Spain, Sayyida's thirty-year reign came to an end. She was deposed by someone—many sources believe it was a step-son of hers, one of the king's sons. Despite having been a beloved ruler and bringing prosperity to her subjects for over a quarter century, she had nobody to turn to in order to protect her claim to the throne. How did the people of Tétouan react to losing Sayyida? Were they devastated or secretly glad? There is no way to discover what the sentiment was in the area during that time. Sayyida's life is scarcely documented in general, but on this topic there is virtually nothing. Most sources note that she was deposed and nothing more.

⚓⚓⚓

Curiously, it seems that Sayyida's model of governing might have made its mark on her part of the world, even if her name did not. In Istanbul, Sultan Süleyman the Magnificent broke with two hundred years of Ottoman tradition and legally married one of his concubines, the woman who would come to be known as Hürrem Sultan, around 1534, during Sayyida's reign. Hürrem Sultan was the first woman to hold power in the sultanate of women. Known in the west as Roxelana, she was born in western Ukraine. She was allegedly a daughter of a priest and was kidnapped and sold to the sultan by Tatars. An ambassador to the sultan's court described her as "young but not beautiful, although graceful and petite." Hürrem worked her way up the concubine hierarchy, and eventually she and Sultan Süleyman fell deeply in love. While he was away fighting a campaign, they exchanged love letters, often in poem form, many of which survive today. Although Hürrem was the second concubine—the mother of the sultan's heir was ahead of her in line—she managed to uproot the first wife and her son, eventually securing her son as heir apparent. She was known as Haseki Sultan (sultan's chief wife), and she exerted considerable influence on him (and consequently the empire). It was said that she "had the bridle of the sultan's will in her hands." The sultan stopped visiting any of his other concubines for physical pleasures and remained monogamously devoted to Hürrem until her death.

Süleyman merged the harem (formerly housed elsewhere) and the rest of the palace, bringing women out of the private and into the political sphere. Wives and mothers of sultans thereafter were allowed to be by the sultans' sides and exert influence in their decisions and affairs.

Hürrem was instrumental in moving women closer to the center of power, yet she is often portrayed as a scheming shrew who bewitched the sultan. However, she was just protecting her son—just as Mahidevran, the first wife, attempted to do. Anxiety about Hürrem may stem from her dual role as mother of a prince and wife of a sultan. Before, women had been mothers first and concubines a distant second. Hürrem's legal marriage made her mother and wife. How could she possibly serve both men at the same time? It was an untenable position that turned the people against her. They simply could not understand why the sultan would break with tradition and legally marry her; they distrusted the amount of power she exerted over the sultan. Also, she was a disruption to the established powerful mother-son bond. Süleyman's own mother, Hafsa, did not enjoy the same amount of power after Hürrem joined the palace as she had before.

Hürrem died before the sultan, who was completely bereft. He was buried next to her in the magnificent mosque built to bury their young son, who died of smallpox. Their elder son, Selim II, succeeded his father on the throne. Selim II was a drunkard who pursued pleasure over affairs of state. His wife was also a part of the sultanate of women. Although his mother had had considerable say in the politics of the empire, his wife Nurbanu, born Cecilia in Venice before being kidnapped by a Barbarossa and given to the sultan at the age of twelve, controlled even more of the empire due to her husband's utter disinterest in ruling. She maintained extensive foreign correspondence, including with Catherine de Medici—who was herself the regent of King Henry III of France. Nurbanu, like Roxelana before her and the women who came after her, all but ruled the Ottoman Empire, despite having no official power. They were more like Western queens than concubines in terms of status and power.

These women were constantly opposed by male advisors to the sultan and had to be extraordinarily careful about how they wielded their power. They could not march off to war like men could; they had to be content with peaceful displays of power, such as charitable works and public buildings. Many mosques, schools, and other monuments were constructed by these shadow sultans. Although historians sometimes dismiss the sultanate of woman as an aberration, Peirce argues that it was an inevitable by-product of the gender politics of the time. Sayyida was certainly a part of the gender politics of the area.

Perhaps Sayyida's example showed Süleyman the Magnificent that women and politics could mix harmoniously, though no evidence has been discovered of a direct connection between her and the imperial sultan. However, it seems significant that as a powerful pirate woman rose in influence in Morocco, the imperial sultan saw fit to end a centuries-old ban and bring women into more power. The sultanate of women lasted for over a hundred years, so Sayyida's influence might have lasted much longer than her own reign did.

How does such a remarkable ruler, consort to the sultan of Morocco, disappear? After her deposition, there is no information on what happened to her. She was presumably stripped of her title, her throne, and her property. Perhaps she was absorbed into her husband's household. Perhaps she was executed. Perhaps she slipped away in the night and took refuge among the many families whom she had helped during her reign. One hopes that after all she had been through in her tumultuous career, she was afforded if not a happy, then at least a peaceful ending. However and whenever she died, she went to her grave secure in the knowledge that she had been a great ruler and had revitalized her new home city of Tétouan.

So why was Sayyida's name kept out of the record? Perhaps her successor made an effort to erase her, as the Vatican did to traditional pagan women goddesses. Maybe the society of her time could accept women having some equal rights to men but not surpassing them as leaders, and so it erased her contributions. Although her life is not well remembered, at least it was recorded at all by the people whom she opposed. It would have been a great loss if her life had fallen through the cracks of history entirely.

After Sayyida's disappearance, the heyday of the Barbary corsairs would last for another hundred years. But just as her reign was ending, a few hundred miles away in the Atlantic another pirate woman was born. Her story was also one of fighting her oppressors and bringing justice to her family, and she would also be called a pirate queen. Grace O'Malley was one of two pirate women who ruled the waves during the reign of another fierce queen: Elizabeth I.

5

The Virgin Queen and Her Pirates

I N HER BOOK *Pirate Queen: In Search of Grace O'Malley and Other Legendary Women of the Sea*, Barbara Sjoholm explains that "to be a pirate [as a woman] is to assert that whatever you fancy belongs to you." This maxim, written to describe sixteenth-century pirate Grace O'Malley, also applies to Grace's adversary: Queen Elizabeth I. Although she never sailed much farther from home than downriver from Greenwich, Elizabeth lived her life and ruled her country in a very piratical fashion, trusting herself above all others and expanding her empire by any means necessary—including dubiously legal ones. She condemned piracy publicly to appease Spain, but privately she supported a fleet of "sea dogs": pirates she employed to steal Spanish treasure, horn in on the slave market, and defend England from her enemies. Besides these sea dogs, Queen Elizabeth tangled with at least two women pirates—one for her and one against her. The English pirate loyal to the queen was Lady Mary Killigrew, and the Irish pirate who struck terror into English hearts was Grace O'Malley.

Elizabeth, one of England's most famous rulers, took a long and winding road to the throne. Daughter of King Henry VIII and the beheaded Anne Boleyn, she was declared illegitimate and removed from the line of succession due to the annulment of her parents' marriage. While her half sister, Mary Tudor, was on the throne, Elizabeth was imprisoned. As a Protestant, she was seen as a threat to Mary's Catholic rule. Mary, despite a famous false pregnancy (possibly an ovarian cyst or tumor, which could mimic the symptoms of pregnancy), died without producing an heir. This allowed Elizabeth back in line, and at age twenty-five, she was crowned Elizabeth I of England.

At the time of her coronation, the mighty British Empire was barely even a figment of her (or anyone's) imagination. After a series of short reigns, England was in desperate need of some stability. The country was broke, torn apart by religious discord, did not have any colonies at this time, and was desperately trying to avoid war with Spain, which it could not possibly afford or survive. In short, England was weak. The country needed a strong ruler to restock the treasury, improve defenses, and expand holdings. In Elizabeth I, England got just that.

Elizabeth understood the adage "You have to spend money to make money," and so she asked Parliament for it often. Her father had used Parliament to bring about the Protestant Reformation in England, but Elizabeth felt that she herself could make the reforms England needed without parliamentary help—if they would just give her the money she needed. According to historian and professor Johann Sommerville, kings and queens were expected to run the country with funds raised by customs and other day-to-day means. Wars and more extraordinary ventures were supposed to be paid for with taxes, which Parliament was hesitant to provide. During parliamentary sessions, they frequently discussed when Elizabeth might marry and produce an heir, much to Elizabeth's irritation. She felt it was not for the government to decide when and whom she should wed. As long as she remained single, she and Parliament remained at odds, which meant that Elizabeth had to find other ways of getting as much money as she wanted.

And who better to provide a little income for Queen Elizabeth than pirates? The shrewd queen understood that Spain regularly shipped tons of treasure from the New World back to Europe and that those slow Spanish galleons could be taken for England's gain. She enlisted the help of a group of expert sailors—privateers—with their own ships to steal Spanish treasure.

Elizabeth's privateers were called her sea dogs. These men gave her the cash to improve England. Their constant attacks on Spain and Spanish treasure ships kept Spain on the defensive and pushed back their eventual attack on England, buying Elizabeth time to fortify her defenses. By some estimates, the sea dogs' interference delayed the Spanish invasion by twenty years. Perhaps their greatest achievement, however, was their instrumental role in the 1588 defeat of the Spanish Armada, which is called the greatest English naval victory ever.

King Philip II of Spain, a Catholic monarch, was weary of Protestant England's attacks on Spain's commerce and was concerned about England's support of the Dutch rebels in the Spanish Netherlands. He planned to conquer England to establish Catholic supremacy and take out an enemy that could threaten his own power. Philip amassed a huge fleet of 130 ships, which included 2,500 guns, 8,000 sailors, and nearly 20,000 soldiers. The idea was to take the English Channel and march an army into England by way of Flanders. The English fleet (thanks to the privateers) was better armed and faster than the Spanish fleet, but Spain's infantry was vastly superior. Philip planned to board the English ships and engage them in hand-to-hand combat if necessary. He was confident that England would be defeated.

On July 21, 1588, the Invincible Armada sailed in range of the English's long-range cannons. For the next week, Spain advanced on England but took serious losses from the English bombardment. By the time they arrived in Calais on July 27, the Spanish knew they would not win control of the channel. Another plan had to be hatched.

While Spain was regrouping, the English sent flaming ships into the now-crowded Calais harbor just after midnight, forcing the Spanish to scuttle all plans other than a hasty escape. The armada broke formation and retreated to Gravelines, a small Flemish port in the Spanish Netherlands. England followed them and fought the Battle of Gravelines, a decisive victory for England that sent the defeated Spanish Armada limping home to Spain around Scotland and Ireland. The return voyage was rough, and many more men and ships were lost during the journey. By the time the remnants of the armada made it back to Spain, about half the fleet and some fifteen thousand men had been lost. This astonishing victory for England established Elizabeth as a monarch to be reckoned with and put England on the map as a rising world power to watch.

How did she pull it off? The English victory was due partly to a key participant in the Battle of Gravelines: Sir Francis Drake, one of Queen Elizabeth's most famous sea dogs. He was a cousin of another sea dog, Sir John Hawkins, who got him into the business. Drake's fame would eventually surpass Hawkins's, though, as he rose from his sea dog beginnings to become the first man to circumnavigate the world. Drake was initially a slave trader, but after an attack by Spaniards in present-day Mexico, he became devoted to Spanish destruction. He carried out a successful raid on the Spanish stronghold Nombre de Dios, and he took many Spanish treasure ships, including the massive prize ship *Señora de la Concepción*, which earned him his knighthood from Queen Elizabeth. He will always be fondly remembered in England, but in Spain he was called "El Dragón." His work in the defeat of the Spanish Armada in 1588, as well as his navigational success, paint him as an English war hero, but it must be remembered that he got his start as one of Queen Elizabeth's pet pirates.

Like Drake, Sir John Hawkins began as a sailor who decided to make his fortune in the slave trade. Hawkins has the dubious honor of being considered the first Englishman to make a profitable triangular trade run. The triangle trade was, as the name implies, a three-stop route: a ship picked up slaves in Africa, traded the slaves in the New World for goods, and then returned to Europe to sell the goods for money. Sir John made a tidy profit for England and his investors with his slave trading, which made Queen Elizabeth very happy. In the eighteenth century, triangle trade would contribute to the rise of piracy in the Caribbean and lead to piracy's Golden Age, so in a way Hawkins is the grandfather of the Golden Age of piracy.

Besides achieving slaving success, Hawkins was also a master shipbuilder. He joined the navy board in 1578, ten years before the defeat of the Spanish Armada at Gravelines, and made improvements in ship design that helped launch England as a world power. Before this time, naval battles were fought by ships ramming one another, with the victor boarding the loser's ship and continuing to fight hand to hand. Galleons were designed to prevail in these types of fights, as they were short and wide with castle-like structures at the fore and aft. They were slow and hard to maneuver, but speed and agility were not high priorities in a ramming battle.

Hawkins saw that, with the advent of long-range cannons, this mode of fighting would not last long. He made changes to the galleon's design to give England's ships the advantage in long-range artillery battles. He lowered the fore and aft castles, which made the ship more stable, and he lengthened and narrowed the hulls, which allowed the cannons to have maximum impact and made the ships much faster and easier to maneuver. Without his foresight and skill, the Battle of Gravelines might have ended differently. While Elizabeth must have been sorry to lose Hawkins as a sea dog, he served her even better as a shipbuilder and navy administrator. She knighted him in 1588.

Besides Queen Elizabeth's most famous and successful sea dogs, there were many other pirates in her employ, some of whom were women. Officially, she could not endorse piracy, and she passed several laws that made it harder to be a pirate, but privately she depended on their financial support. One family, the Killigrews, made pirating a family business, and not one but two women were involved. Lady Elizabeth and Lady Mary Killigrew, mother-in-law and daughter-in-law, were part of a pirate operation that ran for many years out of Cornwall during the 1500s.

Confusion exists about which woman was responsible for what piratical act given the fact that both women had the surname Killigrew by marriage. Many sources combine both women into one. It appears that the mother-in-law was the lesser pirate of the two, while the daughter-in-law was responsible for most of the more legendary acts in the stories. Elizabeth Killigrew, née Trewinnard, was Sir John Killigrew IV's mother. Sir John was the vice admiral of Cornwall, a blood relative of Queen Elizabeth's minister William Cecil, Lord Burleigh, and a pirate. Philip Gosse, author of *The History of Piracy*, calls the family a "veritable oligarchy of corsair capitalists." They did not often go out on pirate raids themselves, but they ran every other aspect of the business. Need a ship? Talk to the Killigrews. Have an official who needs to be bribed? Killigrews can help you with that. Payment dispute with the crew? Killigrews to the rescue. From their home at Arwenack House, the family ensured that stolen goods were properly assessed (with the crown getting its share, of course) and that the lucrative business of pirating for the queen went smoothly. Their illustrious pedigree and fine house made an excellent front for their shady dealings—nobody suspected that the sweet lady and noble lord were notorious outlaws.

Mary Wolverston, daughter of "gentleman pirate" Philip Wolverston, married Sir John Killigrew IV after the death of her first husband. There are no details on how the pair met, or how she made the nearly four-hundred-mile journey from her childhood home in Suffolk to coastal Cornwall. It seems possible that they met through Mary's father's piratical dealings. The couple had five children together.

Given that Sir John was the vice admiral of Cornwall, as well as the royal governor of Pendennis Castle (a nearby fortress built by Henry VIII), he had many responsibilities. According to some sources, Mary used this fact to her advantage and went on some pirate forays while her husband was away. While Sir John appreciated the business aspects of pirating, he did not feel the need to be personally involved. His wife preferred a more hands-on approach and enjoyed going out on raids. The couple hid the stolen goods in their home and paid handsome bribes to make sure officials looked the other way. Pirates who worked for the Killigrews knew they would be looked after by the family, occasionally even sharing meals that were served by the Killigrew women in the main house. When a pirate had an official ship on his tail, he knew to sail right to Arwenack House, where Sir John would row out to the official and offer him a fine hunting trip on land for a few days, courtesy of the Killigrews. The official was satisfied, and the pirate could unload his cargo in safety once the law had moved on. The system operated smoothly, and everyone got what they wanted . . . especially the Killigrew family.

With so many officials in their pockets, the Killigrews got away with some rather egregious behavior. Eventually, they grew so bold that their exploits could not go unpunished. Interestingly enough, it was allegedly an act of Lady Mary's that brought the law down on them at last.

In 1582 or 1583, depending on the source, a Hanseatic ship sailed into the Falmouth harbor right in front of Arwenack House. (The Hanseatic League was a confederation of towns that stretched from the North Sea to the Baltic Sea during the thirteenth to seventeenth centuries.) Due to foul weather, the vessel was forced to drop anchor and send two men ashore to obtain shelter for the crew to weather the storm. These two men, named Philip de Orozo and Juan de Charis in some versions of the story, explained their situation to the kindly lady of the house at Arwenack, who served them tea in front of a cozy fireplace. She explained to them that the ship would be safe in the harbor until the storm blew over and that the crew ought to ride out the storm at a guest house in nearby Penryn. The gentlemen, reassured by the woman and the knowledge that the Hanseatic League and England were at peace, took her up on her offer.

As soon as they were out the door, Lady Mary checked out the ship and decided she wanted it for herself. Nearly sixty years old at this point, she was still young enough for an adventurous caper. She gathered a crew including two of her household servants and sailed out to the ship in the night, muffling their oars with cloth. They climbed aboard the ship, murdered the remaining crew, and loaded the treasure into the boats they had sailed out on. A few of the Killigrew pirates took control of the Hanseatic ship and sailed away with it—to Ireland, according to some sources. When de Orozo and de Charis returned after the skies cleared, only seagulls marked the spot where their 144-ton ship had been.

The furious men registered their complaint with the Commission for Piracy in Cornwall, which was run by Lady Mary's son. Unsurprisingly, the commission was unable to find the culprit. Still upset and unwilling to let it go, de Orozo and de Charis pursued their claim to the highest level in London, where it eventually arrived on the desk of Queen Elizabeth herself. The queen was now in a pickle. She could not ignore the overwhelming evidence (and that Mary's own son had presided over the previous trial) without looking like a fool and possibly provoking hostilities with the Hanseatic League, but she did not want to lose the Killigrews as allies. Could she balance the two interests?

Lady Mary and her two household servants were put on trial for piracy. They were all found guilty and sentenced to death. Lady Mary, however, was given a reprieve at the last minute. Some sources say that her wealthy and well-connected husband secured her release, but the most popular theory is that Queen Elizabeth pardoned her. If the queen did issue the pardon, she seems to have done so in grateful recognition for the Killigrews' pirating services in the past and a hope that Lady Mary would remain available for the queen's needs in the future. After all, Elizabeth seemed smart enough to know not to bite the hand that fed her.

Lady Mary's pardon was not unexpected, all things considered, but another female pirate—this time on the enemy side—was also a recipient of a pardon from good Queen Bess. She is a legendary figure in Ireland, celebrated in song and story but nearly forgotten by history. If not for the English records of her deeds, it would be nearly impossible to authenticate her existence. Her name was Gráinne Ní Mháille, and she was the pirate queen of Ireland.

She is a known pirate, but her deeds were documented mostly through legends. Stories abound about her life, particularly about her childhood. She was born into a family of seafaring chieftains, the O'Malleys, to Dudara and Margaret O'Malley, around 1530. She was most likely born on the mainland in County Mayo but probably spent much of her childhood on Clare Island in Clew Bay, where her family had a castle. The O'Malleys were a wealthy fishing clan who also occasionally did some raiding and unauthorized taxing on the side. From a young age, Gráinne—anglicized to Grace—showed the desire and aptitude to follow her father out to sea.

In some stories, Grace has a brother who has no interest in sailing, but in other versions he is not mentioned. No matter how many siblings Grace had, it was unheard of for a girl to follow in her father's footsteps instead of her mother's. Although pre-Christian Ireland gave women a fair amount of freedom and power, Christianity had stamped out that early equality and ensured that women were kept at home. At most other times in Irish history, Grace would have been confined to home and hearth.

Luckily for Grace, she was born in the sixteenth century. At this time, Ireland was still ruled by chieftains and warring clans instead of a central government. The political situation had been unchanged for thousands of years, but modernization, in the form of the Renaissance on mainland Europe, was barreling on full steam ahead, and Ireland's provincial ways stood no chance against progress. The stripping of Ireland's identity by the English provided Grace the opportunity to step into the disintegrating power structure and claim a large chunk of power for herself.

During any century, she would have needed to be a formidable sailor to survive the dangerous waters off the Irish coast, with enough grit and determination to convince her father she was strong enough to take on the seafaring life. To go to sea was no task for the weakhearted, but young Grace proved her mettle many times as a girl, according to legend. One story tells of a band of eagles that was terrorizing livestock on O'Malley land. Grace, barely taller than the eagles, attacked the birds, killing most of them and scaring the rest away. She did not escape this battle unscathed, though; an eagle clawed at her forehead, leaving large scars she would bear for the rest of her life.

Another tale explains that her parents told her she was not allowed to go to sea because she was a girl. Undaunted, Grace chopped off all her hair, disguised herself as a boy, and joined her father's crew nevertheless. It seems unlikely that her father would not recognize his own daughter, even with short hair, but this story's popularity remains high. One of the many names by which Grace is known is Granuaile, which roughly translates to "bald Grace."

A third legend from her childhood takes place after she was already a member of her father's crew. During an attack by the English on their ship, Grace saw that her father was in trouble. She disobeyed his order to stay belowdecks and dashed into the middle of the fray. She leaped onto the back of her father's attacker and beat him until he relented. She not only survived that attack but saved her father's life as well.

Despite her passion for the sea, she was still the daughter of a chieftain, and she had duties to fulfill on land. At age sixteen, she was married in a politically advantageous match to Donal O'Flaherty, heir to the chieftain of a powerful neighboring clan. The O'Flahertys were a rowdy bunch, so feared by ordinary folk that it was common to hear this refrain in Galway churches: "From the ferocious O'Flahertys the Good Lord deliver us." Grace, with her fierce spirit, was probably not intimidated by her husband's wild nature. She bore him three children, two sons and a daughter.

Donal's nickname was "Donal of the Battles," which seems apt because he loved fighting. While he was waging battles and wasting resources, the people of his clan were starving. Desperate, they appealed to his wife, Grace, for help in feeding their families. Legally, as a woman she could not usurp her husband's role as chieftain, but the clan was all too happy to acknowledge her as the leader in spirit if not in name as long as she saved their children from starvation.

Eventually Grace and Donal might have fought over her assumption of his leadership role, but he was killed before the issue could come to a head. A story details how Donal led his men into battle for a castle that had once been his own but had since been taken over by an enemy clan. This castle, called Cock's Castle, was an island fortress. When Donal was killed in battle, Grace rallied her late husband's troops and staged a retaliatory attack on the castle, retaking it for the O'Flahertys, which Donal had been unable to do. She fought with such bravery and ferocity that the fortress was unofficially rechristened "Hen's Castle."

Despite her clear, demonstrated ability to lead her husband's clan in both battle and peacetime, Irish law prohibited her from ascending to the chieftain position in name. A cousin of Donal's was chosen to replace him. Grace was not going to sink into the role of meek widow when she had been so good at being chieftain, so she decided she was through with the O'Flaherty clan *and* taking orders from others. From now on,

Grace would be ruled by no one but herself. She returned home to Clare Island, but she did not go alone. A group of O'Flaherty men who were loyal to her wanted to continue serving under her rather than Donal's replacement, and they followed her back to Clew Bay. Once she was safely back at home, she gathered some more men, ultimately amassing a crew of around two hundred, took possession of a few of her father's ships, and launched her career as a pirate.

Grace was quite successful in a very short time, due to her excellent sailing skills and her unmatched knowledge of the Irish coast. She sailed in Irish galley ships, which were controlled by both oars and a single sail. Grace was said to have used an Irish *birlinn*, which resembled a Viking longship in construction. Such ships were highly maneuverable and fast when rowed, which gave them an advantage in the plenteous bays and islands of western Ireland. Commonly, these ships had eight to twelve oars, but Grace was rumored to have at least one ship with thirty oars. Like many pirates both before and after her, she was able to use geography to both hide from her victims and escape them after she'd taken what she wanted, be it silk, wine, or silver. English, Scottish, and other European ships had no hope of following her into the maze of small islands and coves along the coast. Maps did not cover Grace's Ireland. To stop her, someone would have to be able to find her. For a while, nobody could.

Eventually, strategic pursuits caused Grace to marry a second time. The man she chose was Richard Bourke (also called Burke), a Connacht chieftain who was in line for the Mac Williamship, the most powerful ruling office in the area. He owned a large fleet of trading vessels and, even more important, Rockfleet Castle. This fortress was better situated to shelter her fleet and crews than her own home base of Clare Island. According to most sources, Grace set out to marry Richard for "one year certain," an odd convention left over from Brehon law. The ancient native civil law code of Ireland, Brehon law was popular in the Middle Ages and on its way out by Grace's time, with large chunks of it being outlawed during the Tudor conquest of Ireland. Under this law, during the first year of marriage, either party could withdraw if it wished and the marriage would be considered officially annulled. Legend has it that Grace waited until she had sufficient control of the castle and then coaxed Richard to go out. She locked the castle gate and shouted out from the battlements as he rode home, "Richard Bourke, I dismiss you!" which was enough to end their marriage. However, the pair continued to present themselves as man and wife and worked together on piratical ventures after this, which suggests that Grace may have kicked Richard out but eventually took him back and did not formally end their marriage. Grace and Richard had a son together, Tibbott-ne-long.

When an English representative visited the western Irish coast in 1576, Grace pledged her services to him, saying that her husband would do essentially whatever she told him to do, which prompted the visitor to proclaim that Grace was "a notorious woman in all the coasts of Ireland." Why she chose to offer herself to the English when she had been devoted to stealing from them is curious. Nonetheless, Sir Henry Sidney knighted Richard before returning home, making Grace Lady Bourke.

Another popular legend about Grace's bravery comes from this period. She was sailing with Richard and her crew when she gave birth to her last son, whom she named Tibbott-ne-long (Theobald or "Toby of the Ships"). The day after he was born, their ship was attacked by the ferocious Algerian corsairs. Her men were unable to hold them off, so Grace, who was resting belowdecks, was summoned. According to the story, she cursed, "May you be seven times worse in one year, seeing you can't manage for even one day without me," and ran up to join the battle. Her disheveled appearance so alarmed the corsairs that she turned the tide of the battle and fought off the enemy. Presumably she returned to her bedroom afterward, grumbling all the while and hanging a Do Not Disturb sign on her door.

In 1577 she was captured for the first time by the Earl of Desmond while raiding his land. She was sent to Dublin Castle, where she was jailed for eighteen months. She was eventually released as a bargaining chip to quell her husband's rebellion, but after her release both Richard and Grace remained as piratical as ever.

The fortuitous timing and location of Grace's birth was a gift that had allowed her to rise to power, but that gift came with an expiration date, and since her birth, the clock had been ticking. Her luck ran out when Queen Elizabeth sent a new governor to Ireland, Richard Bingham, in 1583—the same year Grace's second husband, Richard Bourke, died.

Queen Elizabeth's father, Henry VIII, had first had the idea of making Ireland an English colony, and Elizabeth was determined to make her father's dream a reality. Bingham, cunning and ruthless, was a part of the plan to beat the chieftains into submissive English subjects. He particularly hated Grace and the freewheeling Irish spirit for which she stood. Grace apparently returned the sentiment, conducting three rebellion plots against him before she was captured by Bingham. He was only too happy to hang her, but she was saved at the last minute by a Mayo chieftain who traded some hostages in exchange for her life, a testament to how much she was respected by the chieftains in the area. But Bingham would not be denied revenge on Grace. He confiscated her cattle and horse herds and kidnapped two of her sons: Owen O'Flaherty from her first marriage and Tibbott-ne-long from her second. Owen died in Bingham's custody—some accounts say that he was murdered by Bingham's men. Grace knew that this time there would be no last-minute escape. The time had come for her to appeal to the highest power she could think of—a fellow queen.

In 1593 Grace sent a letter directly to Queen Elizabeth, requesting that her son Tibbott be released. She did not attempt to hide her piratical past, but she did try to paint it in a sympathetic light, claiming that circumstances forced her to take arms to maintain her family and her people. Grace asked that Tibbott and her other remaining son, Murrough, be able to hold their lands under English rather than Irish law. This was a savvy move designed to protect them against the change she knew was coming. Claims under Irish law would be nearly worthless once England's capture of Ireland was complete. If Elizabeth would grant this, Grace would devote her life to sailing against Queen Elizabeth's enemies, answering only to the queen herself, which conveniently cut

Bingham out of the equation. She sent this missive to England, then waited for a reply.

Queen Elizabeth was intrigued by this pirate queen who had appealed to her so boldly, despite her obvious past acts against England. She sent a list of eighteen interrogatories to Grace, which the pirate queen answered shrewdly. Grace offered the least objectionable parts of her life and career to Queen Elizabeth and painted a pretty picture of a smart and remarkable woman, much like the Queen of England herself. Meanwhile, Bingham upped the stakes and charged Tibbott with treason. If he were tried, he would almost certainly be hanged. Grace had already lost one son to Bingham and would not lose another. She could wait no longer, and in July 1593 she set sail to England carrying the answers to the interrogatories, determined to meet with Queen Elizabeth in person. This was an extremely bold move—especially for a well-known pirate. England's ports were adorned with the rotting carcasses of hanged criminals, including pirates. If she went to England, Grace knew she might not come back alive. But her love for Tibbott (and her fleet) was stronger than her love of her own safety. She would speak to the Queen and bring her son home, or die trying.

Against Bingham's wishes, the Queen granted Grace an audience in the fall of 1593. The exact details of what transpired when queen met queen are lost forever to history. Legends abound regarding what each woman wore, who was taller than whom, and what happened when a courtier offered Grace a fancy lace handkerchief. (The story goes that Grace wiped her nose with it and then tossed it in the fire, to the horror of the lady. Grace explained that in Ireland, trash was trash despite the value of the piece of cloth.) A woodcut of the two queens is thought to possibly depict their meeting, but only the two women present know for sure what happened. Many sources claim that the conversation took place in Latin since Grace spoke no English and Elizabeth spoke no Irish, but it is clear from her letters that Grace did in fact speak English, so they may well have spoken English at the meeting. Grace's boldness and Elizabeth's unique sense of humor must have made for a lively discussion.

Whatever these two women—whose lives were starkly different but also fundamentally the same—discussed, Grace was allowed to return home and her son Tibbott was freed. She was also allowed to resume her pirating, this time with Queen Elizabeth's blessing. Bingham was instructed to provide Grace with some kind of pension to maintain her in her old age, much to his outrage. He tried to protest and outright disobeyed the Queen's orders by posting troops on Grace's lands and ordering her to feed them, but he was eventually recalled back to England in disgrace. These two women who had made their way to the top of the man's world and become leaders of their people were able to come together and, for a time, set their world right.

The meeting with Queen Elizabeth—and her victory for her son—is the dramatic climax of Grace's story. She returned home and went right back to pirating, even fighting an English warship. However, her eye was always on her own legacy and the legacy of her son, and so when Tibbott was passed over for the Mac Williamship, Grace hung up her Irish flag and installed Tibbott in command of her ships, instructing him to sail for Her Majesty. During the Battle of Kinsale, the final battle of the Nine Years' War, which ensured England's conquest of Ireland, Tibbott fought on the English side. In 1603 Tibbott was knighted. Eventually he would become the Viscount Mayo. Also in 1603, Grace died of old age, at home in Rockfleet Castle. Queen Elizabeth, coincidentally, died that same year. Grace is said to be buried on Clare Island, at an abbey beside her beloved sea.

This tidbit about Tibbott's defection is perhaps part of why most Irish historians do not fondly remember, and sometimes go so far as to ignore, Grace O'Malley. Although she did sail against the English for most of her career, when it was convenient to do so she changed her allegiance. She put her family first and would do anything to ensure their safety, even betray an old alliance. She was not a woman who fit neatly into a mold of a heroine or patriot. Grace O'Malley was loyal, first and foremost, to her own self and her own freedom, like Jeanne de Clisson before her, another woman who looms larger in folklore than in official history. The inability to easily categorize Grace leaves a sour taste in many Irish historians' mouths.

Yet despite her lack of coverage in conventional historical channels, something about her life burns brightly enough that her legends have endured for so long. Perhaps it is due to her Irish heritage: Ireland is a land of poets and balladeers, and they would be loath to let such a tempting subject slip away uncelebrated in song and story. That might explain Grace's fame compared to that of the English Killigrews. It is true that the Killigrew women worked more behind the scenes than in the spotlight, but their presence in pirate lore is tiny next to Grace's.

That fact also might be due to the Killigrews' lack of a diligent biographer. More official information has come to light about Grace O'Malley in large part due to the tireless scholarly work of Anne Chambers and her seminal book about Grace, *Granuaile*. With a sympathetic advocate to tell her story, how could Grace fail to attract some notoriety? In the past few decades, a number of plays about Grace have been performed all over the world, and there is even a Granuaile Heritage Center in County Mayo. Interest in this pirate's life has never been higher. Her legend continues to inspire women today, just as it must have inspired the pirate women who came after her, during piracy's most infamous and celebrated epoch: the Golden Age.

6

The Golden Age

HE JOLLY ROGER. The fearsome, long-bearded pirate. The sun-soaked days and balmy Caribbean nights. Many of the images that have become synonymous with the word *pirate* originate in the Golden Age of piracy. This era spawned more legendary pirates and epic stories than almost all the other eras combined. Ask people to share a fact about piracy and, if they know one, chances are it will pertain to the Golden Age.

For something talked about so often, the Golden Age of piracy is surprisingly difficult to define. Just placing a time limit on the Golden Age is tricky. Some historians clock it from the 1650s to the 1730s, while others claim only a fraction of that time. Professor Marcus Rediker uses a framework for the Golden Age as 1716 to 1726—a mere ten years—and historian Angus Konstam provides one of the shortest definitions: eight years, 1714 to 1722. Where the line gets drawn depends on a number of factors: whether the buccaneer period is included, which execution actually marks the last great pirate to be hanged, and so on. While all definitions have merit, a generous, wider definition gives the reader the opportunity for a clearer understanding of how the Golden Age came to be and how it evolved.

Three major movements or periods define the Golden Age: the buccaneer period from 1650s to 1680s, the Pirate Round period from the 1690s to the 1700s, and the post–War of the Spanish Succession period from 1713 to the 1720s. That last period is often broken off by itself and called the Golden Age, as seen in Rediker's and Konstam's definitions, while the first two never stand alone as the Golden Age. The first two periods are like rough drafts to the Golden Age's final copy—during these periods the politics and tactics of the Golden Age were developing and changing. Without these periods for context, the Golden Age would appear to have sprung fully formed out of nowhere, like Athena from Zeus's head. While it is true that every age evolves from the age before it, and it's fair to say that the Golden Age evolved out of, say, ancient Mediterranean piracy, the proximity in both time and place to the post–War of the Spanish Succession era render the buccaneer and Pirate Round periods especially influential to the development of "true" Golden Age piracy. For that reason, they are included in this definition of the Golden Age.

So who were the buccaneers, and why do they matter to Golden Age pirates? Well, strangely enough, they weren't originally seafaring pirates at all, but hunters. They were mainly French settlers who lived off the land in Tortuga, part of present-day Haiti, hunting oxen, manatee, and wild pigs, then cooking the meat and selling it to passing ships. The native population had been virtually eliminated a century earlier by Spanish importation of diseases and enslavement of the natives to work in the Spanish gold mines. In the absence of predators or people, the livestock of the Taíno people had flourished, which made Tortuga the perfect hunting ground for the buccaneers. The name *buccaneer* is actually an Anglicized version of *boucanier*, the French word for a person who uses the boucan grill, as they did to prepare the jerky-like meat they sold.

These were famously rough men who dressed in animal skins stained with blood and who lived in primitive campsites. Their weapon of choice was a musket with a long barrel and a broad stock. These they kept in perfect condition because being able to hunt was what kept them both fed and paid. Buccaneers were great shots, much better with a gun than the Spanish soldiers they often came up against. Each crew was out for personal gain rather than the current causes or political movements of their homeland. Allegiance to the Brethren of the Coast superseded allegiance to any country or government for the buccaneers, despite the fact that many buccaneers were privateers in the employ of a nation. This is perhaps why so many buccaneers—male and female—went unrecorded in history. If it were not for historian Alexander Exquemelin, there might not be much known about them at all.

So where did they come from? During this period, Spain was the biggest game in town. Starting with the Treaty of Tordesillas in 1494, Spain had called dibs on the American territories that Columbus "discovered" and defended them with deadly force. Any nation that they were currently at peace with back home in Spain was still regarded as an enemy down in the Caribbean; this was the doctrine of "no peace below the line." No ally was safe once they left the comfort of Europe for the wilderness of the New World. Spain wanted to be the exclusive holder of all the colonies in the Caribbean and was prepared to fight for that right.

And who wouldn't want to control the Caribbean? With sailors reliant on the breezes and currents to make their way from one place to the other, having a good geographical location was key. Currents lined up ideally in the Caribbean: sailors could sail from Europe to the New World and back via the islands. The Caribbean also became a vital stop in the transatlantic slave trade, which rose in popularity during this time. Europeans sailed to Africa with textiles and other goods, which were traded for slaves. Slaves were taken to the Caribbean, and later to the American colonies, where they were exchanged for sugar, tobacco, and cotton. These goods then were transported back to Europe, and the cycle began again.

Spain also sailed its heavily loaded treasure ships through the Caribbean on their way back to Europe from South America. There was a lot of money and treasure moving in and out of the Caribbean at that time—and most of it belonged to Spain. The French, English, and Dutch wanted to establish colonies to get a piece of that action, but Spain had a chokehold on the region. These countries were unable to maintain a full military presence in the area due to Spain's no-peace policy in the Caribbean. What's an enterprising country to do? Enter the perfect solution—the buccaneers. Buccaneers were often officially in the employ of France, England, or the Netherlands, but their primary interest was plundering—no matter if they were paid to do it or not. They used long dugout canoes to attack passing Spanish ships, and they unleashed the brutality they usually reserved for the animals they hunted on the Spanish men. Their privateering was "probably the most important source of capital for the infant colonies of the West Indies," according to author Charles M. Andrews. Provincial governors of the time, rather than attempt to suppress the privateers, actively encouraged them in hopes that the money the privateers collected would stick around in the colonies and increase the colonies' fortunes. These governors believed that the buccaneers were also their best hope of ending Spain's colonial monopoly in the Caribbean. Until the arrival of Bahamian governor Woodes Rogers in 1718, buccaneers roamed where they liked in the Caribbean, knowing they outnumbered and outgunned anyone who might try to stop them.

The English buccaneers migrated south to the Caribbean on their own during the reign of James I. Unlike his predecessor Elizabeth I, who used privateering as state policy and actively recruited her sea dogs, James disliked these lawless men, and the feeling was mutual. No longer welcome as privateers, they headed to the Caribbean, where they turned outlaw. When Oliver Cromwell chartered Port Royal in 1666, these men were invited to sail on behalf of England again. Many became privateers-turned-pirates-turned-privateers, a perfect illustration of the state's complicated relationship with privateers.

Most of what is known about the buccaneers comes from one source: *The Buccaneers of America* by Alexander O. Exquemelin. Although this is a seminal text, it is devilishly hard to track down details on the author. First published in Dutch in 1678, it has been translated into many languages, and very liberally adapted. Each edition and translation of the book changes a bit from the previous one and reflects the time and political climate in which it was published, so it's fair to say the editions don't bear much relation to each other.

Exquemelin's life, much like the lives of the buccaneers he profiled, is wrapped in legends and myths. Very few concrete details are known about him. He may have been English, French, or Dutch, although most accounts agree that he was probably French. He sailed from Le Havre, France, to the Caribbean with the French West India Company in May 1666 and served there as an indentured servant for three years. He escaped a cruel master (or just completed his service, depending on the tale), and he sailed with the buccaneers for some time after that, most likely as a barber and surgeon. As a medical man, he would have had close contact with all the crew, including the captain. His access to the buccaneers allowed him firsthand knowledge of their daily lives and adventures. His descriptions of pirates, second only to Charles Johnson's, have most influenced the modern idea of what a pirate is. But what drove Exquemelin to join the buccaneers? He is not shy about pointing out their sometimes inhuman cruelty. Could he not have found a more civilized post in the Caribbean? Without an understanding of what motivated him to sail with the buccaneers, it is almost impossible to examine his biases in his writing. Further complicating matters, subsequent editions of the book added chapters not written by the author, so it is sometimes hard to determine what was part of Exquemelin's original story. Captain Henry Morgan, one of the latest and most famous buccaneers, sued the publishers of an English edition for libel and recovered £200 in damages regarding embellishments on his life story.

Exquemelin does not mention any female buccaneers in his book. But his work certainly shaped attitudes about buccaneers, which in turn no doubt influenced the authors of the women's stories, so it is worth considering his perspective. His agenda may have been no more complex than to make some money off his adventures after returning home to Europe. No matter why he penned his account, historians have benefited because his glimpse into the world of the buccaneers sets the stage for the Golden Age that came after.

⚓⚓⚓

The most famous buccaneer Exquemelin profiles is better known for the popular rum that bears his name than for his exploits: Captain Henry Morgan. He was born in Wales sometime around 1635 to a farming family, but he decided not to go into the family business and went to sea to seek his fortune instead. He wound up in Jamaica, where he was first a sailor for England and then joined a band of buccaneers. Morgan quickly adapted to their rough-and-tumble way of life, and when he and some comrades scraped together enough money to buy a ship of their own, Morgan was made captain.

Morgan's life was full of adventures, many of which he pulled off only by extreme cunning. His fly-by-the-seat-of-his-pants style is a good example of how the buccaneers lived. As Exquemelin explains, "These buccaneers remain in the bush up to two years. . . . Upon arrival [in Tortuga] they squander in one month all they have earned in the previous two years. The spirits pour like water." These wild men had little allegiance to anyone other than themselves and the pursuit of a good time. They faced hardship and life-threatening danger at sea and on land, so they lived it up while they could. Their rough life did not usually include time for families or wives, which is perhaps why there were so few female buccaneers. The two women profiled here have very few sources, none of which are from the buccaneer period, and although their stories are prevalent, they are likely fictional. The two women have very different stories, and both illustrate different facets of buccaneer life. The first woman is Anne de Graaf and the second is Jacquotte Delahaye.

⚓⚓⚓

Few details exist regarding Anne "Dieu-le-veut" de Graaf's early life. Her maiden name is unknown. According to Klausmann et al. (the only major published source to cover her story in detail, although she is mentioned in other books), she was a Frenchwoman, most likely from Brittany, a hilly peninsular region in the northwest part of France. She arrived in Tortuga during the reign of Governor Bertrand d'Ogeron, which would have been sometime roughly around 1665 to 1675. Why she left France for the Caribbean is unclear. Jon Latimer suggests that she may have been part of a program sponsored by France to ship women to the colonies. The French colonial governors requested that women be sent from France to civilize the men and tempt them into getting married and settling down, finally becoming the plantation farmers France so deeply desired. As a result of these shipments of women, the population of Tortuga was roughly equal parts male and female, which was unusual for a Caribbean colony. The women, however, did not have the desired effect on the men, as very few chose to plant tobacco. At any rate, there was nothing civilized about Tortuga during this era.

Anne might also have been deported to the island; criminals and prostitutes were often sent from Europe to the colonies during this era. Prostitution and piracy have a long and twisted history, and both practices were alive and well in Tortuga. Exquemelin says that the buccaneers went to Tortuga to "celebrate . . . the goddess Venus, for whose beastly delights they find more women than they can make use of." The women of Tortuga were financially dependent on the buccaneers' patronage. While some of these men eventually fell in love with and occasionally married the bawdy women, many more took out their more violent urges on the prostitutes in encounters that were "predatory in nature," John Appleby reports. Rape complaints in nearby Jamaica were "made a jest of even by authority," claim the state papers from the period. Many of the young, poor, and vulnerable women of the Caribbean, plenty of whom had been deported there, were abused and assaulted by the ruthless buccaneers. The Tortuga of Disney's *Pirates of the Caribbean* franchise conjures up sassy tarts who slap an offensive man's cheek, but in reality it was the women who were slapped—and worse. Native women, poor women, and African women were disproportionally affected by these crimes.

Violence against women pervades many periods of piracy—toward captives and paid companions alike. However, this fact is often downplayed in pirate stories, while the more palatable elements—such as the swashbuckling and adventure—are often glorified. Sullivan claims that pirates' appeal lies beyond historical facts, which seems true and accounts for why pirate lovers accept violence as part of the narrative. Klausmann and other scholars have suggested that the heightened violence of this period is part of what prompted later storytellers to insert Anne and Jacquotte into the narrative, or at least tell the women's stories in such a way to counteract the prevailing theme of violence against women of the period.

Anne may have been one of the many prostitutes who plied their trade in the Caribbean. Soon after she arrived, Klausmann says that she married Pierre Le Long, a minor political figure and local scallywag. He died soon after their marriage, possibly killed by pirate Laurens de Graaf. Anne's largest claim to fame is her affiliation with de Graaf, a Dutch pirate who served the French colonies in the Caribbean during the late seventeenth to early eighteenth century. According to Klausmann, he is included in an edition of Exquemelin's *The Buccaneers of America*. De Graaf (also spelled de Graff) appears in numerous other sources as well, such as Benerson Little's *The Buccaneer's Realm: Pirate Life on the Spanish Main, 1674–1688*. Reportedly, Henry Morgan called de Graaf "a great a mischievous pirate."

Klausmann reports that Anne met de Graaf after he had slandered her. Other stories claim that she challenged him to a duel after he killed her husband. In all versions of the story, the initial meeting was a thrilling one. Anne was furious and threatened to kill de Graaf for his offense. She was itching for a fight, which so charmed Laurens that he proposed to her on the spot. Anne is not the only pirate woman to inspire such ardent devotion with her fury—Cheng I Sao would later allegedly attract a husband in the same way. Klausmann says Anne accepted de Graaf's proposal due to his good looks. Jon Latimer claims that the two were never formally married.

Anne was not much of a fighter, according to Klausmann. Instead, she preferred to accompany her new husband on raids as a sort of lucky charm. Despite the fact that women were generally regarded as unlucky aboard a ship, Anne seems to have been well liked by the men of de Graaf's crew because her presence did bring them success. She was given the nickname Anne Dieu-le-veut, which translates to "God wills it." It seemed that when Anne wanted something, she always got it, as if God himself handed it to her.

Laurens and his crew most likely raided in the typical buccaneer fashion. The buccaneers used small boats, such as canoes, to sneak up on their much larger prey in the dead of night. They wrapped their enemy's oars in fabric to immobilize the ship, then boarded. The large, slow-moving vessels were ripe for the plucking by the buccaneers' smaller, faster ones. Like the early Mediterranean pirates, the buccaneers used their size and speed to their advantage. As more and more men in need of employment flooded the Caribbean, buccaneer bands became larger and more sophisticated. They participated in coordinated attacks both on land and at sea, accumulating ever more wealth.

Although the buccaneers were fiercely individualistic, they lived by a code they called "the custom of the coast." This was a skeletal system of government that acknowledged individual sovereignty both on land and at sea. Over one hundred years before the Declaration of Independence, the buccaneers organized a strong government that was in many ways a model democracy. A contemporary author, Charlevoix, explains that "[the buccaneers] had established a kind of Democratic Government; each free person had a Despotic authority in his own habitation, & every captain was sovereign on board; as long as he was in command, but one could depose him." Each ship was a mini world of its own, part of a decentralized power.

These men were loosely allied across racial, religious, and political lines into what came to be called the Brethren of the Coast. These Brethren were mostly English and French Protestants, but they included a variety of people such as some Spaniards, Africans, and nationless outlaws. Based in Tortuga, they were for a time the largest and most powerful governing body in the Caribbean. They shared a "remarkably democratic concept of justice and class consciousness," and onboard a pirate ship was "just about the most democratic institution in the world in the seventeenth century," according to Marcus Rediker. A former buccaneer wrote that "the prizes that [they] make are shared with each other with much brotherhood and friendship." It appears that in spite of their more violent tendencies, the buccaneers respected one another—just not always women. Laurens, Anne, and the rest of his crew most likely lived in relative harmony with one another and the rest of the Brethren of the Coast.

Although Anne was supposedly a good-luck charm, her luck ran out, according to Klausmann, during a battle with the Spanish. Her husband was struck by a cannonball and killed in front of her and the crew. This legend runs afoul of the historical record of Laurens de Graaf's life. Other sources claim that de Graaf, after being reunited with his family who had been taken hostage by the English for a few years, disappeared from the Caribbean and ended his days somewhere in the American South, fate unknown. Only stories featuring Anne include this detail of his death by cannon in the Caribbean. In Klausmann's telling, Anne, horrified at the loss of her husband, nevertheless leaped into command of the ship. Her husband's crew followed her orders and put up a brave fight, giving the Spaniards a long and bloody battle. The Spaniards ultimately prevailed, though, and Anne was captured along with the surviving crew. Her ultimate fate is unknown, although Klausmann and others mention a daughter of Anne's who would grow up into quite a firebrand herself. This daughter allegedly became famous for fighting in a duel with a man—no doubt her mother would have been very proud.

Anne's story illustrates several typical buccaneer characteristics. First and foremost, she was independent. As a widow, she could have spent her life shut away from the world, but instead she challenged a fierce pirate to a duel and ended up joining his crew. Her ability to look out for herself mirrors the buccaneer way. Also, she assumed command of her ship after her captain was taken out, just as Henry Morgan and others did. There wasn't time midbattle to elect a new captain, but her crew's willingness to follow her orders suggests she was fit for the job. Finally, as a woman she was a nontraditional crew member. Buccaneer crews included formerly enslaved people, as well as other outcasts from society. As long as he agreed to the terms in the articles at the beginning of the raid, each man onboard was treated equally. The conditions in the buccaneer crews were far more permissive and tolerant than conditions on land, and especially the conditions back in Europe. Anne's story reinforces the point that buccaneers were a special group that operated outside the confines of polite society.

⚓⚓⚓

If Anne de Graaf has only a small chance of having really lived, Jacquotte Delahaye has an even smaller one. Spanish author Germán Vázquez Chamorro in his book *Mujeres Piratas* (*Pirate Women*) claims that she certainly never existed, but she was added into the lore of the buccaneer period to make the ruthless men more palatable to the modern reader. He argues that although she is fictional, her story has made an impact on history—something that many more real people have not been able to do. Interestingly, Chamorro reports that Delahaye's fictional life corresponds closely with that of a pirate he claims is not fictional: Anne Dieu-le-veut.

Details of Jacquotte's life are understandably few and far between. Some stories give her Haitian heritage, while others claim that at least one of her parents was a Spaniard. Regardless of which country they hailed from, all accounts agree that they were killed by the Spanish when Jacquotte was young. Some accounts claim that this forced Jacquotte into a life of piracy to support herself and her younger brother, who is often described as mentally challenged or autistic. Like Sayyida al-Hurra before her, Jacquotte is, in most versions of her story, motivated by revenge. It is definitely a dramatic scenario: A young girl cowers with her small brother in a corner while their parents are killed in front of them in their own home. The girl vows to avenge her family's deaths and take care of her brother by undertaking a life of piracy. Years pass, and Jacquotte's anger stays bottled up inside of her as she bartends or serves as a lady's maid. Every day her anger grows as she and her brother barely survive on the pittance she makes. Finally, her anger burns so brightly that she can no longer ignore it. It is finally time for a reckoning with those who killed her family. It is time to be able to give her beloved brother more than just crumbs. She summons all her courage and devotes herself to the dangerous life of a buccaneer.

The reality of what drove most people to buccaneering was much less cinematic. These nomadic hunters-turned-pirates were motivated primarily by economic concerns. As discussed earlier in the chapter, Spain's treasure ships sailing from the New World back to Europe were large and slow—perfect targets for a quick, enterprising buccaneer. The opportunity to get rich off of Spain's work in South America was too tempting to pass up for a certain type of independent man. Jacquotte's legend puts a more sympathetic face to the trade of buccaneering. Giving Jacquotte a brother to support as a reason for her buccaneering contradicts the typical buccaneer situation—most lacked any family ties. It almost seems as if her legend was constructed entirely as a counterpoint to the prevailing stories of buccaneer life.

No matter how young Jacquotte ended up among the buccaneers, all tales agree that she quickly rose through their ranks. Some accounts claim she commanded a hundred men. Some claim that she began her life of piracy dressed as a man, while others contend that she took a male alias only after faking her death during a battle. Most agree that she did dress as a man at some point in her career. This fact is complicated by the consistent occurrence of her flaming red hair in the legends. It is described as her distinguishing feature, which made her stand out from a crowd. She is often referred to as "Back from the Dead Red," a reference to her return to piracy after her faked death.

A few accounts of her life claim that she teamed up with Anne Dieu-le-veut, but Anne's arrival in the Caribbean occurs after Jacquotte's death. Perhaps the storytellers confused these two buccaneer women with another Caribbean female pirate duo: Anne Bonny and Mary Read. In any case, the loving wife Anne would have had little in common with the single Jacquotte, who is always depicted as a loner. A quote attributed to Jacquotte (although no primary source could be found) says, "I couldn't love a man who commands me—any more than I could love one who lets himself be commanded by me." Her desire for freedom above all else is emblematic of not just the buccaneers of her era but of all pirates. Only in this does her story run along with and not contrary to buccaneer life.

One of Jacquotte's most epic accomplishments, according to Klausmann, is the capture of Fort de la Roche on Tortuga in 1656. The small, turtle-shaped island of Tortuga, first used by buccaneers in the early 1620s, was a hotly contested spot variously controlled by the French, Spanish, and English, to say nothing of the native Taíno population. French governor Jean La Vasseur was a friend to the buccaneers and happy to have them around, as long as they shared some of their booty. He built Fort de la Roche, also known as de Rocher, in 1639 to defend the island from the Spanish, who had raided it a number of times. The fort was built high on a hill near the harbor, accessible by ladder. Niches were carved in the rock below to shelter the men defending it. It was a nearly impregnable fortress, vulnerable only from a nearby mountaintop. In 1654 the Spanish exploited that weakness and took possession of the island.

In 1656 the fort was wrested from Spanish control by the English, who were friendly to buccaneers. Theoretically, Jacquotte could have aided the English to retake the base. The buccaneers did have a history of helping out their fellow settlers to repel the Spanish, who were hostile to the pirate presence on Tortuga. Jacquotte and her crew might have helped the English gain access to the fort due to their familiarity with the land.

By the 1670s, Tortuga had lost its seat at the center of piratical goings-on in the Caribbean. Buccaneers moved to the nearby town Petit-Goâve and eventually to New Providence in the Bahamas, leaving Tortuga mostly abandoned. Jacquotte Delahaye would not live to see the new island base. She was killed, according to Klausmann, in a shoot-out with the Spanish in the 1660s. With forty Spaniards against only three buccaneers, the obvious choice would have been to surrender, but Jacquotte's death is fitting for a true pirate: going out guns blazing rather than fading into obscurity.

Why are these two women included in buccaneer lore? Their stories do not have much in common with each other. Women of all races and classes had been a part of the Caribbean colonies since their founding but had been left out of their history. While the women were physically mistreated, they were also erased. Surely the lives of those women—uprooted from Europe and all they knew, sent on a journey across the sea, and deposited on an unfamiliar and unfriendly shore—were noteworthy and interesting, yet there is no counterpart to Exquemelin's book covering their exploits. We are left to imagine their lives, while the lives of the male buccaneers are covered in detail. Anne and Jacquotte's stories give women a voice in the narrative and put them back into the story, this time as victors instead of victims. Instead of nameless props in the buccaneer story, these women are portrayed as heroes: women who, despite the unpleasant and tragic circumstances they found themselves in, lived their lives on their own terms and valued personal freedom above all else, just as the male buccaneers did. Whether Anne or Jacquotte really existed, their stories are emblematic of the kind of adventurous women who *did* live during this period and whom history has forgotten.

Instead of going out guns blazing like Jacquotte, the buccaneers instead came to a slow and quiet end like the city of Tortuga itself. By 1690 buccaneering had all but died out. Countries abandoned privateering: first the Dutch in 1673, then the English in 1680, and finally the French in 1697. Spain's chokehold on the region had ended, and other nations had established colonies in the Caribbean, including Jamaica and Hispaniola. The privateers had done their duty so well that they had worked themselves out of a job. When the world ceased its warring, the privateers were a threat to order, and so they had to go. Privateers such as Morgan were rebranded as patriotic heroes, although most of them had been less than heroic. Many buccaneers retired and started families, happily living off the loot they'd won. But some were unwilling to leave the sea just yet. There wasn't much left for them in the Caribbean, so they had to seek new waters to plunder.

Newer research suggests a blurred line between the buccaneers, privateers, and pirates of this era. Timothy Sullivan argues that despite small regional differences, these groups were all one large group: both a subculture and a counterculture. Philip Gosse's *The History of Piracy*, published in 1932, was the first book to look at pirates all together in one work, which allows him to link the three groups. They may appear diverse, but all played a part to stake a claim in formerly all-Spanish territory, and they fused their native European customs with the indigenous cultures they encountered, with various degrees of success. This frontier culture theory unites the different phases of the Golden Age and demonstrates that the buccaneers were neither a distinct section of the Golden Age nor a separate, unrelated period of piracy, but rather the first wave of the Golden Age. The pirates and privateers shared experiences, goals, and methods in the Caribbean. They have more in common than they have differences. The Pirate Round phenomenon further links these two groups into one continuous movement.

The Pirate Round route, used during the second phase of the Golden Age, grew out of the end of the buccaneering period. Pirates started in the New World, sailed across the Atlantic, and continued down around the Horn of Africa to Madagascar. From there, they plundered ships traveling to and from India and the Ottoman Empire, collecting vast fortunes. Thomas Tew appears to be the first pirate to make this voyage, but many others—including former buccaneers—raced to follow his example.

In *Raiders and Rebels: A History of the Golden Age of Piracy*, Frank Sherry describes the great pirate stronghold on Madagascar that advanced the Pirate Round. There, the pirates established their first real republic. From that common base, they were able to organize into a powerful entity that was much stronger than any previous coalitions, including the Brethren of the Coast. Without the restrictions of a privateering license, these pirates were able to attack at will. In the Indian Ocean, the buccaneers-turned-pirates refined their ship-hunting tactics, swelled their ranks, and established rules of governance that would come to characterize the piracy of the Golden Age. Madagascar was the triple-A baseball league where the pirates honed their skills and grew their confidence. Once the War of the Spanish Succession ended and vast numbers of skilled sailors were suddenly unemployed, the pirates were ready for the big leagues—the Caribbean.

The War of the Spanish Succession ended in 1714—the spark that lit the fuse of the final phase of the Golden Age and brought the pirates back in full force to the Caribbean. With the lessons learned in Madagascar and the Pirate Round, the new pirates of the Caribbean were ready to terrorize ships of all nations. They were poised to become the most famous pirates of all time, the pirates people think of when they hear the word *pirate*. These stories are now ingrained in myth and pop culture. Along with the oft-repeated names of Blackbeard and Jack Rackham, many other pirates sailed under the black flag during the Golden Age, at least two of whom were women: history's most notorious female pirates, Anne Bonny and Mary Read.

7

His Majesty's Royal Pirates

FOR MANY PEOPLE, the Royal Navy conjures up images of strapping young men in sharp, pressed uniforms with artfully windblown coifs straight from the set of a historical period drama. For others, it is no more than "rum, sodomy, and the lash," a quote about British naval tradition often mistakenly attributed to Sir Winston Churchill. To the surprise of almost nobody, the actual Royal Navy—particularly during the Golden Age of piracy—bore little relation to either of these images. Life in the Royal Navy was perilous and harsh, and conditions there directly contributed to the outbreak of piracy in the Caribbean.

Today's Royal Navy, the United Kingdom's main seagoing fighting force, can trace its origins back to the middle of the seventeenth century. It was instrumental in establishing the British Empire as a world power and was, for a long time, the most powerful navy in the world. In 1660, just as the earliest part of the Golden Age was getting under way, Charles II took the throne. During the bloody English Civil War, the Commonwealth regime had assembled an efficient and powerful fleet. After the Commonwealth's defeat, Charles II inherited the fleet and used it to build the Royal Navy, which would become the dominant fighting force on the water. Among its first tasks was the destruction of the Barbary pirates who had been terrorizing English shipping. By the end of the seventeenth century, the Royal Navy was a force to be reckoned with, made up of 127 battleships and 49 frigates.

Those ships could not sail themselves, however, and men were desperately needed to fill out the navy's ranks. Men were contracted to the individual ship and were required to stay on until the commission was ended. Of course, the navy encouraged men to stay on after their commissions expired, but it wasn't possible for a nonofficer to join the navy permanently, and many men chose to pursue other careers after their time on a Royal Navy ship came to an end. Recruitment was able to pull in many men, but not nearly enough.

The Impress Service, otherwise known as the press-gang, was an ingenious—although unsavory—solution to this problem. First made legal by Queen Elizabeth, it was expanded in 1597 to include the impressment of "men of disrepute." Popular posters from the time depict armed men snatching hapless grooms from their brides at weddings, and the reality was only slightly less dramatic. The press-gang was employed to force men to serve in the navy, similar to the American military draft. Men could be called into service from land or from sea. Seagoing impressment was done by individual warships instead of the Impress Service. In theory, the Impress Service used the king's power to summon men to serve their country. In practice, it was more like kidnapping—and it disproportionally affected the poor and unemployed. Men could be stolen from ships that were headed home after a job well done and forcibly installed on a Royal Navy ship for an indeterminate period of time. The families of these impressed sailors often suffered: as Frank Sherry notes, "Pay aboard a warship was low and, at best, intermittent."

Another contribution to the rise of piracy was the decrease in privateering. England had long been a fan of privateering and had employed many men and ships to plunder for the Crown, but the newly brokered peace with England's mortal enemy Spain at the end of the War of the Spanish Succession brought the practice of privateering to a sharp halt. France, a former ally, could now be attacked by privateers as a result of King William's War, but the French ships were much faster and harder to take than the lumbering Spanish treasure galleons. So the cessation of privateering and the dismal life of a navy man combined to make a lot of unhappy, restless sailors. These sailors yearned for something more than better pay or more food—they longed for freedom. Sherry writes that "denied, the universal hunger for freedom inevitably breaks out in some form of rebellion. . . . The thousands of disaffected seamen who worked the ships of the world's maritime and naval fleets had the capacity to turn their craving into action." When pirates took a navy ship and offered to take the captives on as new pirates, many common sailors put up little resistance.

Besides making navy life so inhospitable that it drove men to piracy, the navy also did very little to suppress piracy in the Caribbean for many years, further contributing to piracy in the region. England occasionally sent warships to patrol the area when colonial governors requested assistance, but these warships generally didn't deter the pirates, for a number of reasons. First, the Royal Navy felt itself above talking to the local population and refused to listen to the advice of the colonials. As a result, they often had little to no information about the pirates' whereabouts and habits, which would have been very helpful in hunting them down.

Second, some Royal Navy commanders decided to use their time in the Caribbean to make a little extra profit. They would sell themselves out as escorts to the terrified merchant ships of the area for a hefty fee, taking advantage of the merchants' fears of pirates to make a buck. This off-the-books income was quite lucrative—and it would go away entirely if the pirates were wiped out. So the navy didn't try too hard to eradicate the pirates; they were too valuable to the navy. Also, it's worth mentioning that the navy force in the Caribbean was ravaged by disease and malnourishment and hardly in any condition to mount a serious attack. The pirates were much more accustomed to the weather and generally healthier. The sweaty, sunburned Englishmen alternating between vomiting and diarrhea were not much of a match for the hale and hearty pirates. For all these reasons, the pirates were allowed to run free while the navy looked the other way, at least until Woodes Rogers arrived on the scene in 1718.

Given all this information, it seems natural that some of the most famous pirates started out in the Royal Navy or as privateers. Marcus

Rediker goes so far as to claim that nearly all pirates began their careers as navy men, merchant sailors, or privateers, which makes sense because these men would have the benefit of the sailing skills and training that these occupations provided. Although pirates and privateers of this era did participate in land and sea raids, they were first and foremost sailors and considered themselves men of the sea. There was a sharp divide between the burglars of the shore and the robbers of the sea.

One of the robbers of the sea who started in the navy was Henry Avery. He was also known as Long Ben, John Avery, and a score of other names, and he was a midshipman in the Royal Navy during the end of the seventeenth century. He served on the HMS *Kent* and the HMS *Rupert* before his fateful journey on the English privateering ship the *Charles II*. On that voyage the captain failed to pay the crew, which turned out to be a disastrous mistake because the crew then mutinied, turned pirate, and elected Avery their captain. Samuel Bellamy, known as "Black Sam," may also have been in the Royal Navy before his pirating days. Countless other pirates during the Golden Age distinguished themselves as privateers before turning pirate, such as Charles Vane, Thomas Tew, William Kidd, and possibly even Edward Teach, also known as Blackbeard.

⚓⚓⚓

Besides incubating the next generation of pirates, the Royal Navy also had countless women in its ranks during this time. Rediker says, in his essay "When Women Pirates Sailed the Seas," that an anonymous writer in 1762 claimed there were so many women in the British army that they should have their own battalions. The world may never know exactly how many women fought for England because just like with women pirates, the only ones remembered in history are the ones who were discovered after their time in the service. Countless women have slipped through the grasp of history, their secrets forever safe from the prying eyes of people who came after them.

Two of the most famous female navy sailors are Hannah Snell and Mary Ann Talbot. Mary Ann started her life at sea at age fourteen, serving on several ships in various capacities, becoming a prisoner of war for eighteen months, and suffering multiple grievous wounds that could have ended her career before she was discharged at age nineteen when she was forced to reveal her gender. Because she was a woman, she was never able to obtain payment for her service in the navy, although she petitioned for what was rightfully owed her for many years. Mary Ann died in poverty at age thirty.

Hannah joined the military after the death of her daughter, disguising herself as James Gray. She served as a foot soldier and a sailor while pretending to be James and eventually retired, somehow successfully petitioning the Duke of Cumberland for her pension. This victory brought her into the public eye, where she would stay for much of the remainder of her life. She spent her postservice years onstage, performing military drills in her dress uniform to packed houses of curious spectators. An account of her story was published during her lifetime to great acclaim. She contracted syphilis, in those days untreatable, and she was admitted to Bethlem Royal Hospital, known as Bedlam, by her son. She died there six months later at the age of sixty-eight in 1792.

⚓⚓⚓

Besides Hannah and Mary Anne, at least two other women served in the Royal Navy and are particularly relevant: Charlotte de Berry and Mary Read. They both started out in the navy but turned pirate, and they both met sad ends as well. To be sure, there were not many rags-to-riches, joyful stories for women during the late seventeenth and early eighteenth centuries, but it is worth noting that military service did not prevent any of these women from meeting unhappy fates. Becoming a pirate did not enhance these women's outcomes, but it did not seem to harm them, either.

Charlotte de Berry enters history in 1836, two centuries after her alleged birth. She was written about in publisher Edward Lloyd's *History of the Pirates*, a penny dreadful from a man who would become famous for his popular plagiarisms of stories by Charles Dickens. Although she is common in current piratical literature, there does not seem to be a source for her other than the Lloyd book. However, her story—tailor-made to sell as many copies as possible—gives the reader a glimpse into the fervor of the reading public for female pirates. Books are published in order to sell, so Charlotte's story was crafted to have wide appeal. For example, the much-beloved fictional tale of girl-turned-pirate Fanny Campbell (explored in chapter 12) would be published just a few years after Charlotte's story, to the public's adoration.

Why did stories of women pirates have so much popular appeal? Did women, yearning to escape the confines of their society, look to these daredevils for inspiration? Or did the books serve as warnings to virtuous young ladies about the dangers that befell women who stepped out of their traditional spheres? Art can explore cultural anxieties and illustrate flaws in current popular thinking. A study of the murder pamphlets of the seventeenth century explains that "by questioning unruly behavior, [the pamphlets] attempted to restore stability and convince the populace of the importance of performing their gender role properly." However, the stories might have also demonstrated the unreasonable limitations in the typical gender roles, which would have resonated with younger readers who chafed at traditional mores. Perhaps it was a combination of both of these. Lloyd's depiction of Charlotte's story is clearly meant to titillate with its more salacious elements, but also to capture the heart of the female reader. Charlotte's story inspires sympathy even as it increases the heart rate, probably precisely what Lloyd's publishing house intended.

Charlotte, as the story goes, was born somewhere in England, most likely along the coast, in 1636. Even as a young girl, she dreamed of a life at sea. Starting in her early teens, she would sneak out of her home and hang around the docks, dressed like a man. Why? The story does not say. Perhaps she feared for her chastity if she slunk around the docks as a girl—she could be mistaken for one of the many prostitutes who haunted the water's edge. Maybe she did it for safety reasons. It's possible that she was attracted to women and felt she could pursue them only dressed as a man. She eventually met a sailor (one version of the tale calls him Jack, which will be used here for clarity's sake) and fell in love with him—while still dressed as a boy. Once Charlotte revealed her identity to Jack, he proposed to her and they were married, despite her parents' objections to the match.

How could a young couple manage getting married without the support of parents? The banns had to be published and licenses had to be obtained. There was no such thing in the seventeenth century as a civil marriage; weddings had to be conducted through the church. Luckily, in London in the early seventeenth century, "Fleet Marriages" existed for people wishing to get married without the traditional trappings and regulations. They could get married inside Fleet Prison, which claimed to be outside of the church's jurisdictions. There were enough ordained ministers imprisoned there, or living in the sketchy area surrounding the prison, who were willing to bend the rules a bit—for a price. A filthy prison, with leering inmates for bridesmaids and a felon for an officiant, does not seem like an auspicious beginning to wedded bliss, but desperate times called for desperate measures. Many sailors took advantage of these marriages before shipping off. It seems extremely likely that Charlotte and Jack were married in this way.

For a honeymoon, Charlotte followed her husband into the Royal Navy. She claimed to be his brother. Some versions of the story assert that she went by the name of Dick while in the Royal Navy. Dick and Jack were inseparable and fought side by side. Somehow, the lovebirds revealed that they were more than brothers, and an officer on the ship found them out. Rather than kick them both off the ship, this officer decided he wanted Dick for himself. He propositioned Charlotte, but she refused him, remaining faithful to her husband.

Not content to take no for an answer, this officer instead assigned Jack the most dangerous duties during battle in hopes that he would be killed, similar to the Old Testament story in 2 Samuel of David and Uriah, in which David sends Uriah to the front lines to die so he can take Uriah's wife, Bathsheba. However, the officer's dastardly plan was foiled time and again due to Charlotte's bravery and strength; she rushed to Jack's aid more than once in the heat of battle and saved his life.

Fed up with waiting, the officer played his trump card: he accused Jack of mutiny. In the Royal Navy, a common sailor's word didn't stand a chance against the word of an officer, and so Jack was convicted and sentenced to flogging. Charlotte could not step in and take the flogging for her husband, and so the officer finally accomplished his mission of getting rid of Jack. Without Charlotte to save him, Jack died as a result of the flogging.

Flogging was a common punishment in the Royal Navy, according to Colin Woodard's *Republic of Pirates*. The number of lashes was determined by the seriousness of the offense, with the worst crimes receiving up to three hundred lashes, which was thought to be the maximum a person could endure without dying. Variations on this punishment included "running the gauntlet," which involved the prisoner's walking between parallel lines of his fellow crew as they all whipped him, and "flogging around the fleet," a particularly bizarre practice in which a prisoner was tied on a rack on a small boat and rowed from ship to ship in the fleet, receiving lashes at each ship. Ordinarily, lashes were delivered to the victim's bare back in full view of the rest of the crew. The instrument of choice was the cat-o'-nine-tails, a whip with nine thin ropes at the end—each one bearing a knot—that caused considerable damage. After the whipping, the victim would be taken belowdecks to have salt rubbed into his wounds, an excruciating process that helped prevent infection. With discipline like this, it seems little wonder that so many men died in the service of king and country.

After Jack's death, the officer was surprised to find that Charlotte was still not interested in his advances. In fact, rather than seek comfort in the arms of the officer, Charlotte murdered him as soon as the ship was close to shore. After taking her revenge, she snuck off the ship and disappeared into the world of the docks.

London at this time was a city on the brink of a great rebirth. In a decade or so, the Great Fire would sweep through the city, and the rebuilding efforts would create some of the city's architectural marvels such as Christopher Wren's majestic St. Paul's Cathedral. Shipping and trade were on the rise, the population was exploding, and by the end of the seventeenth century, London would rival Paris as a great intellectual and artistic capital of Europe. However, by the water's edge, there was little evidence of this great renaissance. Wapping, where the Execution Dock for the pirates was built, was a fetid maze of crumbling buildings teeming with unfed, unwashed bodies, people who could not afford to live anywhere else. In this world, there was just one rule: survival of the fittest, and the competition was fierce. Here Charlotte tried to blend in with the crowd, working as a waitress in one of the many waterfront cafés.

She attracted the attention of a merchant captain, who kidnapped her and forced her to marry him. This captain was even crueler than the officer on her first ship, and she was raped and abused by him. On the way to Africa, she convinced the crew to mutiny against this vicious man. Charlotte decapitated him and declared herself captain of the ship. The men agreed to follow her lead and turn pirate. They were successful for several, some say two, years. This part of the story seems to be an allusion to the Pirate Round route, which postdates the time in which Charlotte's story is set by a little over a hundred years but would have been known to Lloyd in 1836.

During her travels, Charlotte found love again, this time with a Spaniard named either José or Armelio, depending on the version of the story. He eventually joined her on her ship, and Charlotte married for the third time—this time for love, like her first marriage. However, their honeymoon was short lived, as their ship was sunk in a horrible storm and only a few crew members survived. The marooned survivors had no food and were forced to resort to cannibalism, drawing straws to determine who was to be eaten. Charlotte's husband was the chosen victim.

This macabre process was not an uncommon occurrence at sea. Before ship-to-shore communication existed, ships were alone on the sea, at the mercy of the waves and wind. There were virtually no safety regulations regarding ship construction, navigator qualifications, or emergency protocols. If something went wrong, nobody would come rescue the unfortunate sailors unless they happened to pass by. A sailor knew that when he set foot on a ship he was taking his life into his own hands.

Law books are filled with cases revolving around cannibalism at sea, the earliest recorded one dating back to 1641. It was customary to draw lots to determine who was to be eaten, as was done in Charlotte's case. Cannibalism at sea was so common that it was routinely allowed as a defense to murder in English courts until 1884, with the *R v. Dudley and Stephens* verdict (which outlawed necessity as a defense for murder approximately fifty years after Lloyd published Charlotte's story).

The band of survivors was rescued by a passing Dutch ship, but the rescue came too late for the luckless José/Armelio. Soon after the rescue, the Dutch ship was attacked. Charlotte and her remaining crew—probably reckoning they had nothing left to lose at this point—defended their rescuers, fighting off the attackers. It was to be Charlotte's last fight. She and her crew fought mightily, and they were able to overpower the attackers. While they were celebrating their victory, Charlotte threw herself overboard, her beloved's name on her lips.

Charlotte's story is an odd amalgam of the stories of Mary Read and Anne Bonny, biblical stories, piratical history, and current events at the time of its writing. While it is certainly sensational, it does not feel out of place among more verified pirate women stories. Only one detail fails to ring true: Charlotte's suicide. Only one other pirate in this volume voluntarily took her own life: Maria Cobham, another possibly fictional pirate. Lloyd may have felt that he had to include this detail in order to return things to the status quo; a thrice-married woman who took part in murder and mayhem would not have been able to seamlessly integrate back into polite society. If her tale had ended with her married to an upstanding man and renouncing her former occupation, she might have been allowed to live without reader outrage, but since she killed her second husband *and* refused to give up piracy, she could not be granted a happy ending. Unfortunately for Charlotte, her fate was in the hands of her biographer, a Victorian male with little sympathy for lawless ladies.

⚓⚓⚓

Another pirate who carried on despite being twice widowed was one of the most famous women pirates of all time. Mary Read, usually spoken of as one half of the dynamic duo Mary Read and Anne Bonny, had a rich, adventure-filled life before she ever clapped eyes on Calico Jack and his crew and began a life that "some may be tempted to think the whole Story no better than a Novel or a Romance," according to biographer Charles Johnson. Mary Read, like Anne Bonny, first appeared in Johnson's wildly popular *A General History of the Pyrates*, published in 1724.

If Exquemelin is the second man held responsible for the popular image of pirates, Johnson is definitely the first one. His images in his book have endured for centuries and are said to have inspired many piratical storytellers who came after him. Despite the book's massive popularity, the author of the book is still a mystery. "Captain Charles Johnson" is thought to be a pseudonym. Various theories over the years have posited the author's identity, with a popular but disproven theory attributing the book to Daniel Defoe. Whoever Captain Johnson was, his book was an instant bestseller, capturing the imaginations of readers back in 1724 and keeping them captive up to the present day. The book still sells well and is likely the most referenced primary source of pirate information. However, its accuracy as a source is doubtful; Johnson liked to embellish the facts when they weren't picturesque enough. The book has been reprinted many times in various editions. The first edition had two volumes, the first of which included on the title page a promise to recount the "remarkable actions and adventures of the two female pyrates [*sic*], Mary Read and Anne Bonny." Johnson knew that the inclusion of two women, so recently tried in a very public fashion, would grab the reader's attention. Indeed, the tales of both women seem to have been ripped from the headlines and were practically guaranteed to keep people reading. However, the sensational nature of the stories doesn't mean that they are untrue. Enough of the account corresponds with the court documents and other primary source material of the time that Captain Johnson's account is generally accepted as, if not wholly accurate, then accurate enough. He may have added some details and language to sell books, but the spectacular story of these two women is presented more or less intact.

According to Johnson, Mary Read's mother was married to a sailor who got her pregnant before going off to sea and never returning. Whether he died or just abandoned his wife is unknown. Mrs. Read had her baby, a son, and lived with her husband's family until she became pregnant again, this time by a man she was not married to.

Knowing she would be disgraced if her secret was discovered, Mary's mother left her husband's family and moved in with some friends. Her son died shortly before her daughter, Mary, was born. Mrs. Read had no money of her own; her mother-in-law had been sending money to care for the senior Mrs. Read's grandson. With the grandson dead, the senior Mrs. Read would no longer have any reason to send money to Mary's mother. How would they live? Mary's mother hatched a desperate plan. Why not swap a living daughter for a dead son? She hid her son's death and dressed Mary as a boy, passing her off as her son. It was as if Mary had never been born. This went on until Mary was thirteen years old.

When the elder Mrs. Read died, Mary and her mother had to find another way to make money. Young Mary was hired out—still dressed as a boy—as a footboy to a French lady. Footboys ran alongside a carriage to ensure it did not tip over due to a tree root, pothole, or other obstacle in the road. They also ran ahead of the carriage to ensure everything at the destination was prepared to the master's liking. Footboys were used by only the wealthiest people. They provided a less essential service than cooks and other domestic servants and were primarily for show. Footboys were chosen for their good looks—the woman who hired Mary Read must have found the feminine-looking "boy" alluring. Eventually, Mary's developing body would have given her away, but she left her job before she was discovered. She was fed up with domestic life and was ready to strike out on her own. No more a servant's life for Mary: she was going to sea.

The details of Mary's Royal Navy service are unclear. Some accounts combine her army service and naval service into one. Johnson says only that she "enter'd herself on board a Man Of War, where she served some time, then quitted it," which leaves out a lot of information. Some stories claim that she served as a cabin boy, others as a powder monkey. As a cabin boy, her duties would have included running errands for the officers onboard, assisting the cook, climbing up the rigging when the sails needed trimming, and various other duties, sometimes of a sexual nature, depending on the captain. Mary could have engaged in sexual acts with her captain and still kept up the deception, but she would have had to be very, very careful. As a powder monkey, she would have had to ferry gunpowder from the ship's hold to the artillery on deck during battle. Neither job would have paid well or offered the benefits that she would have received as a footboy.

Besides the low pay, life on a Royal Navy ship was not particularly glamorous. Danger levels were high, and shares of any prizes found were notoriously unequal, with officers taking the lion's share and common seamen getting only a pittance. Crews faced a "poor diet, harsh discipline, exposure, and disease," according to Woodard. Samuel Johnson remarked that "no man will be a sailor who has contrivance enough to get himself into a jail; for being in a ship is being in jail with the chance of being drowned. . . . A man in jail has more room, better food, and commonly better company."

Perhaps more distressing than the lack of food and space was the discipline program onboard a navy ship. Although the king's law reigned, each ship was a microdictatorship in which the captain had absolute power. Sailors were subject to the whims and caprices of their captain with nobody to complain to up the chain of command if they were treated unfairly. Captains punished infractions, real or perceived. It was not uncommon for crewmen to be struck with canes, whipped by crewmates or officers, or hanged. Woodard claims that half of the men pressed into the Royal Navy died at sea. For so many reasons, Mary would have been better off staying on land.

But Mary had her reasons for joining the navy. After being a possession of others her entire life—first her mother's, then the French lady's—she decided to make a decision for herself. In the navy, she would be property of king and country, but at least that was a service she had chosen for herself instead of one that had been chosen for her. At sea, there were no familial entanglements. Working on a British ship would have been the freest period of Mary's life up to this point.

At some point, perhaps Mary grew tired of life at sea or she was discovered. She left the navy and went to Flanders, where she joined the English army. At the turn of the eighteenth century, England was allied with the Dutch forces fighting the War of the Spanish Succession in the Spanish Netherlands, of which Flanders was a part, and which is now part of present-day Belgium. This war lasted from 1701 to 1714, during which Mary would have been aged eleven to twenty-four, if we take 1690 to be her birth year. As she fought alongside her Flemish comrades, she fell in love with one of them.

Johnson spins a misogynistic aside here, explaining how love made Mary a poor soldier, because "Mars and Venus could not be served at the same time," and how she would run into battle without orders to do so just to be closer to the object of her affection. Her behavior was so odd that her comrades thought she had gone mad. Johnson describes how she "found a Way of letting him discover her Sex, without appearing that it was done with Design." When her beau-to-be "accidentally" discovered Mary was a woman, he apparently was delighted that he could have a "Mistress solely to himself," but Mary was so chaste and ladylike that he decided instead to court her as his wife.

What an odd little anecdote this is; it paints Mary as a lovesick fool, gladly placing herself in harm's way for her love. Her sweetheart fares little better; he comes across as a womanizer content to take advantage of Mary's charms before deciding she was ladylike enough to take home to mother. This whole escapade feels out of place in the story. Perhaps Johnson spun this yarn to inject some virtuous behavior into Mary's life to make her more sympathetic to readers. Mary would fall in love once more in her life after her Flanders beau, but that story belongs in the next chapter.

When Mary and the Flemish man married, their fellow soldiers were so moved by their story of love that they threw Mary a sort of bridal shower, offering her gifts and money toward setting up their married household. The army got caught up in the sentiment as well and discharged the two lovers. The couple bought a tavern near Breda (present-day Holland) and named it the Three Horse Shoes. It was very popular with their former comrades and other soldiers, and they did a brisk business until Mary's husband died. Exactly how long they ran the tavern together is unknown due to their unknown wedding date.

To compound Mary's misery after her husband died, the war ended and business dried up. Mary found herself in the same position as her mother had been many years before: husbandless with no income or means to support herself. Once again, she donned a man's clothes and joined the army, but during peacetime she could not gain a position where she could support herself. She left the army and boarded a ship headed for the West Indies, determined to try her luck in a warmer climate.

Generally during this time, people did not go to the Caribbean without reason. It was viewed as a hot, disease-ridden, uncivilized place, not an unwarranted reputation, tolerable only for the potential tobacco-growing land available there. Yet Western powers were competing to establish supremacy in an area where nobody actually wanted to live. Jamaica in particular was the "center of Anglo-Spanish imperial competition in the seventeenth century," according to Amanda Snyder. When England won control of it in 1655, the island was full not of planters but of pirates. Oliver Cromwell added Irish dissidents, Jews, Quakers, convicts, loose women, and other "undesirables" whom he wanted out of the way to the pirates and privateers already there. This motley crew of people earned Port Royal nicknames such as "Sodom of the New World" and "wickedest place in the Caribbean." Of the reported two hundred buildings on the fifty-one acres of land, at least forty-four of them were taverns. A woman of good breeding would not be caught dead there if she could help it, but Mary Read was not a woman of good breeding—she was a woman with nothing left to lose.

What Mary planned to do upon reaching the West Indies is unknown because her ship did not arrive there. It was intercepted by pirates, who kidnapped Mary and forced her to join their crew. She pirated with them until the crew decided to take advantage of Governor Woodes Rogers's pardon and become privateers for the English against Spain. Mary was "resolved to make her Fortune one way or another." When some of the privateers mutinied and became pirates again, Mary was among them.

Pirate ships shared many of the dangers that Royal Navy ships faced, but on the whole were a more pleasant place to be. For one thing, the crews were much larger. David Cordingly explains in *Under the Black Flag* that while a one-hundred-ton legal ship would be crewed by twelve men, a comparable pirate ship would have around seven times that many crew members. Generally discipline onboard a pirate ship was not nearly as aggressive as it would be on a navy ship. Most of all, pirate ships of this era were democracies. Captains were elected by the crew at the start of each voyage. Decisions on where to sail and whether or not to make a raid were decided by majority vote. Rules, division of prize money, and injury pay were all written into a charter that had to be signed by every pirate at the start of a new voyage. This system, developed by the Brethren of the Coast and perfected in Madagascar by the pirates of the Pirate Round, would come to be a hallmark of the Golden Age of piracy. As Cordingly comments, "Liberty, equality, and brotherhood were the rule rather than the exception."

It's not hard to imagine why Mary chose to join the pirates. Johnson claims Mary said she hated piracy and only did it under compulsion, but that appears to be a bald-faced lie. Numerous witnesses testified at her trial that she was as willing as anyone else to join in the raids. She also had many opportunities to get out of the pirating racket and never took them. Despite Johnson's own story that she told Rackham that pirating was for the courageous, which contradicts her own testimony that she abhorred piracy, it seems most likely that Mary was attracted to the freedom a life of piracy offered. As a former navy sailor, she would have recognized that piracy offered a more comfortable life than the Royal Navy. As a pirate, she could make more money than as a servant of His Majesty and also have a say in where she sailed. For a woman whose entire life had been dictated for her, it would have been a practically irresistible offer.

Before long, she was onboard Captain Jack Rackham's ship and about to meet the woman who would help enshrine her name in history, the other half of the dynamic duo of women pirates: Anne Bonny. For Mary Read the best was yet to come.

8

"If He Had Fought Like a Man, He Need Not Have Been Hang'd Like a Dog"

ESPITE THE STRANGLEHOLD CARIBBEAN PIRATES have on popular imagination, their heyday in the period following the Spanish succession spanned roughly ten years. By the second decade of the eighteenth century, the pirates' days of reckless plundering while the law looked the other way were drawing to a close. Several factors brought about the end of this third and final phase in the Golden Age of piracy.

As discussed in the previous chapter, with the signing of the Treaty of Utrecht in 1713, the War of the Spanish Succession ended, and the population of pirates experienced a huge boost. Thousands of skilled soldiers found themselves suddenly unemployed, and many of them migrated to the warmer climates and the more adventurous lifestyle of the Caribbean. However, this rise in piracy caused a corresponding beefing up of national navies as protection against the pirates. No longer needed to fight other nations postwar, the navies were able to focus on pirate hunting. Privateering, the nations reasoned, was all well and good, but outright pirating could no longer be tolerated now that the once-rival nations were at peace.

The pirates now lacked a safe haven where they could base their adventures. By the late 1680s, the former pirate hot spot of Tortuga had turned hostile, passing strict antipiracy laws and increasing the military presence. To make matters worse, party city Port Royal had been destroyed by an earthquake in 1692. All over the Caribbean, the pirate paradises full of taverns, whores, and places to sleep it all off were attempting to turn themselves into more law-abiding communities, which would ironically bring a few of their economies to financial ruin. Once given free rein of the Caribbean, the pirates were now confined to an ever-smaller geographical area. They needed one secure base to keep their trade viable, and they found that base in the city of New Providence.

The last great Caribbean pirate stronghold, New Providence, part of the present-day Bahamas, became home to some two thousand pirates, who in 1713 outnumbered law-abiding inhabitants two to one. An island of about sixty square miles does not seem like a likely pirate metropolis, but it had a variety of features that made it a decent base. Before 1718, governors were selected by the islanders instead of appointed by England, and the British Bahamas happened to lack a governor from 1706 to 1718. Besides the lack of supervision, the island—like much of the Caribbean—was ideally located close to trade routes and good wind patterns. The harbor was too shallow for large warships but just right for the smaller ships favored by pirates. There was an adequate supply of fresh water, timber, wild animals for hunting, and high hills that could be used as lookout posts. These factors, combined with the fact that the pirates were no longer welcome in Port Royal or Tortuga, meant that New Providence was an excellent choice for them.

Nearly every major pirate of the period spent time on the island. They conducted business in the thriving black market, trading slaves, liquor, and other contraband. Ships, cannons, swords, and other weapons could be obtained as well as repaired there. When work was done for the day, the pirates could pass a few merry hours in the taverns and brothels of the island. Benjamin Hornigold, Calico Jack Rackham, Samuel

Bellamy, and Edward Teach, better known as Blackbeard, were known to frequent New Providence during the last years of the Golden Age.

New Providence was a prosperous yet lawless island, which made it a threat to the British colonial presence in the Caribbean. Woodes Rogers, appointed governor of the Bahamas in 1717, intended to flush out the pirates once and for all and make the Bahamas a respectable colony. His efforts ultimately succeeded, but at tremendous personal cost. With his bold plans to pardon pirates and his insistence on maintaining England's sovereignty on the island, he was able to convince the inhabitants of New Providence that he was there to stay, and he meant business. Pirates had three options: decide to abide by Rogers's conditions, make themselves scarce, or die fighting. Rogers pardoned over six hundred pirates, many of whom became pirate hunters themselves and made a living by informing on their former brethren. Many other pirates were captured, tried, and executed, such as Calico Jack Rackham and his crew. Rogers's move of convening pirate trials right in New Providence instead of sending the pirates back to England to face justice further established his supreme authority and convinced the pirates that there was no escaping him.

Ironically, without the pirate economy, the colony fell into ruin, and Rogers was imprisoned for his debts. The man who ended the Golden Age of piracy died in debtor's prison and is for the most part left out of the history books. Today, much of New Providence's livelihood comes from pirate tourism, a fact that surely has Rogers rolling in his grave.

⚓⚓⚓

As the Golden Age was winding down, two fierce pirate women—one famous, one less so—were making names for themselves. Their exploits ensured that the Golden Age went out with a bang instead of a whimper. Although their methods and locations of piracy were very different, these women shared an adventurous spirit and a knack for the nastier bits of pirating. In the Caribbean, there was Anne Bonny, and off the North American coast, there was Maria Cobham.

Anne, like Mary Read, is one of the few pirates whose existence has been verified. She was a main attraction in Captain Johnson's *A General History of the Pyrates*, originally published in 1724, just a few years after her trial took place. Her name also appears in the trial documents of the crew of the *William*, and she is mentioned in a pamphlet and letter written during this time. The main source of information that exists about her life, however, is Johnson's account. As discussed in the last chapter, Johnson's accounts cannot be taken entirely at face value, particularly where the women pirates are concerned. Johnson himself says the section on Bonny and Read strains credulity. In a few key places in Anne's story, it is necessary to push back against Johnson's assertions to see what the famous pirate biographer might have purposely left out.

Anne was born in Ireland, the illegitimate daughter of an attorney thought to be named William Cormac and his maid Peggy. After his affair was discovered, the scandal cost him many of his clients. He was forced to appeal to his wife for an allowance to live on, the wife having been left all of William's mother's money upon her death, due to her son's infidelity. Knowing that his wife would never pay for the upbringing of his bastard daughter, Cormac dressed Anne as a boy and told everyone she was a relative's child whom he was training to be his clerk. When Cormac's wife figured out her husband's ward was not a nephew but in fact his illegitimate daughter, she cut them all off. So William, his maid, and his young daughter set off for America in search of a new start.

William found better luck as a merchant in the Carolina colony, in the area of present-day South Carolina, than he had back home as a lawyer. He became the wealthy owner of a large plantation that Anne became the mistress of at just twelve years old, after her mother's death. She ruled the plantation with her famous fiery temper. Stories abound regarding her punishment of servants, including one brought up at her trial about stabbing a servant with a knife, although Johnson claims this tale is "groundless." The only daughter of a rich merchant, she had many suitors, yet she rejected them all. She so severely beat a would-be suitor who was too forward with her that he was laid up for weeks.

Despite her father's desire to marry her off to one of Charles Town's eligible bachelors, she set her sights on ne'er-do-well sailor James Bonny. When she married him over her father's objections, the heartbroken William disowned her. A prevalent legend states that she retaliated by setting fire to her father's plantation, but the incident is not mentioned in Johnson's account.

James was allegedly interested in Anne only for her father's money, so he was extremely disappointed when he found out she would inherit none of that money. The disenchanted newlyweds took off to New Providence, where James thought he'd try his luck as a pirate hunter. Governor Woodes Rogers's 1718 declaration welcomed anyone looking to make some easy money by capturing some pirates—no questions asked. Anne quickly tired of her uninterested husband and began frequenting the nightlife of the pirate hot spot she found herself in, meeting and quickly falling in love with Captain John Rackham, known as Calico Jack due to his fondness for flashy calico clothing.

John Rackham began his pirating career as a quartermaster under pirate Charles Vane—one of the only pirates who actively resisted Governor Rogers. When Vane refused to attack a ship the crew felt that they ought to go after, they voted Vane out of his captaincy and elected Rackham into power. Such an episode would never have happened on a ship in any national navy—one of the many reasons why piracy was so appealing to many former navy sailors. Rackham fell in love with Anne and, according to one story, offered her husband, James, a large sum of money if he'd release her from the marriage. Given James's desire for money, this proposition might have seemed well timed, but apparently the pirate hunter was offended by the offer and asked Governor Rogers to administer a rarely enforced adultery law and have Anne publicly beaten. Anne and her new lover Rackham ran off to bluer seas to avoid the sentence.

While off pirating, Anne became pregnant with Rackham's child. Rackham sailed to Cuba for his wife's delivery. She had the baby in Cuba, although the exact date is unclear—some accounts place it as late as 1720. What happened to the baby is also unclear; Anne either gave it up for adoption or it died, according to different versions of the story. Whatever happened to the child, Anne rejoined her pirate crew soon after the birth of the baby and continued pirating.

Rackham and his crew were technically privateers, having taken advantage of a proclamation that pardoned pirates provided they turned themselves in. Anne, Jack, and the rest of them did enough privateering to avoid arousing suspicion, but they also did a fair bit of honest-to-goodness pirating on the side. This was not an uncommon situation, and many other pirates did the same thing. The American colonies, for example, looked the other way while pirating was taking place so long as the privateers defended the colonies against opposing forces. This lax attitude had taken its toll over time and the pirates had grown too powerful to control, which is one of the reasons Woodes Rogers was sent to the Bahamas—to end the pirates' domination of the area.

Sometime after Anne rejoined Jack's crew, the pirates picked up another crew member, a slim fellow called Mark Read. According to many accounts, Anne became quite taken with Mark, to the point that Rackham became jealous. Mark was forced to reveal to the pair that "he" was actually a "she": Mary Read. Johnson claims that the rest of the crew never discovered Mary's secret, which seems odd given the trial testimony by the pirates' victims that it was easy to tell that Anne and Mary were women. Perhaps Johnson felt that if he acknowledged that the crew knew about the women, he would have to explain why the crew did not reject them onboard. Regardless of his claims, captives also testified at trial that the women dressed as men only during raids and were dressed as women at all other times.

No matter what they were wearing, it is clear from trial testimony and Johnson's account that Anne and Mary were fierce pirates who took an equal part in the business of pirating. During battles, they participated enthusiastically with guns and swords. At trial, captive Dorothy Thomas claimed that the women "were very active on Board and willing to do any Thing . . . they did not seem to be kept or detained by Force, but of their own Free-Will and Consent." Thomas Dillon, another witness at trial, testified that "[the women] were both very profligate, cursing and swearing much, and very ready and willing to do any Thing on Board." Historian Jo Stanley asserts that the women were "not marginalized but played a central role in Rackham's raids, as integral members of a tightly knit group."

A recurring idea in Anne and Mary's stories is that they were lesbian lovers. It is by no means impossible that these women shared a sexual attraction, but there is no evidence to support this claim. Both women were married to men at various points, and Anne was Jack Rackham's lover, so each woman appeared to have some heterosexual inclinations. Each could have been bisexual, but it is doubtful that they were exclusively homosexually oriented. Mary was said to have fallen in love with a fellow pirate once she joined Rackham's crew and possibly even married him onboard. Johnson details an encounter where the object of her affection angered a fellow pirate, who challenged him to a duel. Mary, eager to rescue her love but unwilling to do it in a way that emasculated him, challenged the other pirate to a duel that was to take place before the one scheduled with her lover. She killed the pirate, thereby negating her lover's duel and saving his life. Like Charlotte de Berry, her combat skills came in handy to preserve her love affair. Johnson, again curiously dismissive when it comes to Mary Read, intimates that the entire duel was an attention-getting charade Mary partook in to get the man to like her. Fortunately he liked her anyway, according to Johnson, and they "plighted their Troth to each other," which they considered to be as good as a marriage. Mary used this union in court to justify her pregnancy, claiming she had never committed fornication or adultery. Johnson describes how, also at the trial, Mary Read refused to identify her husband/lover, which allowed him to claim he was press-ganged into service and was not a pirate voluntarily. This lie spared his life once again and allowed him to go free. Johnson seems keen to set up Mary Read as the "good" girl next to Anne Bonny's "bad" girl, which does both women a disservice in reducing them to stereotypes. It would have, however, enticed readers and consequently boosted sales of the book.

Despite the largeness of their legends, the women were pirates together for only a short time—some accounts claim less than a year. Trial testimony says that they began their official pirating careers on September 1, 1720, when they agreed to sail with Rackham. Anne had been with Rackham for a longer period of time but perhaps was involved only in privateering up to that point, or maybe the date given at trial was inaccurate. In any case, by 1720, Calico Jack and his crew—Anne and Mary included—were successfully plundering many ships in the Caribbean and on the North American coast. Rumors of a pirate crew with not one but two women began to circulate throughout the Caribbean.

Perhaps one of their greatest exploits was the theft of the sloop *William*, stolen in August 1720 out of the Nassau harbor right under Governor Rogers's nose. Owned by John Ham, the twelve-ton sloop was a British warship with one gun deck that could hold up to eighteen guns. It would have been rather small in comparison to other British warships, but it was still a large prize for the pirates. Stealing a British ship was a clear indication that the pirates were not strictly privateers as they had promised, and Governor Rogers was incensed that he'd been duped. On September 5, 1720, he declared that Jack Rackham and his crew, including "two women, by name, Anne Fulford alias Bonny & Mary Read," were enemies to the Crown of Great Britain and sent Captain John Barnet to capture them. From then on, the clock was ticking against their capture.

The date on which the women were captured is unclear. Johnson's account does not mention an exact date. A popular date offered is October 22, 1720, but November is also given. One evening, in either October or November, Captain Jonathan Barnet came across the pirates at Negril Point, Jamaica. He ordered them to surrender immediately.

Legend has it that, it being late at night, the pirate crew of the *William* was belowdecks, drinking, sleeping, and playing cards. Only Anne and Mary were on deck keeping watch. When the women realized they were being attacked, they shouted below in an attempt to rouse the men, but none came to help. Mary Read is even rumored to have fired her gun into the hold, wounding several, in an attempt to coerce her fellow pirates into defending the ship. While the men, including Captain Jack Rackham, cowered down below, Anne and Mary fought like the devil himself, shooting their pistols and brandishing their swords. The women held off the British crew for as long as possible and managed to take down several of them, but eventually they were overtaken. Along with the rest of the crew, they were captured and taken to Jamaica for trial.

The High Court of Admiralty convened in Spanish Town, Jamaica, on November 16, 1720. The men of Rackham's crew who could not deny they were voluntarily pirates were tried for piracy. Those who were believed to be press-ganged or held against their wills, including Mary Read's "husband," were acquitted. In a trial lasting a short amount of time, the remaining pirates were all convicted and sentenced to hang.

Captain Jack Rackham was one of the first to be hanged. His body was shown publicly as a warning to other pirates. He was put on a gibbet, which was a type of gallows used to showcase dead, and sometimes still-living, bodies of criminals in chains, and displayed near the water. The spot near the entrance to the Port Royal harbor where his body hung as it decayed is now known as Rackham's Cay. Before he was to be executed, the condemned man requested one last moment with his beloved to say good-bye. Knowing Anne as he did, he likely did not expect any words of comfort from the fiery woman, but even he probably did not expect her last words to him to be that she was "sorry to see him there, but if he had fought like a Man, he need not have been hang'd like a Dog." One hopes that he went to his death smiling at the thought that even the specter of death could not cow the woman he loved. The stone-cold sass of Anne's statement, more than any other part of her story, has enshrined her legend dearly into the hearts of pirate lovers everywhere.

On November 28, 1720, ten days after Jack's execution, Mary Read and Anne Bonny were tried for piracy. They were accused of having committed "Piracies, Felonies, and Robberies . . . on the High Sea" numerous times. They were not accused of murder, but throughout the trial numerous victims, including captive Dorothy Thomas, testified that they feared for their lives. They also testified that the women were active participants in the raids, threatened captives, and were equally as culpable in all pirate activities as the men were. The women spoke very little and offered no statements in their own defense. It was only after Sir Nicholas Lawes pronounced them guilty and sentenced them to hang that both women claimed to be pregnant.

Numerous scholars, Joan Druett and Jo Stanley among them, have pointed out the irony that these two women who lived like men in so many other respects were able to cheat death due to the womanliest of reasons. However, this analysis is not entirely fair because the executions were only stayed—not commuted—until the children were born. The court was concerned that it did not take an innocent life as well as a guilty one, but it was apparently not worried about the children who would grow up without mothers due to their actions. These pirates would have to serve another sentence—pregnancy and childbirth—before coming to reckoning for their crimes.

Mary Read did not live to see the hangman's noose. She died in prison in 1721, either in childbirth or of a type of typhus known as "prison fever." What became of Anne Bonny is even less certain. There are no records of her execution. Some accounts claim that she was given a reprieve. Another theory says her father, overcome with grief, intervened on her behalf and secreted her away to the Carolina colony, where she lived out the rest of her days as a law-abiding citizen. Perhaps she returned to her home country of Ireland.

Another theory is less popular but infinitely more exciting. Picture Anne in her jail cell one night, furious that she had been caught, and unable to sleep. Suddenly, she hears a muffled thump and a crash in the dark hallway. Someone is jiggling the key in her door's rusty lock. The heavy wooden door is thrown open to reveal Bartholomew Roberts, resplendent in his fine clothes and jewels. Although they have never met, Anne recognizes him from the stories she's heard in port. There's a glint in his eye that speaks of mischief. "Come on, Anne, let's get you out of here. Will you join my crew?" Roberts asks. Anne just stares, in a rare moment of speechlessness. "Why did you come for me?" she asks Roberts, who in turn opens his jacket to reveal that *he* is most definitely a *she*. "We women have to stick together, don't we? Come on!" The shocked Anne follows the legendary Black Bart to the waiting dinghy in the harbor, and by dawn they are on the *Royal Ranger*, sailing toward a lifetime of more adventures, at least until Roberts's death in 1722.

Bartholomew Roberts, one of the most famous pirates of this era, may have been female, according to Klausmann et al. Born in Wales, Roberts captured four hundred ships in a relatively short two-and-a-half-year career. Roberts's introduction to the pirate life was being captured by them off the coast of West Africa. Although initially repulsed by the pirate way, he quickly got onboard, so much so that a few weeks later, he was elected as the ship's new captain. He quickly drew up his own articles—a strict code that forbade gambling, staying up past eight o'clock, bringing women and boys onboard, and allowing one's pistol to fall into disrepair. He is known for never killing a single passenger or crew member of an enemy ship except in battle.

His famously austere life could have been the result of a religious upbringing—or it could have hidden a huge secret. Toward the end of his life, Roberts engaged in a serious emotional relationship with the ship's surgeon, which could indicate he was a homosexual man or a straight woman in disguise. After dying in battle, Roberts was buried at sea, in accordance with his wishes. His body was never examined by a doctor, which adds more fuel to the flame. There is no proof that Roberts was a woman, but then again there is also no proof that Roberts was a man, and there are plenty of things that give an investigator pause. It is tempting to imagine that the most successful pirate of the Golden Age was actually a woman in disguise, but there is simply not enough evidence at present to back up the theory. Unless more comes to light, Roberts will remain on the books as a man.

Anne's fate is ultimately unknown. One of the most famous female pirates of all time simply disappeared, although the circumstances were altogether different than those of other pirate women, who faded into obscurity. If Anne fell off the map, one senses that she meant to do so. This remarkable woman, an illegitimate child turned fierce pirate, would not go gently into that good night. One hopes that she fought her way into old age, regaling anyone who would listen with tales of her adventures.

Why, out of all the pirates in this book, is Anne one of the most famous? She is neither the longest-reigning pirate nor the most successful. No doubt her inclusion in Johnson's *Pyrates* as the "bad girl pirate" aided her ascent. His titillating account of her sordid deeds made her a media darling. She is a popular figure in pirate novels, TV shows, and movies, which has kept her in the public eye. The fact that she was active during the most famous period of piracy, the Golden Age, probably helped her too. She was also white and allegedly beautiful, which never hurts one's prospects for fame. Whatever the reason, there is no doubt her legend lives on and will most likely continue to do so long after others are forgotten.

⚓⚓⚓

While Anne Bonny was being tried for piracy, another woman pirate was just getting started. Maria Cobham, born Maria Lindsey, raised hell all over the Atlantic from 1720 to 1740. She and her husband made bundles of money—enough to retire and buy a fine estate in France. However, her story is far less well known, possibly because it is less verifiable. Maria's story first appears in the anonymous volume *Lives of the Most Celebrated Pirates*, published around 1800. She is also included in *The Pirate Who's Who*, written by Philip Gosse in 1924. Allegedly, a firsthand account of their exploits was written by her husband, Eric, but it has never been located. Given her twenty-year span of activity, it seems strange that she would not have been covered in newspapers or other contemporary material. Her story is often included in twentieth-century piracy books and is mentioned in the *Canadian Encyclopedia*, so she has become part of history regardless of whether or not she actually existed. If she did exist, she would have to be among the longest-lasting and most successful female pirates.

Maria's birthplace and family circumstances are unknown. She enters history as a young prostitute in Plymouth Harbor, a busy harbor on the English Channel in the south of England where, one hundred years earlier, the *Mayflower* embarked for the New World. Prostitution in England at that time took roughly three forms: the high-class courtesans and mistresses, the pimp- or madam-controlled girls who worked in brothels, and the street girls who often worked outside and serviced many clients per day. These street girls were mostly young, uneducated women, many of whom were addicted to drugs such as morphine, laudanum, and opium.

Prostitution was at the time considered a safe way for bachelor men to sow their wild oats without sullying the virtues of their chaste sweethearts. So long as this practice remained quiet and discreet, the authorities were loath to intervene. It is estimated that in the early 1700s, roughly one in five women in London were prostitutes. Catalogs describing the locations, physical virtues, and prices of prostitutes around London were printed and circulated during this time. Not until the late Georgian era did reformers focus on equating prostitution with sin. The Vagrancy Act of 1824 punished prostitutes with up to one month of hard labor. Depending on the political climate, prostitutes were either denounced for their supposedly lustful natures or seen as victims of desperate economic circumstances. This public opinion battle still carries on in the twenty-first century, not only in the United Kingdom but in other countries as well.

Eric Cobham, a pirate captain fresh off a voyage where he stole thousands of pounds of gold, made a brief stop at the harbor that would change his life forever. He met and wooed Maria with stories of the gory business of pirating. Eric, according to the stories, had lived a foul life full of thievery, murder, and deceit, which began when he was very young. These stories enchanted rather than repelled young Maria. She was so taken with his tales of murder and mayhem that when Eric's ship left port a few days later, she was onboard as his wife, most likely as a result of a "Fleet Marriage," like Charlotte de Berry's.

Women as a rule were not welcome on ships, and Eric's crew was not happy about their newest passenger. Maria quickly endeared herself to them. She won their admiration, if not their hearts, by being the cruelest pirate of them all, perfectly willing to plunge her dagger into a man's heart with no hesitation. Pirate stories are seldom without violence, but legends of Maria's bloodthirsty nature are extreme, even for a pirate. She seemed to genuinely enjoy murder—stabbing people in the heart, tying them to the mast and using them for target practice, and sewing them into bags and dumping them overboard. While other pirates killed out of necessity, Maria killed for fun.

One of the more popular stories about her comes from early in her career and involves the capture of the Flemish brig *Altona*. When they captured the ship, Maria took a fancy to the captain's uniform and decided she would have it. In front of the crews of both ships, she made the captain strip. Once he was completely naked and humiliated, she shot him and two other crew members. She put on the uniform, promoted herself to first officer, and just like that her transformation into a member of Cobham's crew was complete. From then on, she wore the uniform at all times, even going so far as to have copies of it made. Nobody dared question her authority—they were all too terrified of her.

As she was coming into her own as a vicious pirate, her husband was becoming ever more disenchanted with their way of life. The swaggering pirate who'd won his bride with gruesome tales now yearned for a quiet, respectable life on the Continent. Twenty years on the sea was long enough for him. Maria, however, was not interested in retiring, but eventually agreed—provided Eric agree to buy her dream home on the coast of France. In order to finance that, the couple would have to pull one last big job and go out with a bang.

Most accounts agree that the couple selected an East Indian ship, the *Middleton*, for their last target. What happened once they took the ship is the subject of several different stories. One account claims that Maria, to avoid anyone's giving them away, ordered the whole crew locked in manacles and thrown overboard. Another story is a bit more sinister but seems like something Maria might have enjoyed. The crew, no doubt aware of their captors' reputation for cruelty, was astonished when rather than immediately murder them all, Maria instead served them a fine dinner and sent them belowdecks to get some rest. All night, the ship reverberated with the groans of the crew as the men died slow and painful deaths from the poison Maria had cooked into the stew. By morning, she had a ship full of corpses, which she tossed overboard. Either way, Maria ensured that nobody would be around to tell their story.

With the money they made from the *Middleton*, as well as the profits from the sale of their ship, the Cobhams were able to purchase a massive, twenty-mile-long estate on the coast of Le Havre, France. The estate's previous owner was the Duke of Chartres. Le Havre's location in the northwest region of Normandy, adjacent to both the English Channel and the Seine River, ensured it was a busy port area where many ships passed. Many wealthy traders were building homes along the coastline around the time the Cobhams chose to retire there. King Louis XV himself visited the area with Madame de Pompadour in 1749. It was a place for the rich and powerful to enjoy the view of the sea—and Eric Cobham intended to do just that.

Apparently done with his life of crime, Eric became a local magistrate. Landlubbing life suited him, and he became, by all appearances, a respectable citizen, presiding at local courts. Occasionally he would take the family yacht out for a spin and do some minor pirating, but he never again took on the "big money and many murders" jobs he and Maria used to get away with. The family had three children and seemed to be settling into life in Le Havre quite nicely.

Maria, however, was not quite so content to close the door on their old life. She became a recluse, reportedly leaving the house only for brief journeys on the yacht. Eventually, she met her untimely end—though just how is the subject of some dispute. Gosse reports that, filled with shame for her lifetime of bad deeds, she took laudanum and died. Other accounts claim that she told Eric she was going to take a walk along the cliffs one day and never returned; her shawl washed up on the beach some days later. Howard Pyle's *Book of Pirates* says that Eric was fed up with his wife's morose behavior and killed her himself. *Lives of the Most Celebrated Pirates* notes that nobody mourned her death because "her temper had nothing feminine in it."

Eric, overcome with guilt over his wife's death, assuming he didn't kill her himself, went to a priest to unburden himself of their sordid past. Over the remaining years of his life, he told the priest everything about what he and his late wife had done, confiding all their secrets. As he lay dying at the estate, he called the priest to hear his last confession. He gave the priest the account he had written about their twenty years pirating and made the priest promise to publish it after his death. The priest, according to the story, kept his promise.

At the time of his death from old age, Eric's children had become members of Le Havre's high society and had no inkling of their parents' wicked past. When the pamphlet appeared, they were horrified but determined to avoid a scandal. With their considerable money and influence, they made sure that every copy of the confession disappeared—save one. The only surviving copy is said to be secreted away in French archives, but it has been so cunningly hidden that it has never been recovered. Nonetheless, the story of the pamphlet somehow got out, and thus the Cobhams' bloody past became part of pirate history.

Maria's story hits a discordant note in the ballad of pirate women— she is one who is hard to root for. Pirates always operate in a morally gray area, but Maria Cobham seems by all accounts to have been a vicious, ruthless woman who was not drawn to the freedom or adventure of piracy as much as the murder. Like Rachel Wall after her, she has very little in her story that readers would strive to emulate. She drives home the fact that piracy, for all the love it is given in popular culture, was sometimes a vile and cutthroat business, not for the weak of heart. It attracted all sorts of people for a variety of reasons, many of which were less than noble. Yes, there were the pirate republics and constitutions that promised equality for all, but there were also the amoral robbers and villains who just wanted to cause mayhem. The line between morally questionable and morally reprehensible behavior is constantly evolving with societal and cultural norms. Piracy straddles that line, pushing readers to reckon with their own moral codes. Seldom is that duality more evident than in the tale of Maria Cobham.

But perhaps Maria was not as vicious as she was portrayed. Lack of a reliable primary source account of her life means that her story has been subject to many retellings and edits over the years. It seems more than likely that details could have been exaggerated. History may never get a clear picture of what Maria Cobham really was like. But perhaps she was as bloodthirsty as has been claimed—is the reader more likely to judge her harshly due to her sex? Many male pirates, such as François L'Ollonais, were noted for their cruelty but were not chastened because of it—if anything, they are admired for it. Should Maria be spoken ill of for the same qualities that are applauded in her male counterparts? If piracy is to be accepted, warts and all, then Maria Cobham should be praised for her long career and great success, as are her similarly dispositioned male cohorts.

Bonny and Cobham entered piracy voluntarily for ostensibly the same reason: the love of a man. Both exit the historical record under mysterious circumstances. With the Golden Age of piracy coming to an end, the world no longer had room for such ambitious and avaricious women. Their crimes would inspire some copycat women pirates in the coming years, but nobody would rise to the level of these two in the West. Piracy lost something important at the end of the Golden Age—call it swagger, call it panache, call it what you will. By no means was piracy over, but the glory days of pirate havens and permissive governments were gone. From this point forward, pirates would look back to the Golden Age and try to recapture some of its grandeur. Anne and Maria, with their larger-than-life tales and remarkable careers, are excellent symbols of that bygone age.

9

Pirates of the New World

EFORE THE UNITED STATES OF AMERICA became a nation, it had female pirates. And it is no surprise, given the variety of people who lived in the American colonies. Political prisoners were shipped from Europe to the Carolinas and Virginia beginning in the seventeenth century. Georgia was founded as a debtor's colony. Run-of-the-mill nonpolitical prisoners were also transported to the colonies—English judges realized they could use the colonies as a storage locker, where malcontents could be disposed of and never seen or worried about again.

In the early 1600s many people, both men and women, were sent to America through the Virginia Company for a period of indentured servitude, during which they would work off their contracts as tradesmen, craftsmen, and laborers in both urban and rural areas. The colonies were full of land suitable for farming but lacking people to do the farmwork. Indentured servitude was, at first, an excellent solution to this problem. Some colonies offered incentive programs that gave landowners a set amount of free land for every indenture they imported. It seemed like a good plan—a person could get a free trip and room and board for the duration of his or her indenture, as well as money when he or she finished work.

Less than half of all indentured servants lived to see the end of their indenture. Conditions were unduly harsh. Women and children as young as twelve were subject to kidnapping to become wives and mothers.

According to Professor Dorothy Mays, women indentures were subject to nearly constant sexual harassment and pressure, often from their masters, yet if they became pregnant it was considered theft from their masters due to the loss of work time, and they had to serve extra years on their contract as a result. Companies seldom followed through with the promises they made to indentured servants, often giving small fractions of the land and money they had offered to the new colonists. Many of these people died penniless and far from home. This practice did not go on long, however; as the seventeenth century came to a close, many employers shifted to a cheaper source of labor: slavery.

The first colonial women pirates were originally British citizens who had come to the colonies either as prisoners or as indentured servants. As the Golden Age of piracy came to an end in the Caribbean a few hundred miles to the south, Virginia tried and convicted a number of pirates, two of whom were known to be women. On August 15, 1727, at a court in Williamsburg, Virginia, Martha Farley (commonly called Mary Harvey or Mary Farley) and a gang of three men, led by John Vidal, were tried for the crime of piracy. Martha's husband, Thomas Farley, who had allegedly coerced her into piracy, was never apprehended and was at large at the time of the trial. Martha had been transported to Virginia in April 1725 for an unknown crime. The men were accused of pirating in the area of Ocracoke Island in what is now North Carolina, and Martha was accused of aiding and abetting them. Exactly what Martha's role was in the pirate crew and whether she cross-dressed or appeared as a woman is unclear, but there are a few clues.

Martha's marriage to Thomas Farley and her acquaintance with the rest of the gang is compelling proof that her gender was known to at least Thomas; however, even if her gender were known, she may have worn men's clothing during piratical outings. According to John C. Appleby's book, *Women and English Piracy, 1540–1720: Partners and Victims of Crime*, Martha pled ignorance at trial, claiming she had no idea what her husband was doing or where he was taking her. She said that he had taken her and her two children away from their friends and forced them to go begging, and that when he took her out on the boat to go pirating, she thought he was taking her back to her friends. She was released due to lack of evidence and out of concern for her children's welfare.

Was she really innocent as she claimed? She would have to have been rather naive to be completely unaware of the nature of the piratical boat trip. The court apparently believed her story, or at least thought her wickedness was outweighed by the needs of her children. Ultimately, Martha's piratical bona fides are uncertain. She could have just as easily been a poor kidnapped wife as a ruthless pirate, and she took that secret to her grave.

A similar situation happened a few years later, also in Virginia. Maria Crichett (or Mary Crickett/Crichett) was transported to Virginia as a felon in 1728, on the same boat as a man named Edmund Williams. A year later, Williams, Crichett, and four other pirates were all tried and convicted of piracy. We know very little about Maria—her style of pirating, her role on the ship, and so on. Like Martha Farley, she might not have even been a pirate at all but simply a woman who was known to spend time with pirates, either voluntarily or involuntarily. That she was tried at all shows that the American colonies were not willing to turn a blind eye to piracy as the Caribbean colonies had done a few years earlier. With Blackbeard dead, pirates were no longer welcomed into polite society as interesting ruffians. Virginia would not stand for it.

Maria was sentenced to death by hanging, like the men, but there is no record that the hangings actually took place. Even if the men were ultimately hanged, she may have escaped the noose like Anne Bonny and Mary Read before her due to pregnancy or another excuse.

What inspired these indentured women to go to sea? Their biographies are frustratingly incomplete. Perhaps the stories of Bonny and Read came to them, through a battered copy of *The General History of the Pyrates* or a story whispered through the servants' quarters. These women and potentially many others who managed to avoid detection may have felt a spark of hope for the first time since their indentures began. If another woman could escape her dreary life and grab her freedom with both hands, why couldn't she? Or maybe they were forced into it by their partners. No matter how or why they entered the ranks of pirate women, they did, taking the torch lit by the women before them and passing it on to the next generation of female pirates.

Thus little is known about these women, and even less is speculated. Despite the fact that they are officially on the record, they are not prominent in pirate lore. They are included in only the most exhaustive pirate history books, and then usually as a footnote or a single paragraph. Maybe their insistence that they took no part in piracy makes them unattractive pirate heroines. But, they might have just been very good actresses determined to save their own skins. Unless more accounts come to light, these women might remain footnotes in pirate history. At least Martha's story is still regularly told in one place: Colonial Williamsburg, as part of a popular pirate walking tour.

About twenty years earlier, in roughly 1700, there was another woman pirate whose story is inextricably intertwined with one of the most famous pirates of all time. Mary Ann Townsend was allegedly wife of the infamous Edward Teach, also known as Blackbeard. According to W. C. Jameson's *Buried Treasures of the Atlantic Coast*, the pair merrily plundered the Carolina coast in the early decades of the eighteenth century. Jameson's book is the only source for Townsend's story, and he does not cite his sources—he also erroneously claims that she is the "only successful female pirate on record." Her ties to Blackbeard give her story a similar feel to Jacquotte Delahaye's; perhaps she was invented to correct an unsavory part of pirate history—in this case, a notorious womanizer. Nevertheless, a legend of this woman may persist on the Carolina coast.

Blackbeard reportedly had up to fourteen common-law wives, according to Johnson's *General History*; ergo any claims that he associated with a particular woman are somewhat believable—she may have been one of the fourteen. He did engage in several partnerships with other pirates over the years, although there are no records of him ever partnering with a woman. Regardless of how Townsend's story came to be, it is entertaining and illuminates Blackbeard's life as much as it does Townsend's. It humanizes the vicious Blackbeard (as many movies and television shows have attempted to do in the twentieth century, such as the 1951 film *Anne of the Indies*) and allows a woman to gain a place at the table of this particular historical banquet, which is pretty heavily male-dominated during this era.

Townsend, according to legend, grew up in Jamestown, Virginia, the niece of a well-to-do government official, who raised her. This part could also be true: the Townsend family has roots in Virginia as far back as the Jamestown colony, so there may well have been a government official named Townsend during the early 1700s. Mary Ann was attractive and well educated, and she was a favorite at high-society gatherings. The story does not mention her parents. On a business trip to Bermuda with her uncle, Mary Ann's ship, the *Shropshire Lass*, was seized by Blackbeard's crew. The crew murdered many people immediately, then forced others to walk the plank.

Here the story differs from historical fact: Blackbeard, for all his cruelty, did not actually make his victims walk the plank. There's little proof that any pirates did. Druett says Captain Charles Johnson included a story in *General History of Pyrates* about ancient Mediterranean pirates telling their captors that they could climb down a ladder and swim for their freedom in the middle of the open sea. In 1837 Charles Ellms's *The Pirates Own Book* mentioned a "death plank" from which prisoners fell into the sea. He may have been working off Captain Johnson's description and adapted it for his own. Robert Louis Stevenson included walking the plank in his 1884 masterpiece *Treasure Island*, which won the practice a permanent place in piratical lore. In reality, pirates were more likely to simply toss a captive overboard, ransom her, or maroon her on an island. The only female pirate said to have made her victims walk the plank is Sadie Farrell, who will be discussed in chapter 12.

According to the stories about her, when it was Mary Ann's turn to walk the plank, the six-foot-tall, red-haired beauty refused to let the pirates touch her. She spit in their faces, cursed them soundly, and even kicked a few. This brave—if uncouth—behavior attracted Blackbeard's attention, and he decided to speak to this girl who showed no fear, even in the face of death by pirates.

Just who was Blackbeard? When most people are asked to name a pirate, chances are his name will spring to their lips. His legend looms largest of all pirates, yet few know much about his life beyond his name and possibly that he had a long black beard. So what is the real story of his life?

Some scholars disagree on the spelling of his name, but he is commonly referred to as Edward Teach. Teach was born sometime around 1680 in Bristol, an English seaside town. He probably attended some school there, given that he was known to be able to read and write. His first piratical activity was to become a privateer during the War of the Spanish Succession, which ran from 1702 to 1713. He sailed under Captain Benjamin Hornigold, who mentored the young pirate-to-be.

As a privateer in the employ of the English navy, Hornigold was able to lucratively plunder England's enemies during the war. But when the war ended, he found himself out of a job and in fact forbidden to do what he had recently been employed to do. Hornigold and his crew, Teach included, became pirates, albeit pirates who refused to attack English ships due to Hornigold's love of his home country. Hornigold gave his young apprentice a ship of his own in 1717, which Teach renamed the *Queen Anne's Revenge*, a name that would come to strike fear into the hearts of many captains across the waters of the world.

Teach sailed all over the Caribbean and as far as Africa. He did not share Hornigold's patriotic views and attacked English ships as well as French, Spanish, and Portuguese ones. His penchant for theatrics, including tying lit matches in his beard to give him the "appearance of Satan," made sure that his reputation preceded him. As long as a crew surrendered quickly, they were most often spared. Despite the legends that proclaim his cruelty, there are no verified reports of him killing anyone, although it almost certainly happened. It seems that his fearsome appearance did a lot of his work for him. Perhaps Mary Ann's crew refused to hand over their treasure and that's what prompted their slaughter. Whatever transpired on the *Shropshire Lass*, Mary Ann enters Blackbeard's legend at that time.

According to the story, Teach was so taken with this spirited woman that he invited her to step down off the plank and into his cabin. She became a captive of the ship but was not treated like a prisoner. She was instead courted with gourmet meals, jewels, silks, and precious metals. Like Anne Dieu-le-veut before her and Cheng I Sao after her, her fierce antics and refusal to be wooed only endeared her more to her would-be suitor. Many a pirate man, it seems, held a soft spot in his heart for a pirate lass who was his equal in temper. Teach, normally a ruffian, curbed his bad behavior around her and was a perfect gentleman. Eventually, he asked Mary Ann to marry him. After a while, she accepted, and the pair embarked on a mutual career of pirating.

The only woman Teach is known to have married is Mary Ormond of Bath, North Carolina. She was around sixteen years of age and the daughter of a plantation owner. Johnson claims that she was Teach's fourteenth wife, although she believed herself to be his first. Her fate, as well as the fate of the other wives, is unknown, although some stories, including Johnson's account, indicate that Mary Ormond was forced to prostitute herself to the members of the *Revenge*'s crew.

Mary Ann Townsend, however, was not offered such a grim fate, but instead a life of luxury by the side of the world's most feared pirate. She begged her husband to teach her all that he knew, and he readily agreed. He also took her into Charles Town and showed her the delights of the town, which included the swamps where his treasure was reportedly hidden. Mary Ann is thought to be the only person besides Blackbeard himself who knew the location of his treasure—despite the fact that pirates were known to spend treasure rather than bury it. After a year under his tutelage, she was awarded a ship of her own to command, the *Odyssey*. Given that she had developed a reputation herself, it was no trouble for her to assemble a crew and begin her solo pirating career—which she did with gusto.

It's possible that during Mary Ann's foray into pirating by herself, Blackbeard decided to undertake another project: respectability. In 1718 he downsized his crew from four hundred to forty by running the *Revenge* aground at Beaufort Inlet, North Carolina, either by accident or on purpose, and abandoning most of his crew along with the ship. It is hard to imagine the depths of self-interest that would lead a pirate to send over three hundred men in his care to their deaths to save himself. This coldhearted behavior lends credibility to the stories that claim Blackbeard abused his wives. Surely someone who would leave his men to die in such a way had little regard for the value of human life. With a much more manageable crew, he appealed to the governor of North Carolina for a pardon for his crimes, bribing him heavily to ensure he would grant it. Teach and twenty of his men were pardoned, and Teach set out to live a country squire's life, living in a fancy house in Bath. Weekends, however, were for sneaking out and pirating. Governor Eden of North Carolina either was unaware of Teach's double life or chose to ignore it, and evidence suggests it was the latter. The hoi polloi of North Carolina found Blackbeard's antics to be charming rather than horrifying, and he was very popular among the wealthy of the province.

Eventually, Teach's flagrant flouting of the law became too much for the law to ignore any longer. North Carolina was hesitant to cramp the style of its newest favorite son, but Virginia had no reservations about going after the pirate. Governor Alexander Spotswood took a hard line against piracy that would remain official policy through the next several governorships, including the years when Martha Farley and Maria Crichett were tried. Lieutenant Robert Maynard was dispatched to hunt down Blackbeard's hideout at Ocracoke Island, with Spotswood's money to furnish the ships needed to navigate the narrow inlet.

In the early morning hours of November 22, Maynard and his two ships, the *Ranger* and the *Jane*, sailed into the shallow waters off Ocracoke Island where Blackbeard's one remaining ship, the *Adventure*, was at anchor. Maynard's ships were small sloops, purposely chosen to look unthreatening and to travel into the small space. They were able to sail almost to touching distance of the *Adventure* before Blackbeard and his men noticed and hailed them. Words were exchanged, and then the battle began.

The *Adventure* fired a cannon at the *Ranger*; this rendered the ship dead in the water and killed many of its men. If there had been any wind that morning, Blackbeard and his men might have gotten away, but the water was calm and could be traveled only by rowing, so the pirates were stuck in the inlet. The *Jane* was also gravely damaged by a direct hit from the *Adventure*. Maynard, on the *Jane*, saw that Blackbeard and his men were going to overtake them, so he devised a desperate plan not unlike the one Henry Morgan had pulled off at Maracaibo decades earlier. He ordered all his men to go belowdecks and hide, weapons ready, waiting for his command. When Teach boarded the *Jane*, they were lying in wait for him.

In the hand-to-hand combat that followed, Blackbeard and Maynard traded furious blows, wounding each other over and over again—first with pistols, then with swords. In total, Blackbeard was said to have taken more than a half dozen bullets and twenty sword wounds before falling down dead, cocked pistol in hand. Maynard cut off the infamous pirate's head and hung it at the front of the ship as proof of his demise and threw his body into the sea. Legend has it that the headless body swam three times around the ship before sinking. His dramatic death suited the life he'd lived and the way that he'd pirated, and no doubt helped boost his status from famous to most famous. A skull that is reported to be Teach's is on display at the Peabody Essex Museum in Massachusetts, drawing many visitors each year.

Somehow, word reached Mary Ann that her husband had been killed. To make matters worse, she found out that there were privateers on her trail who were after the huge reward offered for her—dead or alive. Not one to get bogged down by hysterics or grief, she immediately stocked the *Odyssey* with provisions and took off for South America, never to set foot on North America's shores again. She abandoned her own treasure in the Charles Town swamps, as well as what was left of Blackbeard's treasure stored there, in order to get out alive. There would be more treasure to plunder in South America.

Over the next decade, many stories surfaced about Mary Ann, but Jameson notes that "none have ever been verified." It was said that she ended up in Lima, Peru, where she married a wealthy businessman, presumably one who didn't ask too many questions about her past. Her treasure store has never been recovered, though people go out into the swamps to search for it (along with Blackbeard's treasure) every year.

Could this woman have existed? Possibly, but most likely not. The parts about Blackbeard's buried treasure are the most unbelievable, but the whole story lacks a certain credibility. However, many extraordinary women have been swallowed up by history and it is conceivable that she could be one of them. Also, her role in the legend as a woman who tamed Blackbeard's womanizing ways is telling of what people feel about Blackbeard. There is a desire to make him more humane and less promiscuous. Mary Ann is a new spin on the Blackbeard story, which is continually refashioned as it is retold. It is gratifying to think of a woman at the ruthless pirate's side, matching him plunder for plunder.

⚓⚓⚓

Another American pirate from this period has more historical documentation but frustratingly fewer details about her life. Flora Burn was listed as a crew member on a privateer ship and entitled to a one-and-three-quarter share of the booty the ship brought in, which was an equal share with the other crew members. She operated out of the East Coast of North America at some time during the middle of the eighteenth century. Privateering in America was very common—before, during, and after the Revolutionary War. The American colonies were very lucrative, and all privateers wanted to have a piece of the revenue they brought in for themselves. Privateers were necessary to protect a colonizing country's interest so far away from home.

How did Flora Burn become part of the business? Why did she join a privateer crew? Was she off to rescue her beloved? Did she have a turbulent home life to escape? The most remarkable part of her story is that there is none; she is simply listed as a crew member without much hullaballoo being made about her gender. One has to wonder what kind of sailor she was, how she was esteemed by the crew, and what became of her. We can only hope that more comes to light about Flora Burn and her career.

Flora was probably not the only woman privateer who fought against the British and helped shape America. During the Revolutionary War, American patriots terrorized the British by sea while the American army fought them on land. Where the American foot soldiers were often poorly equipped and barely trained, American naval privateers were good sailors and wreaked havoc on England's forces. The Continental Congress officially approved the rules and regulations of the commissioning process so that the newly conceived United States could benefit from a privateer force as England had done for so many centuries. It is estimated that during the war, around eight hundred ships were commissioned as privateers, which resulted in the capture or destruction of six hundred British ships. American privateer vessels were of every shape and size, from eight-ton whaleboats to six-hundred-ton, twenty-six-gun warships, with crews from a few men to over two hundred. These privateers risked their lives against the Royal Navy and many died. However, they made their mark on the navy—it is estimated that the privateers did $18 million in damage, which amounts to over $302 million today. The United States, like so many countries, owes a large debt to piracy. Without American pirates, there might not have been an America as it exists today.

⚓⚓⚓

The final pirate from this era is one of the more notorious of the American pirates. Rachel Wall, probably the first American-born female pirate, was born Rachel Schmidt around 1760 in Carlisle, Pennsylvania Colony. Her family was devoutly Presbyterian, according to some sources, and they lived on a farm. William Penn's work to establish religious freedom in the Pennsylvania colony meant that the Schmidt family was probably able to worship in peace despite the fact that the Presbyterians were a minority at that time. Rachel must not have taken to farm life, because she married sailor George Wall and moved away to Boston, never to return to Pennsylvania.

Stories on how she met George Wall are varied. The most common one is that she ran away from home and met him on the docks where he worked, and that the pair eloped soon after meeting. Another version is that while attending a family funeral in another part of Pennsylvania, Rachel slipped away to the docks and got in a fight with a gang of girls. When George intervened on her behalf, the pair began courting and married soon afterward. Where George was from originally and where the couple were wed are both unclear. Almost all the accounts agree that they married quickly and ended up in Boston, where she became a maid and he a fisherman.

George was not a particularly devoted fisherman. He preferred drinking and having a good time with his buddies to doing his job. After a particularly lucrative trip, the Walls and friends went on a weeklong bender, partying so hard that they failed to realize that the fishing boat the men were supposed to be crewing had left without them. Thusly marooned, George concocted the idea of giving up on fishing altogether and becoming a pirate instead.

This was not a completely ridiculous idea on George's part. He and his friends had all served as privateers during the Revolutionary War, and so they had gotten a taste for the life. They had sailing skills from their fishing jobs. George had an invalid friend who owned a fishing boat that they could borrow. So long as they brought back some fish each time they took it out, they could slip in and out of the harbor undetected. It was the perfect cover story. So what if piracy wasn't legal during peacetime? If one was a good enough pirate, one would not get caught. Rachel agreed, though some sources say reluctantly, and the fishing boat was obtained for their first pirate voyage.

Their plan required a storm, which fortunately happened pretty frequently in their neck of the woods. They sailed out to the Isles of Shoals and dropped anchor before things got too rough. The Isles of Shoals are actually a small group of islands about six miles off the east coast of present-day Maine and present-day New Hampshire, although in colonial times the area was all part of the Massachusetts Bay Colony. Before the Revolutionary War, the islands were a hot fishing spot, but they were abandoned during the war. After the war there remained a fair amount of traffic that passed by the islands due to their proximity to the mainland. There the Walls and their crew laid their trap.

They rode out the worst of the storm in the harbor at the Isles of Shoals, but once the bad part was over, they sailed back toward the coast a few miles, putting themselves right in the shipping lanes. They purposely misrigged the sails, raised a distress flag, and basically did everything they could to make the ship look like it had been damaged in the storm. And to bait this trap and make the illusion complete, Rachel was called on to do her part. Dressed as a woman, she stood on the deck, weeping and calling out for help. Well, the passing ships could hardly resist a damsel in such distress, and eventually one of them sailed close by to offer some assistance.

When they did, allowing Rachel to board their own vessel, the kindly sailors who'd stopped were rewarded by having their throats slit and their bodies tossed overboard. George, Rachel, and the rest of them took an inventory of what was on the big ship, stole anything of value, and then sank the ship, leaving no evidence of their robbery. After all, ships were often lost during bad storms, and nobody would question a schooner gone missing in the wake of a storm. The first time the Walls pulled this stunt, they got around $360 in cash, new fishing gear, and enough fish to sell their story to their friend on shore. They could sell the fishing gear back home, claiming it had washed up on the Isles of Shoals—probably the result of a ship gone down nearby. It was, in the end, a highly effective and profitable gambit. After her first taste of the adrenaline that came with larceny and murder, Rachel Wall knew she would not be satisfied with pulling off such a heist just once.

The pirates honed this routine over the following years, murdering twenty-four people, looting twelve ships, and plundering $6,000 worth of merchandise and cash, according to Cindy Vallar's essay "Women and the Jolly Roger." If a ship's crew was too large to murder outright, Rachel would request assistance fixing a leak onboard her ship. This tactic divided the crew, who could then be killed in two shifts: one on the Walls' boat, and a second on their own. The Walls made a decent amount of money pirating like this, as well as presumably all the fish they could eat.

The Walls' spree came to an end in September 1782. Rachel and the gang were headed out to sea—presumably to commit another robbery—when the storm became wilder than predicted and broke the mast of their ship. In the squall that followed, all crew members save Rachel were washed overboard and drowned. In an ironic twist of fate, Rachel found herself on the deck weeping and wailing for rescue, only this time her distress was real. Did the ship's captain who picked her up have any inkling that the woman he was ferrying back to Boston was a bloodthirsty pirate known for killing kindly captains? Was he aware that such a woman haunted those very waters? Probably not. After all, Rachel and the pirates left no survivors, and dead men tell no tales.

Back in Boston, the newly widowed Rachel got back her old job as a maid. She was done with seafaring piracy, but she had not entirely lost the taste for larceny. She reportedly snuck down to her old haunt, the waterfront, and pilfered ships at anchor. Ever the clever woman, she targeted the captain's private bathroom as a spot where precious goods would be hidden. She was never caught for these robberies, during which it was said she amassed a sizable amount of loot.

In 1789 she was accused of picking a lady's pocket on the streets. For this crime—and this crime only—she was sentenced to death, despite protesting her innocence. In her last confession, she admitted to her career as a thief but refused to recant her innocence of this particular crime. She also claimed that she herself had never murdered anyone during her piratical outings. She said it was degrading to be executed for a robbery. She was the last woman to ever be hanged in Massachusetts.

Like Maria Cobham, Rachel Wall is hardly a lovable character. Still, the ingenuity of her scheme does require at least a small amount of praise, if reluctant praise. That she was never caught as a pirate is impressive given how successful she and her crew were. However, in the end she still received the same sentence she would have gotten for piracy: a hanging.

The reality of Rachel's life may be far different from how she is portrayed, though. At the end of her life, she presented a picture of a repentant sinner, full of sorrow for her wicked ways. In her last confession, she laid out a laundry list of crimes she had committed but, curiously, did not include the piracy career. The story is told in many credible books, but the original source of that particular legend is difficult to track down. She does mention in her confession that an account of her crimes would "extend [her confession] to too great a length" as they are "too numerous to mention," so it is possible that she left the whole pirate thing out. Whatever really happened, she was a woman who married young, made some mistakes, and in the end, asked for forgiveness.

These American women pirates may have been inspired by Golden Age pirates, but their methods bore little resemblance to those of their Golden Age foremothers. By the turn of the nineteenth century, piracy would be even more different, for male and female pirates alike. But as ever, piracy would endure. Piracy lived on well into the next century and the centuries after that. The trappings of the trade, the treasure sought, and the ships sailed would change, but the fundamental element of piracy—the desire to take something that someone else does not want to give up—would remain ever present.

10

Women on the Edge

S THE EIGHTEENTH CENTURY rolled into the nineteenth, pirate procedure developed further and further away from the Golden Age
model. The United States was entering its third decade, and the
fledgling country was beginning to take shape, developing a distinctive
character all its own. Canada had been under British rule since the
end of the Seven Years' War in 1763, but the American Revolution
had caused strain between the Canadians and their leaders across the
Atlantic. England also ruled the British colony of New South Wales,
establishing a penal colony there in 1788. The world was becoming a
smaller place, with fewer and fewer unknown spots on the map.

Since the end of the Golden Age, pirates were no longer able to
elude the grasp of the law, which had gotten smarter and faster. Countries also no longer needed pirates to act as privateers—they were doing
their own dirty work now through their own national navies. With no
place to hide, Western pirates were forced to adopt new ways of life.
Targets became less valuable as treasure fleets shrank. Pirates may no
longer have wielded cutlasses or fired cannons as they did in their "glory
days," but during the early nineteenth century they remained a solid
part of seafaring life: as long as there exists something to steal, there
will be pirates to steal it.

Two of the most unusual female pirates of the nineteenth century
were Charlotte Badger and Catherine Hagerty. These women started

their lives in England but ended up settlers in a strange new land. Their story is documented in several sources, including Joan Druett's *She Captains*. Charlotte is said to be the first female settler of New Zealand. Unlike the average eighteenth-century pirate who stole gold and other valuable cargo, these women "stole" themselves—their freedom was their own "treasure."

⚓⚓⚓

Catherine Hagerty, Druett claims, is the more interesting of the women, but unfortunately we do not have nearly as much information about the "blonde, nubile, and husky voiced" Hagerty as we do about the "fat" Badger. Other reports describe Charlotte as the attractive one of the pair. Whatever her physical appearance, it is clear that Charlotte Badger was a woman possessed of no small amount of charisma. Charlotte was born in 1778 in Worcestershire, England, a rural county in the West Midlands rumored to be the inspiration for the Shire in J. R. R. Tolkien's *Lord of the Rings* saga. A teenage Charlotte was convicted of picking pockets (though some reports say housebreaking) in 1796. Legend has it she stole a silk handkerchief and a few guineas. In England, picking pockets was considered a felony and was eligible for the death penalty until 1808. Charlotte was not sentenced to death, however, but to transportation for life to a penal colony in New South Wales—present-day Australia.

The Australian penal colony movement was just getting started in 1796. Since prisoners were believed to be inherently mentally defective and incapable of rehabilitation, they had to be either locked up or executed. England's prisons were under scrutiny after reformer John Howard's 1777 study *The State of the Prisons*, which pointed out the often appalling conditions on the inside. Judges were reluctant to cram more people into these overcrowded jails and risk more public outcry and scrutiny from reformers, but they were also loath to execute every common criminal who came before them. It was a pressing dilemma: What was England to do with all its criminals? Apparently the option of letting petty thieves go instead of giving them life sentences was not on the table at this point. Sending the prisoners to America was no longer an option due to the Revolutionary War and subsequent loss of the colonies. England, despite losing the American outpost, nevertheless still seemed to favor the out-of-sight, out-of-mind philosophy, because on January 26, 1788, the country established the first penal colony in Australia.

Charlotte and Catherine endured the six-month voyage to Australia on the *Earl Cornwallis*. Conditions on the ship were deplorable. Convicts were chained belowdecks for the entirety of the trip, and many died on the journey. Charlotte survived the trip and arrived in Port Jackson, Sydney, in 1801. She wound up at the women's prison, the Parramatta Female Factory, where she gave birth to a daughter at some point, father unknown. It is possible that Charlotte's baby was fathered by one of her guards. Children were allowed to remain with their mothers in the Factory until age four, when they were sent to Orphan (and later Infant) Schools. After the separation, many mothers were never reunited with their children.

Parramatta is a riverside city in New South Wales about fourteen miles west of Sydney. The jail at Parramatta was a one-hundred-foot-long building made of logs surrounded by a high fence. The place was modeled on English workhouses and, just like at the workhouses, women endured unsafe conditions and poor treatment. They were not, however, entirely broken in spirit. Sir Roger Therry, a judge from the New South Wales Supreme Court, wrote in 1863 that the women were far more a blight on the local government than the male criminals transported there. He recounted how they destroyed everything that wasn't nailed down in the dormitories and often rebelled to the point that soldiers with bayonets had to be sent in to restore order to the place. "The Amazons," as Therry refers to the women, were not a bit frightened of the soldiers but instead threw rocks at them and chased them out of the factory. Therry's disdain for these criminals is evident in his book, but underneath there does seem to be a note of grudging admiration for their confidence and vigor in the face of such wretched circumstances.

There was a factory constructed above the jail where women did weaving work. It was notoriously overcrowded and women had to sleep in the workrooms among the bales of wool. There were four ways out of the prison: a ticket of leave upon completion of one's sentence, a transfer, a death, or a marriage. One of the more peculiar functions of the Parramatta Factory was as a matchmaking service. A man seeking a bride had merely to obtain a paper from a clergyman or judge proclaiming him a man fit to marry and present himself to the matron. She would then select a number of eligible prisoners and put them in a room with the bachelor, where a bizarre round of speed-dating would commence. The man would ask the women he found physically attractive if they'd ever been married before, and the women would ask in turn about the man's wealth. If both parties were amenable to the match, the matron was notified, a clergyman was hired, and the banns were proclaimed. Once the marriage was performed, the woman was able to walk out of the prison as a free woman, provided she remained on the right side of the law ever after. Thousands of marriages took place in this way. Catherine and Charlotte did not obtain their freedom through this practice, but they somehow caught the eye of someone important at the factory because their sentences were commuted in 1806. They were selected to be shipped nearly a thousand miles as the crow flies to Hobart Town, present-day Tasmania, to become domestic servants.

The two women found themselves onboard the *Venus*, a forty-five-ton brig. These ships were big, with two tall masts, each featuring the square-rigged sails. The mainmast also flew a smaller, triangular sail called a gaff sail. The ship would be primarily constructed of wood, possibly pine. The captives were housed below the main deck, where there would be almost no light or ventilation, similar to what they endured on the passage from England. Possibly the women would have been given separate quarters from the men, but that comfort was not guaranteed and was often not given. This particular voyage housed Charlotte, Catherine, Charlotte's daughter, two male convicts, a guard by the name of Richard Thompson, and the crew.

Once the women boarded the *Venus*, accounts differ on what exactly transpired. Some stories paint the captain, Samuel Chase, as a sadist who regularly beat the women for his amusement. Other stories claim that the women danced naked for the captain nightly and were generally friendly with the crew, causing mischief and breaking into the whiskey stash, which correlates with Therry's account, but both sources could be false or exaggerated. Another recounting says that Catherine struck up a romantic relationship with the first mate, Benjamin Kelly, while Charlotte took up with Lancashire, one of the male convicts. Whatever truly happened onboard, by June 1806 the women had experienced enough of it and decided to mutiny.

On June 16, Captain Chase docked at Port Dalrymple, a town on the mouth of the Tamar River in present-day northeast Tasmania. One story claims he spent the day doing business and slept, for some reason, aboard another ship that night. The next morning, as he sailed back toward the *Venus*, he was horrified to realize it was sailing off without him. Another story says that he was onboard during the mutiny and was flogged by Charlotte, who was dressed in men's clothing. The captain later said that Kelly was the ringleader of the mutiny but that the women were both enthusiastic participants. No matter who incited the mutiny—Catherine, Charlotte, Benjamin Kelly, or someone else altogether—the end result was that ten people sailed away with the *Venus*, leaving the captain behind. Stealing the ship and making off with the cargo, some of which was the captives themselves, made them officially pirates.

Now that the newly christened pirates had made their daring escape, what next? The first order of business was to drop off the ladies. The pirates, despite their rudimentary sailing skills, managed to sail clear across the Tasman Sea to Rangihoua Bay, in the Bay of Islands, New Zealand. Catherine, Charlotte, and Charlotte's daughter were dispatched to the shore. The men did not want to leave them entirely defenseless and hastily constructed a rudimentary structure for them before sailing off into the sunset. Some reports say that their lovers, Kelly and Lancashire, remained on the island with them, while other stories say that they took off with the *Venus*. All sources seem to agree, though, that in about a year, Charlotte and her daughter were alone on the island. Catherine died in early 1807, by which time the men—assuming they had gone ashore with the women—seem to have either left the island or been arrested for their part in the mutiny.

What happened to Charlotte next is a mystery. She might have died of natural causes or been killed by the native Maori population. The Maori had been isolated until American and European sealers and whalers began showing up with some regularity in the 1780s. These Western explorers were greeted with hospitality and enthusiasm, which they routinely abused. As a result, relations between Maori and Westerners had become strained, and at the time of Charlotte's arrival, the Boyd Massacre of sixty-six people by the Maori in retaliation for the whipping of a chieftain's son was only a few years in the future. Reports of cannibalism were not uncommon from this area. In all likelihood, Charlotte and her daughter perished on the island, either due to starvation or a bad encounter with the natives.

Many other possibilities exist regarding her fate. One account tells that in 1826, an American ship visited Tonga, some twelve hundred miles from Bay of Islands. The author of the account arrived at the tropical paradise and was shocked to find two pale faces among all the dark-skinned ones. This "stout Englishwoman" and young girl had arrived in Tonga a few years earlier and were able to translate between him and the natives because they spoke a "Polynesian" dialect fluently. If this woman was Charlotte, as has been speculated, what was she doing in Tonga? Why had she left the Maoris? The account does not say what happened to this woman after the author left Tonga, so the reader is left to speculate. There are so many different stories about Charlotte's life after being dropped off by the *Venus* that it's impossible to sort out which, if any, are true.

The stories told about Catherine and Charlotte concerning their stay in the Parramatta prison were told by the men who kept them there. The stories were colored by the males' perception of these women as criminals and degenerates, something to be looked down on as inferior and borderline subhuman. Many important details, such as how the women felt about their treacherous sea journey, what they thought about the prison marriage program, and why they decided to mutiny against Captain Chase, are left out of the tale. The reader is left to guess how Charlotte and Catherine felt about the odd incidents that dictated their eventful lives. Charlotte's story was always told by men, so in a way the fact that there is no definitive ending to her tale is a blessing in disguise. By disappearing, she took control of her own story and lived the remainder of her life outside of a male narrator's gaze. Wherever Charlotte Badger went, she died a free woman, far from the prison where she had been sentenced to spend the rest of her life. Her piratical adventure earned her a spot in the history of Australia as the first female settler of New Zealand, as well as Australia's first female pirate.

⚓⚓⚓

The next pirate from this period also entered piracy due to circumstances outside her control, but with considerably less joyous results. Margaret Croke was born in Ireland sometime in the late eighteenth century. She married Edward Jordan, an attractive man with "dark hair and eyes, a flashing grin, and very white teeth" in 1798. Edward had a history as a rebel and troublemaker, and he was fabled to have once barely escaped execution by leaping over a prison wall. Ireland at the time was under Anglican control (Irish Protestants loyal to the British crown). Catholics and non-Anglican Protestants, such as Presbyterians, were widely discriminated against by the government. At various times, these minority groups were not allowed to vote, run for Parliament, or be appointed to state jobs, depending on the whims of the ruling monarch. Edward was part of this minority, as well as a landlord's deputy. In his job, he would have had to evict his fellow countrymen from farms owned by an absentee landowner, a situation that made Edward the bearer of bad news for many people and would have made him the unjust target of a lot of abuse. Given this background, and the fact that he was sent to jail by his landlord for "training rebels," it isn't particularly surprising that he did not look kindly on the English. After he escaped from jail, he joined the Society of United Irishmen. He fought against the British at the Battle of Wexford in 1798, a significant defeat for the British.

Margaret either was unaware of this part of her husband's past, chose to ignore it, or wasn't bothered by it because the marriage appears to have been, at first, a love match. The newlyweds lived with her father for a year, enduring the arrest and trial of Edward for not having his papers in order. They moved out of her father's house and tried living in a different spot in Ireland for four years before deciding the New World had better opportunities for their family, which now included several daughters. The Jordans immigrated to the United States, which is where Margaret claims that the marriage turned sour.

The United States did not offer Margaret and her family the new start that they needed, and the family moved again—this time up to Canada, trying out numerous locations and vocations, even giving farming a shot for a brief period, before landing in Percé, on the Gaspé Peninsula in Quebec. Percé was at the time a seasonal fishing village known for its attractive landmarks. Quebec was newly under British control after the failure of the New France experiment. Canada would not gain its independence until 1867. The Jordan family tried farming again in Percé before attempting to get into the dominant industry of the area: fishing.

Edward Jordan went in with a wealthy family in the area, the Tremaines of Halifax, on a fishing boat. He felt that the joint venture would bring them all money, and if the Tremaines would only loan him the money then he would get the boat into seaworthy shape. The Tremaines sent Edward back to Gaspé with the supplies necessary to fix up the ship. Once he completed the repairs, he returned to Halifax, sailing on the jointly owned boat the *Three Sisters*. Up to this point, all parties generally agreed on the sequence of events. From here, the stories begin to diverge.

The Tremaines reported that Edward showed up without the money he owed them. He claimed that he had dried fish back in Gaspé that would satisfy his debt, but the family doubted his story. No longer content to give him free rein to sail wherever he liked with the boat they co-owned, they put their own captain, John Stairs, on the ship as an additional security measure and sent them both back to Gaspé to find the additional money Edward owed them. Stairs would come to play a pivotal part in the Jordan trial. When Edward returned to Gaspé, he and Margaret could not find anyone to loan them the money that they needed. Edward believed that he had been cheated—he felt that he was the true owner of the *Three Sisters* because he had fixed it up. No matter what anyone else said, he was certain he was right.

Margaret was understandably upset when her husband returned to Gaspé. Not only was he once again in search of money, but he also had not brought the supplies Margaret had requested from Halifax. Their children were starving and clothed in rags, and instead of providing for them, Edward got the family into more and more financial trouble. To make matters worse, when John Stairs realized that the dried fish Edward had talked about would cover only a fraction of what Edward owed the Tremaines, he officially repossessed the ship in their name. Now the Jordans were well and truly out of luck: shipless, penniless, and in massive debt.

Stairs, his three men, and the entire Jordan family set sail on September 10, 1809, from Gaspé for Halifax, a distance of nearly 550 miles as the crow flies. Why the Jordan family was onboard for this voyage is not clear. Stairs later claimed he was taking them to Halifax as a favor to Jordan to enable him to clear up some of his debt in person. Edward believed that, on the contrary, he and his family were being thrown into debtor's prison. Having narrowly escaped serving time in jail once before in his youth, Edward was in no hurry to return—and with his entire family this time. Jailing people who couldn't pay their debts was common at the time, and people could remain locked up indefinitely or even be transported. Margaret and Edward felt that they had been through too much to wind up in debtor's prison so many miles from home. So they hatched a desperate plan to keep their family out of jail at all costs.

In the afternoon of September 13, according to Stairs, they launched their attack. They crept stealthily through the ship and wounded or killed the members of the crew, taking them down one by one. Edward was wielding a gun in one hand and an axe in the other, while Margaret's weapon of choice was a boat hook. She reportedly beat Stairs over the head several times with it during the bloody skirmish. Once Stairs realized that two of his men had been killed by the Jordans, he leaped overboard into the freezing sea, clinging to a hatch he'd pulled from the ship, using it as a life raft.

At trial, Margaret told a different version of these events. She claimed that Stairs—who had previously aroused Edward's jealousy by giving Margaret some calico to clothe her children—visited her cabin alone. When her husband discovered the two of them, even though they were behaving innocently, he was tipped into a murderous rage. The scene was so distressing to Margaret that she lost her senses and was no longer aware of her actions. She testified at trial that "to the best of my knowledge I did not [hit Stairs with the boat hook]," but she couldn't say for sure. She said she was afraid for her children and would have acted out of instinct to protect them.

With Stairs in the sea and two men dead, the Jordans had officially taken the ship and turned pirate. Their original plan was to sail home for Ireland and get as far away from Canada as possible. Their only problem was that the approximately 2,500-mile journey could not be made with just the two of them; they needed more crew members. The *Three Sisters* was forced to dock in Newfoundland in order to recruit some new men. Onshore, Edward had some business to take care of and so the voyage home kept being delayed. Edward and Margaret, according to some accounts, only took trips to shore separately, which took twice as much time and further pushed back their departure date. Although they were in possession of a stolen ship and had murdered three men, the Jordans seemed almost hesitant to leave Canada. This departure delay would prove fatal for one of the Jordans.

John Stairs knew he was headed for certain death in the icy waters when he leapt from the *Three Sisters*. Miraculously, he was picked up just three hours after his jump into the water and so he managed to survive the plunge. The lucky captain sailed with his rescuers to America, where he reported the ordeal that he'd been through to the British consul. Word traveled to Canada that the Jordans were in possession of a stolen ship. On October 20, 1809, a warrant was made out for Margaret and Edward Jordan's arrest by the governor of Nova Scotia. A £100 reward was offered by the government, with an additional £100 put up by the Tremaine family.

With everyone on the lookout for the villainous Jordans, they were apprehended almost immediately and put on trial. Governor Prevost was determined to make an example out of the Jordan trial to prove how far His Majesty's law extended—all the way to Canada. After the trial, there would be no doubt as to who was in charge in the country. He convened a special court just for the occasion, spending large sums of money to ensure that everything was picture-perfect for the trial. No fewer than fourteen men sat on the judges' bench. Everything about the trial was meant to impress, and it certainly did, attracting plenty of attention.

At trial, both Edward and Margaret made brief statements in their own defense. While Edward claimed that he was only defending what was his, Margaret gave an emotional speech detailing the long history of abuse she had suffered at Edward's hands. As for the assault on Stairs, she could not recall the exact incident due to the state she was in at the time. Testimony from the two new crew members Edward had hired after the murders corroborated her statements. They painted a picture of a woman trapped aboard a ship with her murderous husband, constantly in fear for her life and the lives of her children. Even Stairs's testimony about her beating him with a boat hook could not overcome this sympathetic image. Edward was found guilty of piracy and hanged, but Margaret was acquitted.

Interestingly enough, many accounts of this story claim that both Margaret and Edward were hanged. The court report, however, clearly states that she was found not guilty and released. There are even some stories that say a collection was taken up by the friendly Canadians to help resettle the widow and her children back in Ireland. No matter where she ended up, Margaret Jordan almost certainly committed acts of piracy and yet walked away from the gallows. The fact she was able to tell her own story saved her, as it had saved many women before her. The public was not ready to believe that a woman could do such daring and heinous acts, and so it was quick to accept any alternate explanation, such as spousal duress. For Margaret, that acceptance was the difference between life and death.

⚓⚓⚓

A final pirate from this time is the totally fictional Gertrude Imogene Stubbs, also called Gunpowder Gertie. Although her story is verifiably made up, it was so convincing that the Canadian Broadcasting Channel told her story on the air as part of the radio program *This Day in History* without realizing that it was fiction. The story was created by British Columbia schoolteacher and historian Carolyn McTaggart as a tool to introduce children to the history of their area. She included many factual references about the period and the geographic area as she told the story to her students, who participated in a treasure hunt on the nearby shores of Kootenay Lake. They loved the story and told their parents, who called the school expressing wonder that such an amazing woman could have lived right in their area. The widespread popularity of the tale convinced McTaggart that Gunpowder Gertie needed a bigger audience.

She worked with a student's father who ran a local magazine called the *Kootenay Review*. On May 8, 1995, Gunpowder Gertie was the cover story of the magazine. Her fantastic life story was printed, without the caveat that it was made up by McTaggart. The author described it as an April fool's joke, though the piece ran in May. Somehow the magazine ended up on the desk of Bob Johnson, host of the popular CBC program *This Day in History*. The Gunpowder Gertie segment aired from coast to coast in Canada on February 12, 1999. A friend of McTaggart's told her about the broadcast, which prompted her to call the radio station and ask about this pirate. When the radio station confessed they'd had a hard time locating sources for their story, she explained that was because she'd made the whole thing up! Host Johnson was initially embarrassed about the mistake, but he later found it quite funny, claiming the story is one of his fondest memories of his time on air. On March 2 that same year, Johnson invited McTaggart on to his program to explain the origins of the story.

Gertie's story is pretty fantastic and chock-full of adventure. According to the story, Gertrude Imogene Stubbs was born in 1879 in England and emigrated with her family when she was sixteen years old to Sandon, British Columbia, Canada. The young girl left behind a beloved grandfather, who had filled her head with stories of pirates. Before she embarked for Canada, he gave her a gift—a small steam-powered boat, which he christened the *Tyrant Queen*, after his nickname for Gertrude. Her new home, Sandon, had recently become a boomtown with the discovery of galena ore there in 1891, and the railroads were racing to connect the city to the rest of Canada. Gertie's father was hired as a train operator for the newly finished Kaslo and Slocan Railway. It seemed the Stubbs family was destined for a happy and prosperous life in their new home.

Unfortunately, tragedy struck about a month after their arrival. Mrs. Stubbs was killed in an avalanche, which also destroyed the family home. The only thing that survived the avalanche was Gertie's toy boat from her grandfather, which floated up to the top of the snow. In addition to having to endure losing her home, young Gertrude witnessed the whole thing but was unable to save her mother. Her father sank into a deep depression and became a heavy drinker. Gertrude was forced to take care of her father, eventually doing his job for him at the railroad when he was too drunk to work, which was most of the time. His death in 1896 left Gertrude orphaned and jobless—the railroad refused to officially hire her because she was a woman, despite the fact she'd been doing her father's job for some time.

Gertrude was penniless after paying off her father's debts. She spent one of Canada's famously harsh winters earning the meager wages that were available to women in those days, barely getting by. At the end of the winter, she had made a wild choice—since she could not make a living as a woman, she would do so as a man. She sheared off her hair, donned some trousers, and set off to make her fortune as a coal hand on a steamboat.

Stern-wheelers, as the large steamboats were called, traveled up and down the rivers of British Columbia, shuttling supplies such as coal, mining equipment, and even livestock. During the height of the Klondike gold rush (1896–99), these ships provided vital material to the northern frontier. Before railways connected Canada to the rest of the world, these stern-wheelers were the most efficient way to move supplies from point A to point B.

Gertrude, due to her extensive experience helping out with the railroad coal engines, was a natural on the boat. She quickly worked her way up the chain of command and was doing fine on the ship until an explosion exposed her secret. During a race with another shipping vessel to determine which was faster, the boiler onboard was ignored and caused an explosion, in which Gertrude was injured. She lost her right eye and sustained other injuries. She was rushed to the hospital, where the attending physician realized that she was actually a woman in disguise. Without so much as a thank-you for her service, Gertrude was fired. Not only that—she was barred from finding another job on a stern-wheeler; all the companies had policies that forbade the hiring of women.

Gertrude, twice fired from jobs simply because she was a woman, decided that enough was enough. She swore vengeance on the shipping lines and said good-bye to Gertrude Stubbs. She became the fierce pirate Gunpowder Gertie. As a pirate she could do the jobs she was not allowed to do as a law-abiding boat worker. In piracy, she was finally able to break the bonds of her gender and work to her full potential.

The first thing she needed was a ship, and it just so happened the provincial police had a top-of-the-line, cutting-edge ship delivered just as she was starting out on her piratical career. In a stunning feat of illusion, she managed to get the patrol boat from the rail yard where it was delivered and into the river without being discovered. The *Witch*, as it was named, was rechristened by Gertie as—what else?—the *Tyrant Queen*, after her grandfather's gift.

The *Tyrant Queen* happened to be a ship excellently suited for piracy. The hull was encased in a protective layer of iron. The propellers were the newly invented ducted propellers, which only had to be halfway in the water. This gave the ship the advantage of having a comparatively shallow draft, meaning it could sail into small nooks and crannies where larger boats could not fit, much like the earliest pirate ships in the Mediterranean. The boat also boasted a steam engine capable of twenty-two knots and a water-cooled Gatling gun. The *Tyrant Queen* was the fastest thing in the water, and the captain was hell-bent on revenge. It was a deadly combination for the shipping companies that had wronged her.

Due partly to Gertie's excellent skills and partly to the vastness of the Canadian frontier at the time, Gertie was practically unstoppable. Her hand-sewn Jolly Roger flag flying, she would sail right up to the ship she wanted to plunder and fire some warning shots with her Gatling gun to show she meant business. Once she boarded the ship, she would rob the cargo—either valuables from passenger ships or gold and silver payloads from mining boats—at pistol point. She and her crew would then load up the *Tyrant Queen* with their booty and zip away, not to be seen again. Because there were no radios, few police boats, and generally very little communication from ship to shore, by the time the authorities got wind of another Gunpowder Gertie strike, she had vanished into the wind again. From 1898 to 1903, roughly the same time as the Klondike gold rush, she patrolled the Kootenay River and surrounding waterways, racking up a fortune in gold and silver.

Gunpowder Gertie could have sailed on forever. She may have continued pirating happily into old age had she not been betrayed by one of her men. Bill Henson, an engine man on the *Tyrant Queen*, was unhappy with his share of the booty. Nobody knows how Gertie divided up her treasure, but presumably she followed the pirate convention of divvying up treasure into shares based on the position held on the ship. So what happened? Did Bill get greedy? Was he of the opinion that they ought to strike more often or choose more lucrative targets? Did he decide that as a man he deserved more treasure than a woman, even if that woman was his captain? The legend is silent on this point.

Henson answered the provincial police's call for information on Gunpowder Gertie. For a handsome reward, he sold her out to the police. A trap was laid for the pirate in the form of a bogus tip about a big payoff coming into town on the SS *Moyie*. The *Moyie* was a real ship, and, at the time, a large, new paddleboat steamer that was active in the Kootenay Lake, well liked by passengers for the elegant dining room and luxurious details. The ship was 161 feet long and could reach speeds up to twelve knots. The *Moyie* served for almost sixty years, finally being retired in 1957. Today the ship is a National Historic Site of Canada and the world's oldest intact passenger stern-wheeler.

When Gertie attacked the ship in the area known as Redfish Creek (near the school where McTaggart taught), she found it full not of unsuspecting passengers but of armed police. Gertie, anxious to avoid unnecessary damage to her ship, prepared to run, but the dastardly Henson had sabotaged a gasket on the *Tyrant Queen*; it blew and made the pirates sitting ducks on the water. The ensuing battle was long and vicious, and the water ran red with blood before the fight was over. Gertrude was captured by the police and tried for piracy. She was sentenced to life in prison and died there of pneumonia during the winter of 1912.

All of Gertie's crew were killed in battle, so nobody was able to tell the authorities where Gertie had hidden her treasure. In the story, she buried it along the water's edge and it waits to this day to be discovered. Historically, very few pirates—if any—actually buried their treasure, preferring to spend it quickly instead, but this detail would have excited the school-aged listeners of the tale, who may have been inspired to explore the area in which they lived. The story would agree with the images of pirates for listeners familiar with *Treasure Island* and *Peter Pan*. The whole story is cleverly constructed to pique listeners' interest and encourage them to look up some of the places and events in a history book. It's hardly surprising that people would mistake this tale for truth and spread it around.

These three women pirates, so different in location and motive, give a cross-section of Western piracy during this century. Only a few more women pirates exist in the history of this century, and all of them hail from America. But the most successful pirate of all time ruled the waters of China during the early 1800s.

11

The Most Successful Pirate
of All Time

WHILE POST–GOLDEN AGE PIRATICAL operations seldom matched their Golden Age counterparts in fame, there was one post–Golden Age pirate who broke that mold and went on to become one of the most successful pirates, if not *the* most successful pirate, of all time. This pirate had at the height of her operation four hundred ships and somewhere between forty thousand and sixty thousand pirates under her command, which was larger than many legitimate navies of the time. She amassed so much wealth that she was forced to keep records of how much she had accumulated in order to keep track of it all—unheard of for a pirate. She negotiated with the Qing dynasty and won. Who was this fearsome pirate? Her name was Cheng I Sao.

If the most successful pirate of all time was a woman, why don't more people know her name? Surely this fact would be enough to dispel the myth once and for all that women can't be pirates. Even though a reader who has made it this far will no longer be surprised that a woman pirate was left out of history, it is remarkable that this woman could rise to such dizzying heights and attain so much clout and still remain unknown, particularly when the story of her life seems tailor-made for an action film adaptation. Perhaps an exploration of her life may yield some answers.

Before diving into her life story, it is important to understand when and where she comes from in Chinese history. Cheng I Sao is very much a product of China, and some knowledge of the country during the late 1800s will enrich a reader's understanding of her. This brief recap is in no way meant to be authoritative, but hopefully it will help put her epic deeds in context.

China is a massive country with nearly every habitat imaginable—mountains, large urban centers, rural farming areas, and coastal regions. The people who live near the sea have always experienced daily life in a markedly different way than people of inland China. For example, it was not unusual for women to work on the water in coastal China during Cheng I Sao's lifetime. Women often piloted sampans, small raft-like craft, up and down the coast, delivering goods from ship to shore and selling necessities to the boat people who lived at sea. Some seafaring families in the South China region spent nearly their entire lives at sea, living and working together on their ship. In the wealthier classes, men and women were able to more strictly observe traditional Confucian values, which kept women indoors while men were free to roam. Outside of the upper class, for everyone to eat, everyone had to work, women included. The relaxed social norms in some coastal societies aided Cheng I Sao's eventual rise to power.

She lived during the Qing dynasty, which also deeply influenced her pirating career. China's Qing Empire (1644–1911) would be its last, but not least in terms of catastrophic events; China would experience famine, several wars, and a full-blown revolution before it was all over. During Cheng I Sao's lifetime, there were only hints of the troubles ahead. China was thriving. Emperor Qianlong's reign was, on the whole, the most prosperous period of the whole dynasty. His strong military defeated uprisings and stretched China's borders, bringing the population to a peak of about three hundred million people. But despite these outward signs of imperial health, things were decaying.

One theory to explain the decline is that China simply got too big too fast and wasn't able to handle the population explosion. The infrastructure and government could not expand quickly enough to effectively rule and protect these new citizens. Another is that there was too much foreign pressure on China as Europeans spread across the continent, establishing India and other countries as colonies. China was unused to having to fight for its spot as the biggest power in Asia. Other sources claim that China's royal court began to follow Emperor Qianlong's example of spending vast amounts of the empire's wealth on personal expenses. People in the provinces struggled to feed their families while the rulers in big cities indulged in luxurious pleasures. However it came about, most scholars agree that the Qing Empire was in trouble by the late 1700s.

Despite the worsening situation for the average Chinese person during this time, Europeans, particularly the British, still desired to trade with China. Legal imports entered China through Canton (modern-day Guangzhou), a southern province on the coast of the South China Sea. This was the only port where foreigners were allowed to trade in China during the nineteenth century, and it was a bustling hub of activity. Along the Pearl River, the Thirteen Factories area was the trading post where the foreigners lived and conducted business with Chinese merchants. British, American, and Dutch traders snapped up silk, porcelain, and tea to take back home and sell at a huge markup. Trade with China was so profitable that Western traders could make 400 to 500 percent profit on one voyage.

Westerners were absolutely mad for tea and would do anything to get it. This gave the Chinese the upper hand, which they used to their advantage. Most Chinese merchants would not trade for European goods and instead accepted only bar silver as payment. Wanting to even things up a bit and offer something to trade themselves that would bring money back to England, the British introduced an irresistible commodity: opium.

The history of the opium trade in China is long and fascinating enough to merit its own book—or several books—and indeed it already has. Suffice it to say that the Chinese empire's attempts to stem the illegal flow of opium into China caused strife and friction between China and England, ultimately culminating in not one but two wars, fought from

1839 to 1842 and from 1856 to 1860. When all was said and done, the Qing dynasty was considerably weakened and China was much less isolated, at least tradewise, from the rest of the world.

Opium was banned in China starting in the mid-eighteenth century. It was smuggled into the country through "country traders," who were doing the dirty work of the British East India Trading Company (EITC). The EITC controlled the growers in India, who were forced to sell their product back to the EITC. They then turned around and sold the opium to these freelance traders, who technically did not work for the EITC, who then took it from British-held India to the China coast. It was quickly sold for gold and silver, which was in turn given back to the East India Trading Company. A significant portion of the EITC's operating budget came from this arrangement. By 1838 forty thousand chests of opium were imported annually—though off the books—most of them through the Canton area.

A unique feature of this area during this time was the flower boat. The seafaring sister to the mainland courtesan house, these floating pleasure parlors housed women who entertained male guests with song, dance, drink, and sometimes sexual services. They serviced the male populations up and down the coast, further adding to the festive atmosphere of the Canton area.

What sort of power could a woman of this place and time expect to have? As already mentioned, women did take part in seafaring work alongside their husbands; however, they were far from equal partners. A woman had one main purpose, according to Confucian values—to bear a son. Women were meant to be wives and mothers, and anything else was secondary. Daughters were valuable only for fetching a bride-price and becoming potential son-bearers for other families. They were treated as guests in their own homes because, upon marriage, they would become a member of another household. Why invest the energy in making a daughter feel special and valued when she would leave once she was married? Sons were laborers, continuers of the family line, and sources of pride. Once a son was born into a family, he remained part of the family all his life. Women of this time in Canton were conditioned not to expect too much. What they *could* expect were arranged marriages, possibly bound feet, and illiteracy.

Although women were expected to work alongside their husbands on land or by sea, their husbands were almost certainly chosen for them by their parents—without either bride or groom's consent. In nineteenth-century China, as well as many other places, marriage was essentially a financial transaction, designed for the all-important purpose of extending the family line by producing sons. It was far too important to be left to the romantic whims of the people involved. Marriages were determined when children were young—sometimes when the bride and groom were still babies. There were four different types of marriages practiced in China at this time, but by far the most common type was a patrilocal, or major, marriage. After marriage, a young bride left her home and entered her mother-in-law's house, in some cases permanently severing ties to her own home and family. She became the lowest-ranking member of the household, moving up in position only when she bore a son who married. Her new daughter-in-law took the lowest-ranking place from her upon joining the family. More rarely, a boy would enter his bride-to-be's home. This second option, called uxorilocal marriage, happened if the bride's family was short on male laborers. However, most of the time, it was the woman who left her home and was absorbed into her new husband's home, seldom able to visit or even contact her own parents and family again.

If a woman was not married, she still had a chance to enter into a man's household as a concubine. The concubine system is often misunderstood by Western culture. It was used primarily as a way to produce sons. If a wife did not produce a son for the family, a concubine could be added to the family to give the husband another chance to sire a son. Despite frequent portrayals in movies, television, and literature of young, pretty concubines usurping the role of the first wife, in eighteenth- and nineteenth-century China the wife's position in the household was sacred. The concubines were there for one purpose only—to produce an heir for the head of the household. The Chinese did not practice polygamy as the West understands the term, with multiple wives of equal or ranked status.

Whether wife or concubine, a woman of this time was likely to have bound feet. The practice is as inscrutable as it is painful. First practiced in the eleventh century, foot binding involves forcibly breaking a young girl's toes and folding them under her feet. The arch of the foot is then broken and folded upward, so that the toes now point toward the heel. The foot is wrapped tightly in bandages, which are changed daily or weekly depending on one's status, until the foot has healed into this origami-like construction that results in the "three-inch golden lotus," a hobbled foot that requires a woman to walk in an unsteady, mincing gait. It was a symbol of wealth—bound feet often prevented women from working, so to have bound feet meant that you were rich enough not to have to work for a living. First practiced by the elite, foot binding eventually made its way down into the lower classes, where it prevented daughters from participating in the most arduous field work. It became a symbol of refinement and ladylike elegance. It was also considered erotic by men of the period, who enjoyed the wobbling gait of bound women. Chinese love manuals had copious notes on how to use the bound foot as a pleasure tool, complete with explicit artwork. Male arousal came at a huge cost for these women: this incredibly painful process often caused a host of medical problems. Women with bound feet suffered from muscular atrophy, infection, paralysis, and even death. According to one estimate, as many as 10 percent of girls with bound feet died due to infection resulting from the practice. While it is unknown how many Cantonese women bound their feet, it was most commonly done by the Han ethnic group, which makes up the majority of Canton's population. It is not known for sure whether any of the Chinese women pirates had bound feet.

Women—whether they were wives, concubines, or unmarried daughters, bound feet or not—were seldom educated during Cheng I Sao's lifetime. In nineteenth-century China, children were instructed into their adult roles in the household at a very early age, sometimes as young as seven years old. Girls would be taught the domestic arts such as cooking, housekeeping, and sewing, while boys were taught the family trade, whatever it might be. Schooling was reserved for boys so that they could do well on the civil service exams. Test preparation was exhausting and expensive—if a family could not afford it for their bright son, sometimes a wealthy relative would foot the bill so that the honor would benefit the entire family. A Cantonese seafaring woman from this time would probably be of limited literacy, if she could read or write at all.

From these humble circumstances, a fierce pirate would rise to prominence. Although many stories circulate about Cheng I Sao, relatively little information can be verified about her. It is not known, for example, whether she knew how to read or whether she had bound feet. Historian and foremost Cheng I Sao scholar Dian Murray has identified two primary source documents from the period: Yuan Yun-lun's book *Ching hai-fen-chi*, published in Canton in 1830 (and badly translated by Charles F. Neumann in 1831 into *History of the Pirates Who Infested the China Sea from 1807 to 1810*), and *A Brief Narrative of My Captivity and Treatment Amongst the Ladrones*, written by Richard Glasspoole, an officer of the East India Company. There are many other sources claiming to have information on Cheng I Sao's life, but for the most part, they are interpretations and embellishments of these two books. Over the years, many stories have come to be taken as true, despite the fact that there does not seem to be much, if any, historical basis for the stories. Western translation of Chinese sources, the lack of a uniform romanization system for Chinese names until 1850, and a tendency for authors to fill in gaps in their accounts have resulted in many possibly apocryphal stories being added to Cheng I Sao's legend, despite the fact that her story is so exciting that it needs no embellishment.

Her real name has been lost to time. Cheng I Sao is translated to "wife of Cheng I." She is called many names, including Ching Shih and Zheng Yisao (in the modern Pinyin translation), but the two accounts from her time do not mention either of these names. She was born sometime around 1775, most likely in Canton. The sources provide no information on her parents or how she spent her girlhood. Her story begins in 1801 when she was working in a Cantonese flower boat and met and married the pirate Cheng I.

There is no evidence in the primary sources that she was a prostitute; however, it is an often-repeated part of her story in secondary sources. There were certainly many floating brothels in Canton during this time. There is a pleasant fiction, repeated in F. O. Steele's *Women Pirates* as well as numerous other sources, that tells of the future lovers' first meeting. The pirate Cheng I, having decided it was time to take a wife, ordered some prostitutes to be kidnapped and brought to him for perusal. Cheng I Sao (as she would come to be called) was the most beautiful of the captive women, and the fierce pirate immediately asked her to marry him. When she was untied in order to give her answer, she sprang at him like a banshee and attempted to claw his eyes out. This display of violence only served to further endear her to him, and he promised her jewels and fine silks if she would please be his wife. As a counteroffer, she requested half of his fleet and wealth. He accepted, and then she accepted, and the pair wed in 1801. This story appears to stem from an unverified source and is almost certainly untrue, however delightful it may be.

Soon after their marriage, the newlyweds became embroiled in the Tay Son rebellion happening in present-day Vietnam. The Tay Son leaders paid the Chinese pirates to fight for them and transformed them from a hodgepodge group into a professional band of fighters, who for the first time were united and fighting together. Although the brothers responsible for the Tay Son rebellion were ultimately unsuccessful and were overthrown in 1802, the lessons that the Chengs learned in Vietnam would not be lost on the couple. Immediately following the rebellion, the Chinese pirates were abruptly out of a job and returned home to fight each other for a while. But in 1805, Cheng I devised a scheme that would bring the pirates together into a strong confederation. The pair used their influence and leadership skills to herd the formerly warring pirate bands in the area into a strong, unified fleet. This fleet had seven captains, all of whom reported to Cheng I. The subfleets were classified by the different colored flags they flew: red flag fleet, black flag fleet, green flag fleet, and so on.

The Chengs had quite a successful operation for two years, continually adding ships to the fleet and booty to the coffers. Cheng I died in 1807, leaving his wife and his fleet behind. Sources disagree on how he met his end—some say he drowned during a storm, but others say he died fighting. In any case, his death left a big hole in the pirate fleet's structure. To avoid the collapse of the organization, somebody would need to step up and lead—someone whom the other pirates respected and trusted.

Cheng I Sao herself claimed the commander position and assumed control of the coalition. Her ascendancy to the throne was not as radical a decision as it might appear at first glance. Chinese culture of the period did allow men and women to sail together. The seafaring life was perilous, and people often died while working. It was standard procedure at the time for the surviving spouse to assume the responsibilities left behind by the dead spouse. This was essentially the same thing, only with a much larger fleet and the higher financial stakes to go along with it. So Cheng I Sao's rise to commander might have raised a few eyebrows, but it was most likely accepted as legitimate by the majority of the sailors. Her first official duty was to appoint a new captain of the most powerful fleet in the group: the red flag fleet. She appointed a promising sailor who also had the honor of being her adopted son, Chang Pao.

Chang Pao was captured by Cheng I as a young man and put into service in one of his fleets. Pirates were not above the occasional pressgang; it was not only the Royal Navy that made use of this recruitment technique. Somehow young Chang Pao caught the commander's eye, and he was adopted by Cheng I as a son in order to establish the all-important family bond that was necessary for business interactions in China. Some sources speculate that Cheng I developed a homosexual relationship with Chang Pao while he was grooming his protégé. Whatever the nature of Cheng I's relationship with Chang Pao, his wife would continue her late husband's custom of showering the young man with praise and privileges. Eventually, she married him. Whether she entered into that union for love or power (or some other reason entirely) only she knows.

Together, the couple formalized the relationships between the remaining fleets of pirates, making them a more cohesive force. Under Cheng I Sao's leadership, the fleet grew from fifty thousand to seventy thousand men, which she maintained for the remainder of the decade. This confederation outmanned and outgunned anyone who tried to stand up against it, including imperial forces. The coast was virtually unguarded, which left an opportunity for Cheng I Sao to set up a "protection" scheme that collected money from fishing boats and other shippers in exchange for protection from other pirates. This system kept vessels safe, provided restitution if the fleet failed to prevent an attack, and generated enough money to sustain the huge fleet and its men.

The importance of this massive achievement cannot be overstated. Cheng I Sao essentially built a navy and developed a program to keep it running. The logistics of such a feat are staggering. A woman with no training in military tactics or management mounted a formidable force that had China quaking in its boots. She also led pirates on pillaging expeditions to wealthy villages, according to some sources—extending her protection scheme to the shore. Cheng I Sao also decided to try her hand in some military battles, demonstrating her fleet's ability to best the high military officers. No other pirate in history—male or female—is known to have had as many ships or as many pirates under their command. While most pirates were an annoyance to the governments they pillaged, Cheng I Sao was an absolute terror to China, influencing diplomatic relations with foreign governments as well as domestic trade.

Nobody seemed able to stop her. The Chinese navy was utterly useless in holding her back and had to overcome its deep-seated reluctance to work with Britain in order to negotiate to borrow a ship, the *Mercury*, to be used to defend Canton from Cheng I Sao. The British ship was unable to damage her fleet as the Chinese had hoped it would, so the Chinese had to negotiate again with a foreign power—this time the more-familiar Portuguese—for six men-of-war. Still, Cheng I Sao could not be cowed. Her forces outlasted a blockade off the coast of Lantau Island. She was able to deflect the vessels that were sent to destroy her and sail away on the wind. The big showdown to end piracy that China had hoped for never came; when some Cantonese officials sailed out to watch the show, they saw their own ships being destroyed instead of Cheng I Sao's.

One of the accomplishments for which Cheng I Sao is best known is the code of conduct that she enforced in her fleet. Since the buccaneer era, many pirate ships had articles to be signed by everyone aboard, detailing rules and the division of loot. Cheng I Sao's code, however, contained some unique features. For starters, it was particularly strict and punished many offenses with death, including going to shore twice without permission, disobeying the orders of a superior officer, and holding back treasure out of the common stock.

Rape of female captives was also punishable by death. Men were permitted to marry captives if they chose to do so, but a pirate who purchased a wife from among the captives must under the code remain faithful to her, under penalty of death. If a man and a female captive had consensual sex, whether they were married or not, the man would be beheaded and the woman tossed overboard with weights tied to her legs. Even among married persons, Cheng I Sao viewed sex as a distraction that kept men from focusing on their jobs. It would bring jealousy and chaos onboard, which she could not afford in her fleet. According to Richard Glasspoole, this code was strictly enforced. Cheng I Sao had a giant operation to control, and so she needed things to be orderly. This code was a means to hold her vast fleet together and keep it the primed fighting force that it was, capable of taking down anyone in their way.

Perhaps the most controversial aspect of the code is its authorship. While a plethora of sources attribute it to Cheng I Sao, the earliest Chinese sources and, according to Dian Murray, the sources most likely to be factual say that Chang Pao wrote the code. Perhaps Cheng I Sao wrote it but chose to promulgate it under her husband's name to offer it more legitimacy, although the leader of one of the world's most powerful fleets probably did not lose too much sleep over appearing legitimate.

Given that she was Chang Pao's foster mother before she became his lover, and even after they were married she remained his direct superior, it's plausible that even if he *did* write the code, she would have asserted a lot of influence over the ideas that he included. No matter who penned the code, Cheng I Sao was the one responsible for enforcing it, and it remains a major symbol of her reign as Pirate Queen.

Cheng I Sao's pirating spree could not go on indefinitely. However, her end was not particularly dramatic or bloody—a rarity for any pirate, male or female. It was internal dissension that led to the surrender of the force. Kuo P'o-tai was the leader of the black flag fleet, the second-largest fleet after the red flag fleet. These two big fleets often worked together, both in the protection racket and in battle. Supposedly, Kuo P'o-tai was gunning for the red flag fleet position and for more power, and the formerly friendly partnership broke down. He went to the Chinese government, which had put out an offer of amnesty in an attempt to finally stop the pirates. His surrender prompted Cheng I Sao to think about surrender as well, which she eventually did.

After an unsuccessful conference between Chang Pao and a government official in February 1810, Cheng I Sao took the lead on negotiations. She was smart enough to realize that they could not continue pirating until age and infirmity took them to the afterlife and that they might as well go out on top with the government's blessing.

Cheng I Sao, so the story goes, stepped off her ship and traveled to the governor general's headquarters completely unarmed. With her were a number of other women and some children, also unarmed. What a sight they must have made, approaching the fortress of the general. One can imagine nervous soldiers, armed to the teeth, straining their eyes watching for the fearsome pirate leader to appear on the horizon. But she chose to enter negotiations unarmed, and let her powerful track record speak for her—a smart move that immediately gave her the upper hand in negotiations.

She pushed aggressively for a settlement in which the pirates were able to keep all the money they'd won, avoid jail, and obtain jobs in the military if they wished. For Chang Pao, she obtained a ranked position in the navy and permission to keep a private fleet of his own. Also part of the settlement was a large sum of money, paid by the government, which was to be used to help the pirates transition into civilian life onshore. In just two days, she emerged victorious from the negotiations and the surrender began. The government hardly had a choice other than to offer her what she asked for, since they had proved so ineffective in stopping her pirating activities. She held all the power and she knew it, so she used it wisely to the great benefit of her fleet.

Never in the history of piracy was there a large-scale surrender like this. Governor Woodes Rogers issued his large pardons decree during the Golden Age, but those were granted on a case-by-case basis, not en masse through a single pirate ambassador. Queen Teuta also negotiated a surrender for her band of pirates, but she lost a lot more in the discussion than Cheng I Sao did. It is a testament to how desperate the Chinese government was to get her out of the water that they agreed to Cheng I Sao's terms, which amounted to almost a total victory for the pirates, complete with government-sponsored pensions for the retiring pirates. The fact that Cheng I Sao was able to negotiate this might be her most impressive achievement of all. Some pirates were killed in battle, some killed by the law that caught them, but Cheng I Sao's pirates would die warm in their beds, covered in cozy quilts bought on the government dime.

After her triumphant victory, what became of Cheng I Sao? She lived with Chang Pao in Fujian Province until his death in 1822, but after that, sources begin to diverge again. Many claim that she returned to her biggest talent—accumulating wealth—although the stories differ on just how she made her money. Some say that she returned to her first profession and ran a large brothel. Others claim that she started a successful gambling house. No matter what she actually did, by all accounts she led a mostly law-abiding life after the death of her second husband and died in 1844 at the age of sixty-nine.

Why isn't more known about Cheng I Sao? It seems that, with her record, she should be a household name along with Blackbeard and Captain Morgan. Yet she is seldom more than a side note in piratical texts. It could be because many of her accomplishments are hidden under the banner of Chang Pao. It seems that Chinese-language sources simply do not find her as fascinating as Westerners do, due to China's general tendency to view continental concerns more pressing than maritime ones. Pirates are not the cultural and pop heroes in the East in the way they are in the West. Whatever the reason, she remains frustratingly obscure, though Dian Murray's work has shed a great deal of light on her story and brought her more attention. Hopefully additional information on Cheng I Sao will turn up as more scholars become involved in the research.

Over half of the nineteenth century remained when Cheng I Sao died, during which piracy would undergo still more changes and stylistic adaptations. During her lifetime, she briefly revived (and arguably surpassed) the grandeur of the bygone Golden Age, but her death plunged the pirating world back into the post–Golden Age doldrums. The pirates who succeeded Cheng I Sao did not come anywhere close to emulating her style or her success. They did, however, continue to update the ever-changing definition of what it meant to be a pirate, with their own legends of daring deeds and wild exploits.

12

Veterans of the American Wars

P IRACY CONTINUED TO EVOLVE in America, mirroring America's own evolution. As the young country approached and passed its one-hundredth birthday, it barely resembled the land it had been in 1776. Manifest Destiny, the belief that American expansion from coast to coast was both just and inevitable, was the name of the game, and the United States was growing in leaps and bounds as it tried to stretch from sea to shining sea. During the period between 1845 and 1900, eighteen states were added to the Union, including the giant states of California and Texas.

The addition of land and people to the country was a controversial enterprise. Many northern states opposed these new states, claiming they were bought with unnecessary bloodshed and unjust tactics. They also were vehemently opposed to adding more slave states to the country; they were very concerned about being outnumbered by slave states. Despite their fears, the South and West's clamor for more land was answered. It seemed that nothing could halt America's progress from coast to coast, though a great civil war would slow down the momentum.

The two women pirates from this tumultuous era in American history are as different as can be, reflecting the multitude of new roles that could be taken on by women during this time. America was going full steam ahead into the future, never to return to its preindustrial days. The women of America were similarly moved to evolve and change, turning their gazes away from home and hearth and toward their fellow women and dreams for tomorrow. It should come as no surprise that the women pirates from this era were also "new" American women, both ambitious and bold.

Sadie Farrell, known as Sadie the Goat, is one of the strangest examples of the American dream ever imagined. According to Herbert Asbury's 1928 book *Gangs of New York: An Informal History of the Underworld*, Sadie ran around robbing people during the mid-1800s in New York City's bloody Fourth Ward near the East River. Asbury's book is the sole published source of information about her, although legends abound. She is not featured in any police documents or newspapers from the period, which leads to the conclusion that she either never existed at all or was never caught. The truth, as in so many of these stories, may never come to light, but her legend looms large nevertheless.

According to Asbury, Sadie was born sometime around the mid-1800s and grew up poor among the pickpockets and lowlifes on the Lower East Side of Manhattan. The city at that time was a seething mix of too many immigrants in too little space, particularly down below Broadway. The formerly fancy Fourth Ward, once home to George Washington and John Hancock, had gone to the dogs; Asbury says a wave of immigrants chased the wealthy people north. The "ramshackle tenements [housed] a miserable population steeped in vice and poverty." Gangs ruled the streets and battled with one another often, and the gangsters of the Fourth Ward were the worst of all of them—killers and thieves more than common troublemakers.

It is no wonder that the area was full of strife, because the immigrants to America during this period were often met with cold welcomes. Americans knew the country needed more laborers to run its mills and factories, but they resented the influx of new cultures and ideas that came with those laborers. The Chinese Exclusion Act of 1882 is an example of the kind of obstacles immigrants faced. The only welcome for immigrants to New York during this time was from the political machines, such as Tammany Hall. These groups capitalized on the immigrants' need for friends to help them understand the country's bureaucracy and customs. They would help the new Americans . . . for the price of a vote.

William M. Tweed and his cronies got rich off this scheme to the tune of $25 million to $45 million. They controlled almost every part of New York City politics during Sadie's lifetime and could influence anyone they pleased. "Boss" Tweed was the East Coast's answer to Billy the Kid—a wild outlaw who both fascinated and repelled. Tweed saw an opportunity and took advantage of it, growing rich off the backs of others. Tweed was eventually brought to justice around the same time that Sadie's pirating days came to an end. His clear control of city politics could have made an impression on the young Sadie, who saw the evidence that if you were clever and tough, the rules didn't necessarily apply to you.

If Boss Tweed didn't tickle Sadie's fancy as a young woman, perhaps tales of another outlaw did. This period spawned the myth of the cowboy—perhaps the most American symbol of freedom and self-reliance there is, a landlubbing pirate. The pay was very low and the living conditions were worse, but cowboy life has become immortalized as adventurous and exciting. Outlaws such as Billy the Kid made their money robbing stagecoaches, particularly from 1866 to 1876. News of their exploits spread across the nation and could have made it to New York during Sadie's early career. The cowboy way of life was not particularly concerned with following the law, and this spirit was palpable in the western towns of the time. It seems likely that Sadie would have been inspired by the stories of these rough men making their own way in the world, even though their world was so very different from her own.

Sadie was a small young woman, but she was also scrappy, and she learned how to disarm her opponents without engaging them in hand-to-hand combat. Using the element of surprise, she would head-butt her mark in the stomach, knocking the wind out of him. Her male partner would knock the guy out and rob him. The Fourth Ward offered endless pickings, as it housed the South Street Seaport, a bustling port where sailors could be found at all hours drinking, paying for sex, and otherwise making merry. Asbury asserts that for at least twenty-five years,

Water Street was "probably the scene of more violent crime than any other street on the continent." The seeming pleasure district held danger around every corner—and some of that danger was Sadie.

Sadie was no stranger to violence. As a teen, she could not have missed the New York Draft Riots. In July 1863, President Lincoln instituted the military draft. Men with means could buy out of it for $300, approximately $8,000 in 2016 dollars. New York City, which according to Iver Bernstein had "a history of sympathy for the South and slavery," was not in favor of conscription, and many in the city felt that the draft fell too hard on the Irish and the working class. Many New Yorkers had recently lost their lives in the bloody Battle of Gettysburg, and those left alive were not eager to volunteer for what looked like the losing side. While the draft was in process on July 13, rioters interrupted the proceedings and unleashed hell in Manhattan for four days in what would become the bloodiest urban insurrection in American history. With mobs of men shooting and fighting in the streets, factories were closed, weapons were stolen, bridges were burned, telegraph wires and railroad tracks were torn up, and an orphanage for black children was burned down. Neighborhoods set up barricades reminiscent of the French June Rebellion some thirty years earlier.

Although the rioting was meant to protest the draft, it quickly turned racist and ugly. The poor white mob (mostly Irish) felt that they would bear the brunt of this draft, and so they turned on the only group lower in status than they: poor blacks. Reports from those four days describe beatings, mutilations, and lynchings of black people. (New York still lacks a memorial for those killed in the riots.) Eventually the Union army marched in and put an end to the fighting, but not before over one hundred people lost their lives and $3 million to $5 million in property damage accumulated ($60 million to $100 million today). A month later the draft was quietly reinstated, with a fund for poor men to buy their way out furnished by Boss Tweed.

Sadie would have seen the newspapers with RIOT! spelled out in bold, capital letters. She could have followed the coverage that, for a few days, ran before the coverage of the *actual* war. And if she crossed over to the East Side, she could have watched the barricades rise. There was plenty of property damage in her own neighborhood. She may have seen it right outside her door. The entire event must have left an impression on Sadie, although the violence seems to have inspired rather than frightened her. At the very least, she learned that when the rules don't make sense, drastic action and even force can be used to strike back against them.

Sadie did well enough for herself, making small-time money but gaining excellent street cred. She must have made many enemies during her time on the street, but the only major one reported in Asbury's book is Gallus Mag, co-owner of the Hole in the Wall pub. "Gallus" was another name for suspenders, a most unladylike accessory that the trouser-clad Mag was fond of, hence her nickname. (The bar, by the way, still stands today under the name Bridge Café. Although it was badly damaged by Hurricane Sandy, it plans to reopen and is said to be one of the oldest bars in New York.) Mag was a six-foot-tall Englishwoman who served as bouncer of the bar. Asbury says she was "the most savage female [the police] had ever encountered." She was famous for biting the ear off any patron who was especially rowdy. She kept these ears in a special pickle jar on top of the bar for all to see. One night in the spring of 1869, Sadie got into an argument with Mag and lost an ear herself, which merited its own special jar with her name written on it. Disgraced, Sadie decided she needed a new haunt and a new hobby.

Other women might have decided to throw in the towel and get a legitimate job, such as in a mill or factory. During this era industrialization had made many new jobs available, and many of them were expressly for women. Across the country, women left their homes in droves to work in mills and factories. These jobs offered women some autonomy and allowed them some money, which they could use to buy things such as flour, soap, and clothes. The textile mills became their own communities, where women both lived and worked under the watchful eye of the supervisors. Despite the long hours and low pay, the mills offered women an escape from their families and childhood homes. The independence that could be gained at the mill was an intoxicating option for some women. "Mill girls" could take advantage of lectures organized for them, as well as night school classes, although most girls were too exhausted to do so. It is possible that Sadie would have found refuge in the sisterhood of the mill, but given her personality as related by Asbury, it appears more likely that she would have been dismissed for fighting or some other form of "immorality." Luckily, she did not attempt to gain employment through a mill or any other legitimate means.

Sadie walked a long way after her fight with Gallus Mag, crossing out of her own territory and venturing into the west side of the city near New York Harbor. While wandering around the city, she witnessed the Charlton Street Gang clumsily trying to take over a ship in the North (present-day Hudson) River. They were the only gang that worked the Hudson during that time, and their headquarters was an old gin mill at the foot of Charlton Street. When Sadie watched them that night, they were uncoordinated and easily overtaken by the ship's crew, who promptly kicked them off the ship. Sadie, presumably bleeding heavily from her new head wound, convinced the gang that what they really needed was a change in their leadership. If she took over their gang, she could lead them into piracy. For some reason, possibly because of their recent embarrassing failure or because Sadie's reputation was big in the area, they accepted her proposal, and within a week they had captured a boat, hoisted the Jolly Roger, and sailed up the river, looking for places to loot.

Where Sadie learned to sail is not known. River navigation is not as difficult as ocean navigation, but she would have needed some skill in order to pilot a craft up and down the river. Maybe some of the boys in the gang had some sailing skills and guided Sadie through the work. Some sources say that at this point, she became a real pirate enthusiast and read up on other pirates and their tactics. She tried to emulate old pirating strategies but sometimes mixed fact and fiction. For example, Sadie is one of the only pirates who is said to have made her captives walk the plank—something she might have picked up from *Treasure Island*. She was a real pirate in that she sailed, stole, and occasionally kidnapped and murdered, but she was also acting the part of a pirate—imagining herself as a Blackbeard or a Long John Silver.

To be sure, adventure was in the air during this era. Sadie was not the only person who suffered from delusions of grandeur. Untold numbers of Americans followed their dreams all the way out to California to strike it rich after gold was discovered at Sutter's Mill in 1848. These forty-niners caused a population explosion in the West that resulted in boomtowns with hastily erected buildings and slapped-together law enforcement attempting to keep order in towns filled with adventurous men with nothing to lose. The "anything goes" spirit of these towns sheltered all sorts of semi-illegal activity; in some places saloons outnumbered all other buildings two to one. Very few struck it rich panning for their fortunes. The people who really prospered during this time were the ones with enough forethought to start supply businesses: selling food, clothes, and other provisions to the prospectors. Some of these merchants would become major players in the transcontinental railroad effort that would consume the nation in a few short years.

If Sadie had not joined the Charlton Street Gang, perhaps she would have eventually disguised herself as a man and gotten a job working on the railroad. The transcontinental railroad was another big dream of this era—one that would be completed in Sadie's lifetime. It was built in several large sections, each controlled by a separate railway company, and then joined together with a ceremonial golden spike driven by Leland Stanford, former grocer, major backer of the railroad project, and founder of Stanford University. Irish and Chinese immigrants, Mormons, Civil War veterans, and many others labored under backbreaking conditions to lay the tracks. This difficult job was one of the few available to many of these men, especially immigrants. Without their labor, the railroad would have been impossible. When held in contrast to the other great dreamers of the time, Sadie's desire to become a pirate does not seem outré.

For a while, all of Sadie's dreams came true. Under her leadership, the Charlton Street Gang was able to pillage several houses and villages up the river as far north as Poughkeepsie. The prize target to rob was the seaport itself, but it was too heavily guarded. They also attempted to rob large ocean steamers, but they weren't able to do that, either. Sadie and her gang took valuables from mansions along the river as well as from less-armed merchant ships. They were able to fence their stolen goods in various pawnshops back in New York—no doubt aided by Sadie's underworld connections. For several months, Sadie and her pirate band made a good amount of money this way. The chief of police, George W. Matsell, described how Sadie and other river pirates operated: "The river pirates pursue their nefarious operations with the most systematic perseverance, and manifest a shrewdness and adroitness which can only be attained by long practice. . . . In their boats, under cover of night, they prowl around the wharves and vessels in a stream, and dexterously snatch up every piece of loose property left for a moment unguarded."

Eventually, the landowners along the river decided they had endured enough and banded together against Sadie and her boys. Farmers greeted Sadie's arrival with guns, and a seaborne police force impeded her from robbing any more ships. Sadie reportedly lost too many crew members, either to the police or to gunfire, to be able to continue pirating. She abandoned her ship and returned to her old stomping grounds of the Fourth Ward, where she was now hailed as "Queen of the Waterfront."

Before she slipped out of history, Sadie had one final encounter with Gallus Mag. Some sources claim that Sadie went to make peace with the bouncer, while others claim that the Hole in the Wall had seen too many murders in a month and was about to be closed for good and Sadie wanted to pay her respects to her former favorite watering hole. Whatever the reason, Sadie returned to the bar and made up with Mag. Mag, no doubt moved by Sadie's generosity of spirit, returned Sadie's ear to her. Sadie allegedly wore this ear in a locket around her neck for the rest of her life.

What happened to Sadie after that is unclear. A happier version of events has her opening her own bar with the profits from her pirating days. In other stories, she fades into obscurity, disappearing from the pages of history. Perhaps she was murdered in an alley by some young thug who was clueless about her legendary pedigree. Stranger things happened in the Fourth Ward. No matter how she died—or if she ever lived—she certainly lives on in New York City and pirate folklore, appearing in some form in at least four novels, as well as a character based on an amalgam of her and Gallus Mag in Martin Scorsese's 2002 film *Gangs of New York*.

Asbury writes about Sadie as if she were his charmingly eccentric niece. He seems fond but does not present her as particularly competent or frightening. His account of her is a slice-of-life story to inject a little levity into the blood-soaked Fourth Ward lore. He is much more effusive about Gallus Mag, whom he paints as a ferocious she-devil. However, he does say Sadie had "inspired leadership" that "breathed new life into the gang," and that her "ferocity far exceeded that of her ruffianly followers," so he does not entirely dismiss her. If anything, he's not quite sure what to make of her, and many readers may find themselves in the same predicament. Who was this woman who wasn't afraid to go toe to toe with murderous criminals yet had enough whimsy to fly a Jolly Roger? If she existed, it is a shame that her life was not recorded more copiously.

Another pirate who became famous during this era is Fanny Campbell, eponymous hero of Maturin Ballou's 1844 novel *Fanny Campbell, Female Pirate Captain: A Tale of the Revolution*. Her story takes place during the Revolutionary War but deals with the more modern themes and issues of the period in which it was written. Although her tale is fiction, it was so popular that numerous modern sources add Fanny Campbell to the roll of real pirates as if her swashbuckling tale were factual. Her story is interesting not just as a pirate story but also as a story of a model American woman from a nineteenth-century perspective. Her values and spirit may have been intended to remind women of their place in the home, but her story inspired just the opposite reaction.

Fanny's story is a rip-roaring adventure, full of twists that delighted readers then, and it would still entertain today. According to the story, she grew up outside Boston, Massachusetts, and was quite the tomboy. She loved to ride horses and was a cool hand with a rifle. Despite her unorthodox hobbies, she attracted the attention of the boy next door, sailor William Lovell, and they were betrothed when William was nineteen and Fanny eighteen. Although the besotted bridegroom-to-be offered to give up the sea for Fanny, she loved to hear his stories of adventure and insisted that he do no such thing. She promised to marry him after he returned home from his next voyage.

As luck would have it, William's ship was captured in Cuba, and he was imprisoned there. When word of this reached Fanny, she had no choice, apparently, but to disguise herself as a man, call herself Mr. Channing, and sign on to sail with a ship, aptly named *Constance*, as a minor officer heading to England via Cuba. Her plan was to use her Yankee ingenuity and American perseverance to liberate her beloved from the Cuban authorities.

Where did Fanny get all this pluck? American women during this period were certainly becoming more ambitious. By 1850 roughly one-half of American women could read and write. Over the next fifty years, more changes would come for American women. The many machines invented during this time made the lives of upper and middle class women easier, though by no means easy. Entire days were still consumed with domestic tasks like laundry. Still, new machines did speed up housework. With more time on their hands, women were able to obtain more education, as well as more leisure time. Some of this leisure time was spent on sports, which necessitated fashion changes. Toward the end of the nineteenth century, bustles and crinolines went out of style in favor of less-restricting garments that allowed women to move more freely.

Fashion was not the only area in which women were becoming more mobile. Several notable women emerged during this period who embodied the can-do spirit and limitless potential of Manifest Destiny and American industrialism. Women began making their way into the male-dominated professions such as medicine and law at this time as educational opportunities began to open up. Elizabeth Blackwell was the first woman to receive a medical degree in the United States, in 1849. In 1879 Belva Lockwood became the first woman to argue a case in front of the US Supreme Court.

There were also women pioneers and explorers during this era, shocking the world with their derring-do and discoveries. Maria Mitchell discovered a comet that would bear her name in 1847. After traveling extensively throughout the United States and Europe, she went on to become a teacher at the newly formed Vassar College. Nellie Bly, a journalist for the *New York World*, went undercover to expose the horrors practiced on patients at a mental institution in New York in 1887. Her work prompted a grand jury investigation, a massive Department of Public Charities and Corrections budget boost, and many other improvements to the field of mental health.

Finally, there were the social reformers. These women—some part of the suffrage movement, some not—agitated in whatever ways they knew best in order to better the world they lived in. They paved the way for the reformers who would dominate the coming century. Though their methods and desires were different, these women shared much with their pirate sisters—they sought to disrupt the existing laws and take something that the larger world did not want them to have. Sojourner Truth was an abolitionist and women's rights activist. Born into slavery, she won a court case against her former master to get custody of her child after she escaped. She traveled the country speaking on women's rights to hundreds of audiences, delivering her famous "Ain't I a Woman?" speech in 1851. Mary Harris "Mother" Jones was a labor and community organizer who was known as the most dangerous woman in America at one point due to her skill in organizing workers into unions. Harriet Beecher Stowe was an abolitionist and writer who penned *Uncle Tom's Cabin*, a novel about the horrors of slavery that touched the hearts of millions. When she met President Abraham Lincoln, he is reported to have said to her, "So you are the little woman who wrote the book that started this great war." Although many of these women were not famous yet during the time Ballou was writing the book, the heady perfume of powerful women must have hung heavy in the air while he worked. Nobody becomes a force to be reckoned with overnight, and many of these women were growing in their strength and prowess as Ballou was developing his lovable heroine. He may have been influenced by these barrier-breaking women as he worked on his book. Fanny's adventures exemplify how, in the right circumstances, an ordinary woman can become extraordinary.

For example, Fanny must have listened very intently to her fiancé William's stories about sailing, because onboard the *Constance*, she fooled everyone into thinking she was a boy and became a well-liked sailor among the crew. So well liked, in fact, that when news got out that the captain was a crook who intended to sell the entire crew into English service once they arrived in England, she was able to lead the crew in a mutiny for their freedom. Mr. Channing became Captain Channing, and all the people onboard became pirates due to their capture of the ship. Where would the new pirates like to go most? With Fanny at the helm, their first stop would definitely be Cuba.

On the way, a hostile British ship called the *George* was passing, and the captain noticed that something was amiss on the *Constance*, so he attacked. The British ship proved no match for Fanny and her merry crew, who captured the *George* and took it along with them on their journey to Cuba. Once they arrived, they easily freed William, as well as another American sailor. As they sailed for home, Fanny called William into the captain's cabin and revealed her secret: that it was not a brave male captain who rescued him but his own dear fiancée. William was shocked but took the news in stride, claiming, "I never saw you look more interesting." He did, however, promise to keep her secret from the rest of the crew.

There were a few other mishaps during the voyage, like the American Revolutionary War breaking out and the ship turning privateer, but eventually, Fanny and William were able to sneak off to shore, where they married and lived happily ever after. William returned to a life at sea while Fanny stayed home and raised many children, never losing her pleasant disposition.

Modern audiences might find the ending of her story a bit of a letdown. It would have been more satisfying to see the lovers sail off into the sunset together, ready to live the life of pirates evermore. The book was still hugely inspiring to nineteenth-century readers, however, due to her acts of gender-bending and role defiance. One woman wrote of her experience reading the novel, "All the latent energy of my natures was aroused. . . . I was emancipated! And could never again be a slave."

This story was meant to capture women readers' hearts but also to hark back to a simpler time. Although Fanny is daring, it is for a very noble and feminine reason—to rescue the man she loves and to do her duty to her country. During this rapidly changing time in America, portrayals of women who, despite great skill and courage, chose to stay home and have babies could be safely given to women as role models by men who feared a feminine uprising. The book also served as an admonition to men: do your manly jobs, or women will do them for you! Fanny's cross-dressing was threatening to a nineteenth-century audience, now that women were beginning to figuratively wear the pants in and out of the home, but her pure motivation and conventional happy ending ensures that the social order was upheld.

If the ending to Fanny's story is disappointing, there is a real-life story from this time that has a much more satisfying ending, although its battles are still being fought today and will continue to be fought well into the twenty-first century: the beginning of the fight for women's suffrage. During this time, more than half of the members of social justice groups—such as abolitionist societies, temperance unions, and poverty alleviation groups—were women. With all this education and social activism on behalf of others, women soon identified a major stumbling block to really improving their own lives: the lack of a vote. Women's suffrage became an important crusade during this period.

Two women who were banned from an abolitionist convention would go on to create their own convention, which is often hailed as the spark that lit the women's rights movement. Elizabeth Cady Stanton and Lucretia Mott organized the Seneca Falls convention, held in New York on July 19–20, 1848. This two-day event involved many speakers and presentations, including a speech from Frederick Douglass, and produced a Declaration of Sentiments, which was modeled after the Declaration of Independence and written primarily by Stanton. This document asked that women be given "immediate admission to all the rights and privileges which belong to them as citizens of these United States." Many people thought that women were abandoning their traditional roles and as a result would cause the collapse of society. The Declaration of Sentiments formally announced to the nation that American women wanted to be treated equally with men and that they were tired of waiting for it.

After the Civil War ended, various groups were formed, including the National Women's Suffrage Association (NWSA), headed by Stanton and Susan B. Anthony, and the rival group, the American Women's Suffrage Association (AWSA), founded by Lucy Stone and Julia Ward Howe. The NWSA was the more militant and unorthodox of the two groups and favored women being included in the Fifteenth Amendment to the Constitution. The AWSA felt that the vote could be obtained through a state-by-state campaign. The two groups battled it out for several years before finally merging into a single group and renaming themselves the National American Women's Suffrage Association (NAWSA) in 1890. Many books have been written on these groups and their roles in the women's suffrage movement, and new studies are being produced to this day, proving that interest in this topic is alive and well in America, perhaps because many of the inequalities these founding mothers faced are still being dealt with by today's American women.

Many of the original founders of both parties, including Elizabeth Cady Stanton and Lucretia Mott, did not live to see the day when women won the vote. Women's suffrage was not passed until 1920 by President Woodrow Wilson, due to the combined efforts of NAWSA and the younger, more unconventional National Women's Party (NWP). Were it not for the foundation laid by the women of the late nineteenth century, the women in the early twentieth century would not have won the fight for voting rights. Woman suffrage was achieved well before the time of the fictional Fanny Campbell, and Sadie Farrell most likely did not live to see it either. Although these two women pirates were not suffragettes themselves, their efforts to follow their dreams—even if those dreams took them away from what society demanded of them—

place them very much in the American suffragette movement in spirit if not in fact.

Sadie the Goat is the last known American female pirate. As the twentieth century began, American pirates moved inland and became tycoons of industry and progress. The nation would endure two world wars and numerous other military conflicts in the next one hundred years, and there would be little time for seafaring mischief in that part of the world. However, as the twentieth century dawned, China was the place to be for a woman pirate.

13

Evil Incarnate
and the Dragon Lady

T HE WOMEN PIRATES OF twentieth-century China are extremely different from each other depending on what part of the century they
came from. As life in China changed, the pirate's life changed as
well. However, too much emphasis cannot be placed on the revolutions
taking place in China and their role in the pirates' lives, because the
pirate women were, like Cheng I Sao before them, from the rural coastal
areas, where reforms did not have a chance to permeate as much. China's
massive size prevented the government from having equal effect in all
regions of the country; the farther away from the seat of government
one went, the less the head governing body held sway. So despite the
revolutions going on in Beijing and other cities during the twentieth
century, the countryside and coasts were less affected by change.

A caveat before entering into these pirates' lives and the context in
Chinese history of those lives: much of what the Western world knows
about Asia, and China in particular, has been filtered through many
layers of translation and bias, not to mention governmental interference
from both East and West. Propaganda flows heavily to and from China,
and it can be hard to know exactly what daily life was and is like for
the average citizen there. The reader must take all Western accounts of

non-Western countries with a healthy dose of skepticism, knowing that the "real China" is just as nebulous a concept as the "real America."

Around the turn of the twentieth century, the first of the women pirates from this era was born, as the bloody Boxer Rebellion was beginning. China was suffering from a terrible drought, starving citizens, and an adult population riddled with opium addiction, as a result of the British opium trade. The people believed that the foreign interference in their affairs was the culprit for their suffering, and they wanted foreign influence out. When Empress Dowager Cixi purged China of European influence, Europe and other interested nations struck back, sending a force of twenty thousand troops to defeat the Chinese. In the face of the Chinese defeat, the empress dowager realized that she must either modernize China—breaking with a millennium of dynastic tradition—or watch the Qing dynasty perish. Although she had opposed an ambitious reform plan previously—the Hundred Days of Reform decreed by the Guangxu emperor, her adopted son, in 1898—she realized that China must change or perish. Her reform campaign was ultimately too little too late to save the dynasty and her reputation as a leader. Although the reforms were strong and they did help China become a world power, they were not initially successful.

Cixi is often portrayed negatively as a usurper of power and the instrument of the Qing dynasty's downfall. In the respect that she is maligned in history, she is similar to many of the pirate women. Only recently, as the result of author Jung Chang's work, has another side of Cixi's story been told. Chang's research and book portray Cixi's rise from concubine to de facto emperor of China. She demonstrates that Cixi brought China up-to-date with the modern industries it had been lacking, such as railways and electricity. She did this while ruling the massive country in the face of extraordinary challenges, such as nearly perpetual war with foreign powers, internal rebellions, drought, and famine. Although the Qing dynasty, and indeed the dynastic system, ended soon after she died, Chang argues that Cixi left China in a much better state than she found it.

When Cixi died in 1908, she left behind a discontented China and a three-year-old emperor, Pu Yi. China's government was viewed as corrupt and unable to provide. Warlords built armies in the countryside while the cities languished without strong leadership. The women pirates grew up amid this political unrest and upheaval, which likely contributed to their disregard for authority. China could not protect its people from foreign powers, so why should the people respect their country? By 1912 the new government of the Republic of China would force six-year-old Pu Yi to abdicate, making him China's last emperor. The dynastic system, which had served China well for over a thousand years, came to an unceremonious end.

While the Qing dynasty was officially ending, a pirate woman's story was just getting started. In the 1920s, Lai Choi San took advantage of the uncertain government situation to slip under the radar as a government official—who moonlighted as a pirate. Lai Choi San's story comes from just two sources, primarily from one account: Aleko E. Lilius's book *I Sailed with Chinese Pirates*, published in 1931. The journalist of dubious repute (he was alternately self-described as being Finnish, Russian, American, and English and was brought up on fraud charges in Singapore and the Philippines) gained the trust of female pirate Lai Choi San—some sources say through a go-between at a brothel he frequented—and sailed with her on an expedition in the late 1920s off the coast of Macao.

Lai Choi San, as Lilius writes, was the only girl born to a family of four sons. Her father, a sailor, took her on expeditions as his servant-girl, and she grew to love the sea. Her father befriended a pirate captain and moved up the ranks to his second in command. When the captain died, Lai Choi San's father became the captain of the pirate fleet, numbering seven junks at that time. After her father's death, Lai Choi San took over the fleet and added five more junks. She is portrayed by Lilius as ruthless, cruel, attractive, and intelligent.

Lilius recounts several stories about Lai Choi San that give the reader a glimpse into her working life. Onshore in Macao, she dressed gorgeously, adorned with jade, a white satin robe, and gold rings. He writes that she was "rather slender and short . . . not too Chinese [looking]," which one supposes was meant to be a compliment. Her physical attributes are emphasized to make her an interesting subject for a story—nobody was going to buy a book about an ugly lady pirate. Once she was on a boat, however, she took off her shoes and dressed in pants, no longer an elegant lady but all business. She was always in the company of her *amahs* (serving women) and never addressed her crews directly, giving orders to them through the captains. She did not often venture out to sea with her crews either, preferring to run her business from the shore, but when she did sail, she remained in her private quarters, where no crew member was allowed to enter.

Lai Choi San was living this glamorous double life in the wake of World War I. The war was a mixed blessing for China, because it gave China a temporary respite from Western interest while the West had their hands full with fighting. However, rural Chinese warlords battled each other for dominance, attempting to take over larger areas of land. Japan continued to eye China with an eye toward occupation. People were becoming angry that Japan was not being repelled with greater force by rulers Yuan and Sun.

On May 4, 1919, three thousand students gathered in Tiananmen Square to protest the secret treaties signed during World War I between Europe and Japan, as well as the Treaty of Versailles, which gave formerly German-occupied Shandong Province to Japan, instead of back to China as promised. These students claimed that the corrupt Chinese government was incapable of protecting China. After the protesters turned violent, authorities intervened and many of the protesters were jailed. News of the protests spread, and people all over China sympathized with the protesters, continuing to protest and strike until the students were released and the three corrupt cabinet officials were fired. This May Fourth movement, as it came to be called, coalesced into a group that would become the Chinese Communist Party (CCP), which was officially formed in 1921. Throughout the war and the protests that followed, Lai Choi San was able to conduct her business unnoticed by a government that was busy elsewhere.

And what exactly was Lai Choi San's business? Technically she was an "inspector"—fishermen and other boat owners paid her to guard their ships from other pirates. When a pirate ship attacked one of the ships under her protection, she had to sink it or chase it away. Lilius tells of a man who compared Lai Choi San to Robin Hood, but the comparison doesn't seem to hold much water, given that she was paid handsomely for her services, with fees bordering on extortion. When a captain did not pay up, or attempted to organize with other captains to protect themselves, Lai Choi San kidnapped and tortured them until their relatives paid up. One wonders who offered the bigger threat—the pirates or the protectors from pirates.

Lilius spins an entertaining yarn about the woman he calls the "Queen of the Pirates," portraying her as a beautiful, shrewd business-woman, a mother, and a commander. But is any of it true? He does include photographs in his book, which prove that there were some women on a ship, but not that they were commanders or pirates. Lilius's account of his time with Lai Choi San seems possible enough, but the rest of the book gets much stranger and less credible. Other than Lilius's account, there is only one other source that documents her story, and it's a report of her death by a war journalist. He reports that during the Sino-Japanese War, a pirate fleet was sunk, and the captain (Lai Choi San) went down with her ship. This story is not without controversy. Klausmann reports in *Women Pirates and the Politics of the Jolly Roger* that other sources claim she was captured in 1939 by the international coast guard and sentenced to life in prison. Nobody can say for sure where she was born, where she died, or if she ever lived at all.

If her story is fiction, what possessed Lilius to write it? Obviously he (and his publishers) thought the tale would make money. In the late 1920s, American sentiment toward the Chinese was less than charitable. The Exclusion Act of 1882, not repealed until after World War II, prohibited Chinese from immigrating to the country, and the Chinese already in America, even people born there, were subject to prejudice and violence. Lilius's story took advantage of the existing xenophobia displayed toward the Chinese by portraying a cruel and heartless woman readers could feel good about hating. Lilius makes clear in his account that Lai Choi San is an exotic Other—a curiosity to be gaped at and perhaps secretly fantasized about. It was escapism and guilty pleasure all rolled into one. While contemporary readers enjoyed the entertaining story, no doubt the real Lai Choi San would have not been amused by his depiction of her.

Real or not, Lai Choi San has a lasting legacy—she is said to be the inspiration for "The Dragon Lady" in the American comic, radio, and television series *Terry and the Pirates*, which ran in some form from 1934 to 1953. She is also said to have influenced the stock character of the coldhearted beauty, a twist on the femme fatale. Whether or not this is a fair characterization—as well as whether or not the trope is even appropriate in today's society—is up for debate.

⚓⚓⚓

Lo Hon-cho (sometimes referred to as Honcho Lo) is another early twentieth-century Chinese pirate about whom there is a dearth of sources. Her story comes to us from a press report from Hong Kong in 1922 that details her capture. According to this report, her husband was a pirate and she inherited his fleet upon his death. She and Lai Choi San both inherited their fleets from male relatives—this was apparently common in twentieth-century Chinese pirate stories. She is described as "pretty" and "the most murderous and ruthless of all" China's pirates. She was a colonel in the Chinese Revolution and was said to have sixty junks. She pirated on land and sea, sometimes attacking villages and taking young girls captive, later selling them into slavery. She is one of the only female pirates who was reported to kidnap and sell women. She was betrayed by one of her colleagues and captured in 1922. This brief report is the only evidence currently available about her life. How did she feel about pirating? What was her preferred pirating style? What was day-to-day life on her ship like? Unless other sources come to light, the reader must imagine these answers for herself.

After World War I, China fell further into turmoil. The country had endured the war, but Republic of China leader Sun Yat-sen's death had left it once again without a strong leader. Enter Chiang Kai-shek, whose mission was to unify China. He felt that nationalism was the only way to go and sought to eliminate the Communists inside his government, even if it plunged the country into civil war. In 1927 he launched an attack against the Chinese Communist Party (CCP), forcing them to flee on foot from Jiangxi to Yan'an, a trek of about six thousand miles. A young librarian from Hunan Province led what would become known as the Long March, where nearly seventy thousand people died during the yearlong journey. His name was Mao Zedong, and he would become the most influential leader in twentieth-century China's history.

In 1945 China was poor, tired, and devastated by the series of wars that had plagued the country. The Chinese people blamed Chiang Kai-shek and the Nationalist Party for their state. Inflation had gotten out of control, forcing people to use wheelbarrows full of money just to buy rice. In 1946 China once again fell into a civil war: Communists against the Nationalist Party. The people saw Mao and his new ideas as a chance for liberation from the corrupt Nationalist regime. By December of that year, mainland China had fallen to the CCP, and by 1949 China was a fully Communist country.

⚓⚓⚓

In between China's civil wars, a fierce woman pirate rose to prominence. Huang P'ei Mei is listed in the Klausmann book as a woman pirate who commanded fifty thousand pirates. She was active from 1937 to the 1950s, with a varied career that included fighting for China against the Japanese, fighting against the Communists, and working with the Office of Strategic Services (OSS) during World War II. With such an impressive track record, it doesn't make sense that there aren't more references to her or available documents chronicling her exploits. She may be a composite of several different women, a wildly exaggerated account of one woman, or a whole-cloth fabrication. Or she may have been and done all the things that are credited to her and somehow flown under the radar. Perhaps the truth about her is written out in glorious detail but tucked away somewhere in a basement, in a folder marked CLASSIFIED.

There are several other female pirates from this same period who are known in name only. Ki Ming, P'en Ch'ih Ch'iko, and "Golden Grace" come up over and over in lists of pirates from twentieth-century China, but no English-language stories are told about them, nor are there sources that document their lives. It is possible that there are Chinese-language sources for these pirates that have not been translated into English, but so far, this list of women pirates tells the reader only that pirate women were very popular in China in the early twentieth century, and at some point someone was invested in getting their names out there into the world. More research is needed into the lives and even the existence of these women.

How would these women have pirated? The style in the early 1900s had changed due to the advent of steam-powered ships. Sail-borne pirates could not compete with steamers and so were restricted to capturing smaller ships, such as fishing boats. These did not produce the huge hauls of Cheng I Sao's day, and so the pirates were forced to adapt their tactics. Several sources tell of bands of pirates (including female bands) gaining employment on some of these large steamers, as waitresses or porters. Other pirates would pay for passage on these ships as well. The band would bide their time until they sailed near the waiting pirate ship. When the clueless passenger ship approached the predetermined point, the pirates would announce their true purpose, strip everyone of their valuables, and load the people onto the waiting pirate boats and take them ashore to be held for ransom. These carefully planned heist-style operations happened at least twenty-nine times during the period between 1921 and 1929. Perhaps Ki Ming, P'en Ch'ih Ch'iko, or Golden Grace were responsible for some of these attacks.

Huang P'ei Mei disappears from the stories just as Communist China began to ascend. In 1954 the CCP drafted a new Chinese constitution in which Mao Zedong was basically the head of everything. Though China maintained the illusion of a multiparty system, in reality the CCP ran all aspects of Chinese life. Mao's ambitious plans for China were utopian and made people hopeful. His revolution had been bloodless compared to other revolutions. Foreign powers looked to China with interest to see how Communism would play out.

⚓⚓⚓

Mao's rule was in its infancy the same time that a woman pirate was in *her* infancy. This pirate, who was born in Fujian Province of China, would redefine piracy for the new millennium. Her name was Cheng Chui Ping, although she was known mostly as Sister, and she did not command a ship, nor hunt for riches. She made her money offering the chance for riches to others; she facilitated the passage of illegal immigrants from China into the United States as a "snakehead," or human smuggler.

Cheng Chui Ping grew up in the early days of Mao's Communist China. So much has been written on this period that it is difficult to come up with any sort of coherent summary, let alone an unbiased one. Mao was focused on land reform and eliminating the warlords, a threat to his power. He established his goals by implementing several ambitious plans and executing or "reeducating" people who stood in his way. The most conservative estimates claim that at least three million people were murdered by the CCP for opposing the party. Control was Mao's mantra, and he put the issue of solving class problems over everything else.

But despite his auspicious beginnings, Mao eventually made missteps that would lead to his fall from grace. His One Hundred Flowers Campaign, in which he urged intellectuals to come forward with their ideas, backfired spectacularly as the academics did come forward but with criticisms of Mao's regime. His moneymaking program, the Great Leap Forward, was a disaster. People were too busy attending mandatory party meetings and study sessions to harvest grain, so they lied about production rather than risk Mao's wrath. As a result, China suffered a famine in which twenty million people starved to death, a disproportionally large number of them children.

Mao's absolute control was badly shaken due to the famine. He needed to do something drastic to assert his dominance. He launched the Great Proletarian Cultural Revolution in 1966. The orders of the Cultural Revolution were carried out by Mao's Red Guards—school-children and teenagers who were indoctrinated to be devoted to Mao and Communism. They traveled in packs and wreaked havoc on anyone and anything that appeared to oppose Mao. They became so powerful and ungovernable that Mao was forced to officially disband them in 1968, only two years after their inception.

Cheng Chui Ping came of age during Mao's Great Leap Forward and was a leader for the Red Guard in her village as a teenager. She told Patrick Radden Keefe, author of a biography of her entitled *The Snakehead*, that her childhood was brutally hard, but it taught her that only hard work helps you get ahead in life. Her father became a snake-head in the 1960s, and she would follow in his footsteps decades later, turning her back on China to live in the United States.

It is possible that Cheng Chui Ping chose to leave China due to its restrictive policies toward women. During her lifetime, massive changes were made to cultural norms involving women, but even the more pro-gressive ideas of the latter half of the twentieth century could have left this independent woman searching for other options. The Republican government banned foot binding as a symbol of China's backward-ness—Dowager Empress Cixi had also banned it years earlier. How could a country grow to its full greatness if half of its people could hardly walk? Female infanticide, which was widespread at the time, was also banned. The Nationalists, and in a much larger way the Commu-nists, sought to eliminate everything that was old and traditional and forge a new path, which included awarding women status more equal with their male peers. The 1950 Marriage Law abolished the practice of purchased and arranged marriages and made divorces at-will. Before this, arranged marriages had been virtually universal. The 1950 law also granted women some property rights, but in practice, these did not take effect immediately, particularly in rural areas. The goal of these laws was to empower the younger generation so that they could work for a new China. Women were liberated not due to their inherent equal nature or any other altruistic reason but because equality was not a Confucian value, and the CCP wanted to establish itself as a new, non-Confucian regime. Communist women could be workers, just like Communist men.

This deconstruction of gender seems that it would have been a welcome change for the average Chinese woman, particularly due to the common perception that women were not valued in society. The cultural values from the Qing dynasty discussed in chapter 11 were still held strongly in early twentieth-century China. As Chang Yu-I puts it in her memoir *Bound Feet & Western Dress* (as dictated to her granddaughter, Pang-Mei Natasha Chang), "In China, a woman is nothing. When she is born, she must obey her father. When she is married, she must obey her husband. And when she is widowed, she must obey her son. A woman is nothing, you see." Traditionally, women did not bring income into their own family as a worker. They had few rights of inheritance or property. Consequentially, there was little motivation to treat a daughter well. Education, preference, and even food were given to sons before daughters.

The CCP offered women a place in the workforce and in society. Women were expected to work just as hard as men—in offices and on farms. Clothing was gender neutral, and every effort was made to eliminate the differences between women and men. However, this did not work as well in practice as it did in theory. Although women were given more liberty to leave the domestic sphere, many young girls were married off to CCP officials essentially as gifts to the men. Women were still expected to raise children and maintain the home, but now they were expected to put in a full day of work, too. As Mao exhorted women to "hold up half the sky," their identity as women was being erased.

When Sister Ping chose to emigrate to the States, she picked a good time. In the 1980s it was easier than ever for a Chinese person to enter the United States legally. The one-child policy, introduced in 1979, was disliked by the antiabortion administration, and the United States offered asylum to couples of childbearing age for this reason. The one-child policy is perhaps what China is most known for in the West, although misconceptions about it abound. China, always a huge nation struggling to feed its people, became extremely concerned about its population explosion and wanted to slow its growth. Over the last half of the twentieth century, population laws changed often, according to what the government thought would control the population as opposed to what women wanted, which was access to birth control. Families had a difficult time knowing what was legal and not legal. In the 1990s, the proliferation of ultrasound machines brought a new phenomenon to China—sex-selected abortions. The result of years of the one-child policy is striking: an estimated forty million girls are "missing"—women who should be in the population, if sex-selective abortions and infanticide had not taken place. This phenomenon has led to trafficking of women to replace the missing women so that Chinese bachelors have access to brides.

Besides asylum offers for couples, federal policies were relaxing for the first time in decades. Yet legal immigration to the United States was still difficult, and the process could take years. Many perceived that the chance for a better life in America now rather than later was worth breaking the law for, and Sister Ping offered them an opportunity to take that chance.

Sister Ping entered the United States legally in 1981, claiming she planned to get work as a domestic servant. Eventually she obtained naturalization papers and set up a convenience store in New York City's Chinatown. Her store became a gathering place for the Fujianese community, many of whom sent money back home through Sister Ping. It could be done through the Bank of China, but that carried a large fee and took weeks. Sister Ping was cheaper and more efficient.

This cheaper and more efficient way of doing things also extended to her people-smuggling business, which came about in the mid-1980s. There were many people offering to smuggle people into America at that time, for a variety of prices and by a variety of methods. Sister Ping had a reputation for being safer than most as well as fair. If a family member died during the journey, she was rumored to pay funeral expenses. She also allegedly forgave the debts of some people who couldn't pay their fees once they arrived in the States. The journey was always perilous. The risks were always high. But Sister Ping inspired confidence that she would do her best to make sure people got to the United States safely. Whether she really was this benevolent woman or a greedy and cruel human trafficker depends on, as always, who is telling the story.

As Sister Ping's smuggling operation was expanding, the harsh Communist regime in China that people wanted to escape was waning. Toward the end of his time in power, Mao's control of his party was slipping. The more people he exiled from the party, the more the people protested the loss of those officials. When Mao died in 1976 at the age of eighty-two, it wasn't too hard for Deng Xiaoping to slide into the spotlight and take control of the Communist Party.

Deng was a committed Communist, but he did not share all of Mao's beliefs. With Mao dead, he was free to enact reforms to rescue China from economic and political circumstances. Deng quickly reinstated many of the old party leaders who had been purged under Mao, and together they set about modernizing China. Deng felt that the answers lay in looking abroad rather than continuing in isolation—a huge departure from Mao's philosophy. He rolled out his reforms slowly in order to give each program a chance to work.

A new Chinese constitution was ratified in 1978. This document emphasized decentralization, depoliticization, and democratization. These new goals would help undo some of the damage Mao's regime had done and would improve the lives of Chinese citizens. Despite the changes on paper, however, freedoms in China were still scarce. It was difficult to legally obtain a passport, the media was still tightly controlled, and foreign art and literature were heavily censored. Corruption still existed in the government, and inflation made it almost impossible for the rising economy to raise standards of living. People still yearned to break free of the oppressive government and start a new life in America, which, coupled with the infamous Tiananmen Square massacre in 1989, is why Cheng Chui Ping's business continued to boom.

Besides all the political changes that benefited the average Chinese citizen that occurred from the 1980s to the turn of the century, many changes during that same period specifically benefited women's lives. In 1980 a new marriage law passed that raised the minimum marriage age to twenty-two for men and twenty for women. In 1988 China enacted labor regulations that protected women on the job during pregnancy and lactation. In 1995 China hosted the Fourth Annual World Conference on Women. Legislation protecting women from marital violence was enacted in 2001. But no matter how wonderful life becomes in any given country, the grass is always greener somewhere else, and China is no exception to that rule. Though many aspects of life in China were improving, people still wanted to immigrate to the United States. Sister Ping's business remained in demand throughout the 1990s.

When she was eventually caught by the FBI in 2000—due to her involvement in the disastrous *Golden Venture* shipwreck in which ten passengers lost their lives and the deplorable conditions of the smuggling ships were exposed—the American press had a field day vilifying her. She was portrayed as an unfeeling dragon lady, the press likely trading off the stock character popularized by Lai Choi San. One headline read EVIL INCARNATE. Even after her trial, she was still called inhumane and brutal by the FBI, who claimed in a 2006 press release on their website that with her sentence, "justice [had] finally been served for the many victims of Sister Ping." It cannot be denied that she made money smuggling people and that some of those people died. It cannot be denied that the journey to the United States was dangerous and the conditions were inhumane. Even without the rumors of her gang of men beating up people who couldn't pay their fees, there is much for which to convict Sister Ping.

Yet in China, she is considered a hero. There is a statue erected of her in her hometown of Shengmei. She was compared to Robin Hood, and her generosity was praised by the people whom she helped to enter America. The *New York Times* interviewed many people who traveled to the United States under her care, and did not quote a single disparaging remark about her in the piece. No one expressed regret over coming to America. They claimed they knew the risks and dangers and they chose to come anyway. Many expressed admiration for Sister Ping, and one wished to be more like her.

Cheng Chui Ping was eventually sentenced to thirty-five years in prison for smuggling. She died of cancer in federal prison in April 2014. When news of her death reached Chinatown in New York, the temples were packed with mourners. A multitude of grieving supporters called her restaurant in Chinatown, Yung Sun, to offer their condolences to her family.

Cheng Chui Ping's piracy bears almost no relation to Lai Choi San's or Lo Hon-cho's, but then again, the China of the 1920s bears almost no relation to the China of the 1980s and 1990s. This dynamic century saw China move from ancient dynasties to modern governments, and the evolution of piracy in the area reflects that.

Sister Ping's story is unusual among all the pirates in this book for several reasons: she did not actually sail on ships, she did not seek treasure, and she did not steal from other parties. Unique among the pirate women, however, is the fact that she actually told her own story. While some women, such as Margaret Jordan, spoke at sentencing, Sister Ping's account through Keefe is the closest thing to a female pirate biography that currently exists. Writer Patrick Radden Keefe sent written questions to her in prison, which she answered through a translator. At her trial, she spoke in her own defense at sentencing. Her version of her life, along with the version of those who loved her, is remarkably different from the account told by government officials and documents. She is a fitting pirate to close out this chapter because she shows how a set of events can be portrayed in shockingly different light due to the biases of the storyteller. How many of the pirates in this book would have benefited from the chance to tell their own stories? Unlike Margaret Jordan, Ping's summation of her deeds was not enough to convince a court of her innocence, but at least her story was told in her own words and added to the record. People can examine both versions and draw their own conclusions, rather than be forced to accept a secondhand account because no other version exists. This underscores the crucial need for historians of all races, creeds, orientations, and genders, so that as many versions of events are recorded as possible.

As the world moves into the twenty-first century, what will piracy look like? Will the trade evolve past Somali hijackers and turn into something else entirely? And who will be the next great female pirate? For now, the world can only watch and wait—until someone decides to take to the seas themselves.

14

The Pirates of the Silver Screen

ESPITE THE MANY EXCITING tales of the exceptional lives of so many women pirates, movies showcasing their adventures are not available. Of the hundreds of pirate movies made over the years, there have been a mere handful that profile female pirates, and even fewer of those portray characters based on real pirates from history. The most accurate example of a movie chronicling a female pirate is *Anne of the Indies*, which is very loosely based on the life of Anne Bonny. This movie premiered in 1951; it has been over half a century since the silver screen has been graced with a pirate movie starring one of the women from this book.

Why? The women's stories are very cinematic, and there's no doubt that stories about pirates can perform well at the box office. One of the earliest pirate films, *Captain Blood*, made $2.5 million at the box office in 1935 and cost only $1 million to make. Disney's animated classic *Peter Pan*, prominently featuring Captain Hook and his pirate band, was the highest-grossing film of 1953, earning a reported $7 million and multiple cinematic rereleases. *The Princess Bride*, also featuring a pirate as a major plot point, was a box office success and made millions more in VHS and DVD sales as the film became a cult classic. Disney's juggernaut *Pirates of the Caribbean* franchise has, to date, grossed over $1 billion with four films (and a fifth in the works). Pirates are bankable—but Hollywood has refused to cash in when it comes to women

212

pirates, even fictional women pirates. Why? Surely A-list women are lining up to make these swashbuckling superhits?

A brief aside—pirates appear in all forms of media, including books, plays, operas, and novels, as well as films. However, there have been virtually no bestselling books written about women pirates, although quite a few romances exist, which sell very well but lack critical acclaim; only one opera, Gilbert and Sullivan's *Pirates of Penzance*, in which the lone female pirate, Ruth, is well outnumbered by Frederick, the Pirate King, and a crew of male pirates; and one Broadway musical about a woman pirate, Boublil and Schönberg's *The Pirate Queen*, based on the life of Grace O'Malley, which closed amid boos from critics and audiences alike after a measly eighty-five performances. As rare as women pirates are in Hollywood films, they appear more often there than in any other major medium, and for that purpose this chapter will focus on movies.

⚓⚓⚓

The first major Hollywood film featuring a female pirate, *Anne of the Indies* (directed by Jacques Tourneur, 1951), is allegedly based on the life of Anne Bonny. (Bonny appears as a character in the 1945 film *The Spanish Main*, but the movie is not about her.) The character is named Anne, but beyond that there are few similarities to the real Anne Bonny. Captain Anne Providence, played by a future wife of Howard Hughes, Jean Peters, enters the film brandishing a sword. She and her crew have just captured an English ship and are forcing the hapless prisoners to walk the plank. Anne's backstory is explained by clunky exposition: her brother was killed by the English and now she is avenging him by wreaking havoc on every English ship she encounters. In this, she resembles Sayyida al-Hurra or Jacquotte Delahaye more than Anne Bonny. The real Anne Bonny had no such noble motivation for turning pirate; she simply liked causing mayhem. Captain Providence spares a French prisoner's life—after smacking him across the face for calling her "Mademoiselle"—by offering him a spot on the crew. This act of mercy proves to be the first step in her undoing.

Later that night, the pirates are dividing up the loot from the English ship, every man and woman getting his or her fair share as outlined in the articles. Anne offers the Frenchman, Pierre, a piece of the treasure. The crew learns that Pierre has a map to Captain Morgan's legendary treasure haul from the sack of Panama City. (Henry Morgan *did* sack Panama City in 1671, but most of the treasure was snuck out on a ship before his arrival, so the loot gained from the sacking was disappointingly small.) Anne decides to pursue the treasure, but she wants to gather some resources from her mentor and surrogate father Blackbeard first.

Despite Blackbeard's warning that Pierre is possibly a shady character, Anne and Pierre fall in love. She tries on the fancy dress from the treasure stock, and Pierre has to lace the corset up for her. Anne asks him to show her how a Frenchman makes love to a lady. What follows is a scintillating love scene, with Anne's normal bravado only barely masking her fear of rejection and her inexperience in the art of love. Her desire and curiosity have outpaced her knowledge, and despite her copious power in other arenas, it's clear that in this particular area she is powerless. Pierre has awakened a womanly side of her she has denied all her life, and she is compelled to explore it, in spite of herself.

Anne's love for Pierre is, tragically, all for naught. Blackbeard reveals that Pierre is a spy for the English and has killed many pirates, perhaps even Anne's brother. Pierre's smooth talking convinces Anne that it's a lie, and she draws her sword against Blackbeard, turning her back on her family to defend her love. Blackbeard leaves, vowing not to forget this insult. Later, we learn that Pierre is not only a spy—he's married. His assignment was to lead the English to Anne and her ship, the *Sheba Queen*, in exchange for the return of his own ship. When Anne finds out, she immediately hatches a plan to kidnap Pierre's wife and sell her as a slave, because hell hath no fury like a pirate woman scorned.

Anne captures Pierre's wife, and Pierre shortly thereafter, and plans to maroon them on an isolated island, where they (and their love) will slowly starve to death and wither in the hot Caribbean sun. It is some seriously cold revenge, but there's something delicious about watching a woman become so completely unhinged on-screen. After watching a million wilting, retiring women acquiescing to men's demands, it's electric to watch a woman call the shots, especially in such a heartless way. To wish her success would be cruel, but it's hard to deny that watching her scheme is a treat.

Anne relents at the last minute and decides to spare Pierre and his wife. As she is setting them free, Blackbeard arrives. Anne knows that if he sees them, he will kill them, so she puts herself between the fleeing lovers and Blackbeard to give them a chance to escape. Despite his reluctance to fight his adopted daughter, Blackbeard, because of his promise to avenge his insult by Anne, fires on the *Sheba Queen*. Anne is killed in the ensuing battle, leaving the movie as she entered it—waving her sword defiantly in the midst of battle.

Is it disappointing to watch a badass pirate die for the love of a man who will never love her back? Yes. But Anne is no fading flower Camille. She doesn't die for love in a cloud of perfume and dainty handkerchiefs; she dies in a blaze of gunfire. It's refreshing to watch a nuanced portrayal of a woman battling between what is ultimately her love of career versus her love of a man. Despite being made in 1951, the themes of this film still resonate today.

Director Tourneur is best known as a B-horror-film director for RKO Pictures. *Anne of the Indies* was one of the earlier features he made as a freelance director. It did marginally well at the box office domestically but was a huge hit abroad, inspiring a string of Italian lady-pirate movies, such as *Queen of the Pirates* and *Queen of the Seas*. Italian cinema apparently does not share Hollywood's fears of female pirates.

Anne of the Indies gave the pirate woman film such a promising start that it appeared likely that Hollywood would make at least a few more. The fictional female swashbuckler Spitfire Stevens did appear in the 1952 blockbuster *Against All Flags* (in the 1967 remake *The King's Pirate*, the character was downgraded to a love interest), albeit in a supporting role to Errol Flynn's Brian Hawke, but it would be almost fifty years before a female pirate in the lead role graced the silver screen again.

Anne of the Indies might not have been made at all if it had been pitched ten years earlier or later. There was a run of big-budget Hollywood films in the late 1940s and early 1950s that featured women headliners. Movies such as 1945's *Mildred Pierce* and 1950's *All About Eve* and *Sunset Boulevard* all starred women in stories primarily about women. These leading women, however, despite being complex characters, all come to tragic ends. Critic Molly Haskell says in *From Reverence to Rape: The Treatment of Women in the Movies* that in the 1950s, a director might use women as "the repository of certain repellent qualities which he would like to disavow. He projects onto her the narcissism, the vanity, the fear of growing old which he is horrified to find festering within himself." Anne, who dies for love, belongs in this group of strong women who are crippled by the woes of their directors. They are pictured as grotesque for doing what the director fears he himself will do. In mid-twentieth-century Hollywood, women could be strong or happy, but not both. In many ways, this premise is alive and well in the present day (see *Blue Jasmine, Inception,* and even the *Twilight* franchise).

⚓⚓⚓

The relationship between women and Hollywood has always been a fraught one. In its early days, Hollywood was content to cast women as prostitutes, mothers, femme fatales, and love interests, but seldom as leads. The best a woman could hope for was to become one-half of a power couple, like Astaire and Rogers. Rarely was the success of a film laid solely across a woman's shoulders. Films about women with complicated personalities, who were unlikable, or who gained fulfillment from an unconventional lifestyle were (and sometimes still are) seen as box office poison, something audiences would not shell out good money to see. Male characters could be conflicted, multifaceted, or even antiheroes; portrayals of women were limited to either pretty virgins or sexual temptresses. Even offscreen, actresses (and actors too) were expected to adhere rigidly to social norms based on their studio's idea of what their image ought to be. Women were often expected to behave as doting wives and/or loving mothers. There were exceptions, such as Katharine Hepburn and Mary Pickford, women who turned their star power into money power and were able to command some autonomy over their careers, but by and large, women in classic Hollywood were objects for men to fall in love with or be hurt by, not characters worthy of stories themselves.

The New Hollywood period (roughly late 1960s to early 1980s) did bring an improvement in the availability of compelling roles for women. Free from the censors of the old Hollywood production code and studio system, movies could now talk about and depict subjects previously forbidden—including female sexual desire. However, the collapse of the studio star system was a double-edged sword for women; the actresses had greater freedom but less power as the director, not the film star, became the major attraction. Two examples from the beginning and the end of this period demonstrate the evolution experienced in the New Hollywood. The women's liberation movement, which was also happening at this time, brought the idea of women's issues to the forefront of the nation's consciousness. The idea that women might want to see their own stories on-screen began to take hold in the popular imagination.

⚓⚓⚓

Bonnie and Clyde (1967) begins with a close-up of Bonnie's red lips. Bonnie, played by Faye Dunaway, is a waitress from a small town who escapes her boring life by taking up with the gangster Clyde. She's sexually aroused by the violence and danger in their lives and is frustrated when Clyde cannot perform sexually. Bonnie busts the molds of traditional female roles in cinema by being a sexual, "bad" woman who nevertheless is sympathetically portrayed. She does not take a backseat in the violence but participates fully, and she is not spared the gory gangster's death. Bonnie, with her bad-girl antics yet secretly soft heart that yearns for love, is clearly a descendant of *Anne of the Indies*'s Anne Bonny. Due to the later period in which *Bonnie and Clyde* was made, Bonnie is allowed to express her sexual desire more explicitly, a luxury not allowed Anne, whose desire must be read between the lines. This film, in no small part due to Bonnie's unconventional depiction and

Dunaway's performance, shocked audiences but went on to be a major box office success and was nominated for ten Academy Awards, winning two.

Much later in the New Hollywood period, brave divorcée Erica in *An Unmarried Woman* (1978) brought a simple yet revelatory story to the silver screen: regaining one's life after being left by one's husband. It's a common tale, yet it had never before been given such fully realized cinematic treatment. Viewers follow Erica from her idyllic existence in Manhattan with her stockbroker husband and gorgeous apartment down to rock bottom as the husband leaves her for a younger woman. Erica claws her way back to happiness with the help of her girlfriends, long lunches with bottles of wine, a female therapist, and a series of blind dates. She falls in love again, this time with a painter, but she ultimately decides to embrace her single life and put herself first rather than following the painter to Vermont. The idea of an everyday woman's trials and tribulations being worthy film fodder was groundbreaking. Here was a character whom mainstream audiences could identify with, freed from any partnership of validation from a man. Bonnie, fierce as she was, needed Clyde. Erica needs only herself (and maybe her girlfriends). Actress Jill Clayburgh was nominated for the Best Actress Academy Award for her work in this film. Although Erica does not seem like she would last ten minutes on a pirate ship, she is nevertheless a more progressive character than either Anne or Bonnie due to her rich emotional life. Rather than her emotions making her "weak" or cluttering the narrative, they *are* the narrative—much to the delight of the women who flocked to this movie over and over again.

Despite *An Unmarried Woman*'s giant leap forward in the portrayal of women, Hollywood did not suddenly unleash a torrent of women-centered films, pirate themed or otherwise, after its release. Women had continued to show up in pirate films after *Anne of the Indies* as love interests, kidnapping victims, prostitutes, and even (rarely) as pirates— Anne Bonny had a minor role in 1954's *Captain Kidd and the Slave Girl*, for example—but not until 1995 would Hollywood produce another film starring a female pirate. This film was an infamous flop that once held the *Guinness Book of World Records* title for largest box office loss. Given that it sink not just the careers of two of its stars but a production company as well, it's hard to overstate just how big of a disaster this movie was. This epic flop was 1995's *Cutthroat Island*, starring Geena Davis as a pirate named Morgan.

⚓⚓⚓

The plot is part of the reason the movie was such a colossal failure, so don't try too hard to follow it. Basically, a woman named Morgan Adams who offers such bons mots as "I took your balls," referring to the musket balls she pinched from a would-be attacker, lives as a carefree scoundrel until she witnesses her father's murder at the hands of his brother, her uncle Mad Dawg Brown. (Yes, it's spelled D-a-w-g.) Following his final instructions, she scalps her still-warm dad to obtain the treasure map, which is, inexplicably, tattooed on his scalp. She learns that this scalp tattoo is only one-third of the treasure map and that her father's two brothers (Dawg included) have the other two-thirds. She convinces her father's crew that she ought to take over as captain and lead them to the treasure stashed on the eponymous Cutthroat Island. Reluctantly, they agree to give her a chance at being captain of the *Morning Star*.

The map is, unfortunately, in Latin, and so the pirates must obtain a Latin reader to begin to parse the map. One is found at a slave market, the doctor/scholar/fencer/petty thief/slave Will Shaw, played by Matthew Modine. Morgan wins him at auction in a pretty unconventional way: by stabbing her fellow bidder in the leg and threatening to stab him somewhere more private if he doesn't give up. As with watching Anne Providence's cold-blooded revenge plot, it is pleasurable to watch a woman take what she wants on her own terms, propriety be damned, even if her actions aren't exactly commendable.

Despite being a liar, Will does in fact read Latin, so the crew sails on to get part two of three from the nonvillainous brother Mordechai. However, Dawg has beaten them to it, and there's a violent tavern brawl in which Morgan gets to show off some amazing fighting skills, and gets shot by her Uncle Dawg, while Will somehow obtains Mordechai's piece of the map and hides this fact from Morgan. Back onboard the *Morning Star*, Will, in his role as "doctor," removes the musket ball from Morgan's hip and puts the moves on her. For some reason, they kiss, but he ends up in the brig for some offense that's not important to the plot.

Things start to get really convoluted at this point. Morgan's crew mutinies, the *Morning Star* gets caught in a huge storm, and Dawg is still chasing them but somehow Morgan and the loyal part of her crew end up washed up on Cutthroat Island—lucky, no? They trek into the jungle to locate the treasure, still without a complete map. Dawg also arrives on Cutthroat Island but is robbed of his piece by Will, who is not part of Morgan's entourage at this point. Morgan stumbles upon Will, who is neck deep in quicksand but in possession of the map. She rescues him, they make up for whatever they were fighting about, and they set off for the treasure. Morgan and Will find the incredibly fake-looking treasure only to have it immediately stolen by Dawg, who forces them to jump off a cliff into the raging sea below.

Will is captured by Dawg *and* the English navy, which made a brief appearance in the beginning of the film but has been totally forgotten by now. They have teamed up to bring Morgan down. Morgan, however, has no intention of being kidnapped and has swum back to the *Morning Star* and recaptured it from the treacherous mutineers. They attack Dawg's ship, where Will is now a prisoner. The obligatory sea battle is actually really impressive; it's not hard to see where the film's budget was spent. There are some sufficiently heart-pounding moments, and not all of them are ruined by the wooden dialogue. Morgan and Dawg square off in a climactic final battle that spans the entirety of the ship. Watch this section on mute for best results. Morgan manages to best Dawg, sink his ship, and even cleverly steal the treasure back from him. In the final moments before Dawg's ship sinks, she ties a barrel to the treasure haul so that, even when the ship goes down, she will have a marker to follow to the sunken treasure's location. In the end, the *Morning Star*'s crew rejoices over their victory and sets sail for Madagascar, while Morgan and Will kiss.

Few movies have earned such a reputation for being a failure, and few authors who desired to be taken seriously would attempt to mount a defense of *Cutthroat Island* (although notably Roger Ebert gave it a mostly positive review, calling it "satisfactory"). The leads lack any shred of chemistry, the plot is well worn, at best, and the script is laughably bad. *Cutthroat Island* spelled ruin for all parties involved. Geena Davis lost her reputation as a bankable lead, Matthew Modine's career failed to take off as it might have, and director Renny Harlin has had only modest success since the movie. Carolco, the production company on the film that had previously produced such hits as *Terminator 2* and *Total Recall*, went bankrupt, partially as a result of this movie. *Cutthroat Island* cost a reported $115 million to make and earned $10 million at the box office. By most measurable markers, this film was a mess.

Yet *Cutthroat Island*, behind the awful jokes and the strange plot, offers something sorely missing in the Hollywood pantheon: a female action hero. Geena Davis reportedly did her own stunts for this film, and there are a lot of them. She fights with swords, swings from chandeliers, jumps through windows, rides horseback, and jumps off cliffs, just to name a few. After watching countless men perform these stunts in countless action films, there is something viscerally positive about watching a long-haired, undisguised woman do the same. Morgan conceals a large collection of weaponry in her garters. She flirts with men to disarm them before she attacks them. She is, in short, a woman who uses every tool in her considerable arsenal. Unlike Anne Providence's repressed and hated femininity, Morgan's femininity is just one more asset she uses to win. She is not a particularly well-drawn character or even a good one, but in her there are undeniable sparks of something greater.

Only four years before Geena Davis starred in the biggest woman pirate box office bust ever, she starred in a colossal hit that is also one of the most feminist movies of all time to be produced by a major studio: *Thelma & Louise* (1991). This film centers around not one but two women, best friends who take off on an impromptu road trip after shooting an attempted rapist. Their exploits as they cross the country become wilder and wilder as they shake off the confines of their small-town lives. Eventually, the women decide to kill themselves rather than turn themselves in, and they drive off a cliff in a blaze of glory. Written by a woman, Callie Khouri, this film communicates truths about what it means to be a woman that resonated with its audience at its premiere and still do today. This movie unapologetically validates women's experiences of being persecuted and endlessly pursued by men and throws the traditional male buddy road trip movie model on its head. The film was nominated for five Academy Awards and won one. However, the feel-good feminist vibe of this film did not herald a sea change in movies about women any more than *Anne of the Indies* did. In 2011 author Raina Lipsitz called it "the last great film about women" and claimed it could never get made today, citing the fact that she could name only three movies in 2010 and 2011 that passed the Bechdel-Wallace test (the criteria being that the work must depict at least two women having a conversation that is not about a man) and that none had the substance of *Thelma & Louise*. Davis, a champion of strong portrayals of woman in film, almost certainly would have gone on to make more movies headlined by strong women had her career not been torpedoed by *Cutthroat Island*. In 2007 she did go on to found the Geena Davis Institute for Gender in Media, which examines issues such as the ones explored in this chapter.

⚓⚓⚓

Cutthroat Island's resounding defeat would render pirates a box office taboo for the next eight years. Many studios assumed that pirate films had worn out their welcome in the cinemas. In 2003, however, a silver-tongued, crack shot, rum-soaked pirate named Captain Jack Sparrow swaggered onto the silver screen and reignited the public's love of pirate movies. He brought with him the last (to date) major female pirate, Elizabeth Swann. Disney's *Pirates of the Caribbean* franchise (consisting so far of 2003's *The Curse of the Black Pearl*, 2006's *Dead Man's Chest*, 2007's *At World's End*, and 2011's *On Stranger Tides*, the last of which did not feature Elizabeth Swann) has been a colossal success, in no small part due to the complicated gender roles occupied by its leads. The series has quietly but surely uprooted the traditional attributes of male pirates and female captives and presented audiences with something entirely new.

The plot of the *Pirates* series contains more twists and turns than the amusement park ride from which it derives its inspiration, so only the portions of the plot that feature Elizabeth, particularly Elizabeth as a pirate, need be discussed here. In *The Curse of the Black Pearl*, Elizabeth begins the film not yet a pirate but instead the damsel in distress. A wealthy governor's daughter, she is kidnapped by pirates as part of a plan to recover some stolen (and cursed) Aztec gold. Near the end of the movie, Elizabeth and the film's (male) hero kiss as the sun sets behind them. Yet even among these stereotypical feminine trappings, there are clues to the fierce pirate she will become. The first scene of the movie shows her at the bow of a ship, singing a pirate chantey. When she is kidnapped, she demands a parley with the ship's captain instead of simply allowing herself to be taken. She is well versed in pirate terminology and lore and is able to defend herself as a result. The film also contains a scene of Jack forcibly cutting her out of a corset to save her after she almost drowns. She is literally so constricted by her traditional femininity that she faints, falls into the water, and nearly dies, only to be rescued by a pirate who isn't afraid to liberate her from her whalebone prison. When her true love, Will, is captured, she offers herself up as a prize to the man who will go and save him. In the end, she uses a fake fainting spell as part of a plan to save her friend Jack from the noose. Like Morgan from *Cutthroat Island*, Elizabeth is not afraid to use her feminine charms to outwit and overpower men.

Elizabeth is still a respectable woman at the beginning of *Dead Man's Chest*; indeed the movie opens at her wedding to blacksmith Will Turner. However, her entry into holy matrimony is thwarted when Lord Beckett arrests the bride and groom for aiding and abetting the escape of one Captain Jack Sparrow. Will is given a chance to pursue Jack in order to persuade him to barter his compass in exchange for their lives while Elizabeth must remain in prison, deprived of her wedding night.

Elizabeth escapes the prison (thus marking her official status as an outlaw) and stows away aboard a ship, convincing the crew to take her to Tortuga to find Captain Sparrow. Once Elizabeth is reunited with Jack, sparks fly between the pair as they search for Will (and Davy Jones, but that's another story). Elizabeth flirts with Jack to obtain information from him and to coerce him into doing the things she wants. In the end, she kisses him as a distraction while she chains him to the mast as a sacrifice to the kraken, the sea monster that's been plaguing their journey.

What is to be made of Elizabeth's behavior in *Dead Man's Chest*? As Jack notes, Will was sent to obtain Jack's compass, but Elizabeth is the one with all the bargaining chips. Her goal is to save her fiancé, but she is not above a little cheating to do it. She ruthlessly leaves Jack to die, but she saves the lives of the rest of the crew in doing so. This woman is miles away from the prim, virginal governor's daughter from *The Curse of the Black Pearl*. She is not in command of a ship, but she spends nearly the entire film at sea as part of a crew, she holds her own in battle, and she uses her cool head to calculate optimal outcomes in times of great stress. She is well on her way to becoming a fearsome pirate.

At World's End finds Elizabeth a full-fledged outlaw, dressed in men's clothing, infiltrating the enemy's lair, and wielding a comically large arsenal of weapons on her slight person. Kissing Jack was the kiss of death to her old life; she can never go back to respectability again. She is on a mission to rescue Jack from Davy Jones's locker and unite the pirates against the encroaching East India Trading Company, which in real life probably contributed to piracy's growth more than it thwarted it. Once Jack is rescued, she trades herself for the safety of the *Black Pearl*'s crew by agreeing to become a captive on pirate Sao Feng's ship, the *Empress*. Just before Sao Feng's death, he names Elizabeth the new captain of the *Empress*. Here, for the first time in a major motion picture since the comically bad *Cutthroat Island*, a female pirate captain appears on screen.

Her captaincy grants her a spot on the pirate Brethren Court (very loosely modeled on Captain Morgan's Brethren of the Coast), where the eight pirate lords are gathered to discuss how to deal with the threat of the East India Trading Company. Jack wants the pirates to sequester themselves in the hidden fortress of Shipwreck Cove, while Elizabeth thinks they ought to join together and fight. A new pirate king must be elected before the decision can be made. Every pirate votes for him- or herself, causing a deadlocked vote, until Jack votes for Elizabeth and she becomes king. As king, she declares war on the East India Trading Company and rallies the pirate captains to ready their fleets.

The pirate lords and their ships gather for what might be their final battle. Cutler Beckett and the EITC have Davy Jones's supernatural power on their side, as well as the superiorly trained fighting force. Before they rush into the fray, Elizabeth offers a rousing, passionate speech. She knows that they face almost certain death, but insists that they must fight with all their power against the enemy. "They will see what we can do . . . by the sweat of our brows and the strength of our backs and the courage of our hearts!" She defiantly raises the pirate flag, and the other ships, cheered by her fortitude, do the same. It is a triumphant moment, a climax (in a film admittedly full of climaxes), and a glorious motivational speech that so often is given by male heroes but here is entirely, wholly, Elizabeth's moment.

The battle rages on. Will, sensing the end is near, asks Elizabeth to marry him midbattle. Barbossa, a fellow pirate, performs the ceremony on deck (pausing occasionally for cannon fire and swordplay by all involved in the rite), and the couple—bloody, filthy, and so different from who they were when they got engaged—fill the screen as the music swells for a kiss. The pirates win the war, defeating the EITC, and Will and Elizabeth eventually sail off into the sunset.

Many quibble with the ending of *At World's End*, claiming that in spite of all she's been through, Elizabeth is now confined to land as a housewife, the very fate she was trying to escape at the start of the film. After becoming the pirate king, she still chooses domesticity and a family over her career. But at least with this marriage, it was Elizabeth's *choice*. She chose Will—not just once when they were young and infatuated, but again as the double-crossing, unfaithful, amoral pirates they had become. Their marriage is a marriage of equals. Even if one does not accept this theory, the entire arc of Elizabeth's character cannot be discounted. In a series rich with twists and turns, Elizabeth is offered the same chance at heroism, redemption, and morally complex choices as her male counterparts. She is not watching the battle safely from shore—she's the one calling the shots. Elizabeth is more nuanced, more well spoken, and ultimately more powerful than Anne and Morgan combined, and one can only hope that the success of these films will demonstrate to filmmakers that sophisticated women pirates not only *can* engage audiences, they absolutely *do.*

⚓⚓⚓

Modern Hollywood has come a long way from its beginnings, but the trend of shying away from movies centered on a woman is pervasive. Movies made from the 1980s to the present day still generally avoid focusing on complex female protagonists. There are occasional Oscar-bait biopics featuring physical transformations of attractive female stars (Charlize Theron's portrayal of serial killer Aileen Wuornos in 2003's *Monster* or Nicole Kidman's nasally enhanced turn as Virginia Woolf in 2002's *The Hours*), and some sci-fi badass heroines such as Sigourney Weaver as Ellen Ripley in the *Alien* franchise and Daisy Ridley's Rey in *The Force Awakens*, but everyday women going through everyday life is still not seen as a worthy cinematic enterprise. The quest for female equality in movies, as well as in everyday life, seems to have frustratingly stalled as time goes by, never able to capitalize on any momentum it gets. Meryl Streep's 1990 speech to the Screen Actors Guild shares many similarities with Cate Blanchett's 2014 Best Actress acceptance speech: both actors pointed out that women's films are not niche, women deserve equal pay for equal work, and women's films can and do make money. Despite the many voices shouting these truths over the years, Hollywood has been slow to listen. Why that is might be due to who is at the top of Hollywood.

In a 2013 study, the New York Film Academy examined the top five hundred highest-grossing films from 2007 to 2012. In these films,

30.8 percent of all speaking roles were given to women. Only 10.7 percent of these films had a balanced (half-male, half-female) cast. Roughly one-third of women with speaking roles appeared either in sexually provocative clothes or naked. Despite the fact that women buy movie tickets at equal rates as men, women are clearly not represented in the movies in equal numbers.

Besides not being represented on film in equal numbers, women are still consistently not being paid in equal amounts to their male counterparts. *Forbes* puts out a yearly highest-paid actor and actress list and keeps the two genders separate. It's easy to see why when the lists aren't combined: according to the 2014 rankings, only two women would crack the male top ten. The lowest-paid ranked man, Chris Pratt, would earn a spot in the female top ten. The top female earner, Jennifer Lawrence, made $28 million less than the top male earner, Robert Downey Jr. According to the Institute for Women's Policy Research, in everyday American jobs in 2015, women earned eighty cents to a man's dollar, and the amount is even less for women of color. It appears that Hollywood underpays women as well.

And that's just on-screen. Behind the camera, women writers, directors, and producers are even more scarce. The same New York Film Academy study reported that the ratio of men to women working on a film is five to one. Just two of the five hundred top-grossing films were directed by a woman. The Directors Guild of America Women's Steering Committee found that from 1949 to 1979, 0.19 percent of major motion pictures were directed by a woman. In eighty-five years, only one woman has ever won a Best Director Academy Award: Kathryn Bigelow for 2008's male-dominated *The Hurt Locker*. Academy voters are 77 percent male. Only one film directed by a woman, 2013's *Frozen*, has ever grossed $1 billion. Women of color are even less represented than white women. Although many Hollywood executives claim that the best films, regardless of gender of the director or screenwriter, get financing, it strains credulity to believe that in the ratio of best-directed films, male to female is, at the time of this writing, eighty-eight to one.

Confronted with these stark numbers, it is not hard to see why Hollywood has not churned out a number of pirate women block-busters. It is hard for women to tell stories in Hollywood, and it is hard to get movies made about strange, wild, ungovernable women. Pirate women hardly fit any mold or exist in any easily classifiable role. They are violent, they are sexually liberated, they are women of color, they are queer women, they don't follow the rules, they don't apologize, and they do not often get happy endings. They are Thelmas and Louises, Ericas and Bonnies, and there is simply not a lot of room for them in the current cinematic landscape.

This helps to prove why the world *needs* female pirate stories. As has been demonstrated throughout this book, what gets said about a person is controlled by the person telling the story. When men talk about women, women are not portrayed as fully as they could be. This goes double, of course, for women of color and other minority groups. It is vital for the advancement of tolerance and equality that stories—deceptively simple but a powerful part of what people learn and take to be true—are told *by* the people who they are *about*. For this to happen, women and other groups that have long been silenced must be allowed to tell their stories their own way. This will not be an easy feat; inspiration, as well as support, will be needed. Who better to inspire these pioneers than women pirates? After all, women storytellers will be, in essence, stealing something from someone who doesn't want them to have it, which is essentially piracy.

These pirate legends have endured for so long, on- and offscreen, because people want to hear them. The outlaw's irresistible appeal is a testament to the hunger for freedom and the desire to get away with things that one ought not get away with. Pirate women deserve a spot next to their more famous male counterparts because yearning to escape the confines of an ordinary life and to live on one's own terms is not an exclusively male feeling. Indeed, women may have *more* reason to reach outside of their traditional roles than men do. Women deserve, when they get this feeling, to know that they are not alone, and that they have famous foremothers whom they can look up to and whose footsteps they can follow in. The pirates in this book can inspire any woman who has ever wanted something more and dreamed of finding her own place in the sun. Hopefully their stories will inspire the next generation of explorers, scientists, inventors, politicians, peacemakers, and other innovators and guide them on their journey from "what has always been" into the land of "what can be."

Acknowledgments

A PIRATE CAPTAIN CANNOT SAIL her ship without her crew; I too would be rudderless without the support of many wonderful people. I am deeply in debt to far too many people to thank everyone by name—if you feel you ought to be on this list, you definitely are! Thank you from the bottom of my heart.

Thank you to my excellent agent, John Rudolph, who first had the idea that lady pirates deserved a book all their own. You have expertly guided me through the writing process every step of the way, and I will be forever grateful. Thank you to Jerome Pohlen, Ellen Hornor, and all of the lovely people at Chicago Review Press. It was a pleasure making this story into a book with you. I also owe a big thank-you to the whip-smart Jia Tolentino, who first gave my lady pirates a home at *Jezebel*.

A book like this required a staggering amount of research, and I could not have done it without the expert advice and counsel of a few brilliant people. Thank you to Dian Murray, who gave invaluable critique on Cheng I Sao. Carolyn McTaggart explained to me how Gunpowder Gertie came to life. Cindy Vallar helped me visualize what this book could be very early on and was a deep font of wisdom for all sorts of persnickety research questions throughout my writing. Thank you! Madeleine Smith, Caterin Obando, and my mom babysat my son so I could do all that research in the library, so heartfelt thanks to all of you. I also must thank all the wonderful librarians at Georgetown

University and the Library of Congress (and heck, librarians everywhere) for all their help.

Thanks to all my friends who have held my hand, been my cheerleader, and sent me baked goods through the mail to lead me through (in alphabetical order): Alicia Carpenter, Laura Dupuy, Cara Narkun, Trystan Popish, Dauren Velez, and especially my longtime reader Bob Sorokanich. Eric Ray deserves extraspecial thanks for providing endless statistics and commentary, proofreading/fact-checking, and talking me off the ledge more than once. Eric, I wish I knew as much about the sea as you do, but I am at least smart enough to have you as a friend. All of you are heroes, and I could not have made it without you!

I have to thank my incredible family, without whom I would never have been brave enough to try to be a writer in the first place. Thank you, Mom and Dad, thank you, Victoria, and thank you, PJ. You guys are the absolute best. I am so lucky to have such an awesomely loving and supportive family.

The biggest of thank-yous goes to my wonderful husband, Tom, who, when I told him I was not going to be a practicing lawyer but was going to write a book about pirates instead, never told me I was insane and instead became my staunchest ally. You suffered many dinnerless nights, listened to long diatribes about subjects that you had no interest in, and performed endless hours of solo child care so I could do this thing. A thousand thank-yous, my darling. Without you, this would not have been possible.

My final thank-you is for my son, Theodore, who was created roughly the same time as the first draft of this book. You are a wonder, my little prince, and you inspire me to make the world a more compassionate, inclusive, and beautiful place so that you can grow up in it. I love you so very much.

To Find Out More

General Resources

Cordingly, David. *Under the Black Flag: The Romance and Reality of Life Among the Pirates.* New York: Random House, 2006.

Defoe, Daniel. *A General History of the Pyrates.* Mineola, NY: Dover Maritime, 1999. (Previously published as Johnson, Captain Charles. *A General History of the Robberies and Murders of the Most Notorious Pyrates.* London: C. Rivington, 1724. There are numerous editions of this book.)

Druett, Joan. *She Captains: Heroines and Hellions of the Sea.* New York: Simon and Schuster, 2001.

Gosse, Phillip. *The History of Piracy.* Mineola, NY: Dover, 2007.

Klausmann, Ulrike, et al. *Women Pirates and the Politics of the Jolly Roger.* Translated by Nicholas Levis. Montreal: Black Rose Books, 1997.

Stanley, Jo, ed. *Bold in Her Breeches: Women Pirates Across the Ages.* Kitchener, ON: Pandora, 1996.

1. Dawn of the Pirates

Appian. *Roman History.* Translated by Horace White. Vol. 2, Book 10, §7. Cambridge, MA: Harvard University Press, 1912.

Blundell, Sue. *Women in Ancient Greece.* Cambridge, MA: Harvard University Press, 1995.

Herodotus. *Histories.* Translated by George Rawlinson. Book 8. New York: Everyman's Library, 1997.

Omerod, Henry A. *Piracy in the Ancient World.* Liverpool, UK: C. Tinling, 1924.

Polyaenus. *Stratagems of War.* Translated by Richard Shepherd. 2nd ed. Book 8, chapter 53. London: Gale ECCO, 2010.

Polybius. *Histories*. Translated by W. R. Paton. Rev. ed. Vol. 1, Book 2, §4. Cambridge, MA: Harvard University Press, 2010.

Semple, Ellen Churchill. "Pirate Coasts of the Mediterranean Sea." *Geographical Review* 2, no. 2 (August 1916): 134–51.

2. Gatekeepers of Valhalla

Grammaticus, Saxo. *Gesta Danorum*. Translated by Oliver Elton. New York: Norroena Society, 1905.

Ingram, Rev. James, trans. *The Anglo-Saxon Chronicle*. New York: Everyman Press, 1912.

Jesch, Judith. *Women in the Viking Age*. Rochester, NY: University of Rochester Press, 1991.

Jochens, Jenny. *Women in Old Norse Society*. Reprint ed. Ithaca, NY: Cornell University Press, 1998.

Moen, Marianne. *The Gendered Landscape: A Discussion on Gender, Status, and Power in the Norwegian Viking Age Landscape*. Oxford: Archaeopress, 2011.

Symeon of Durham. "Historia Regum" in *Symeonis monachi opera omnia*, 3-283. Edited by Thomas Arnold. Vol. 2. Cambridge: Cambridge University Press, 2012.

3. Medieval Maiden Warriors

Bentley, Richard. *A Brief Note upon the Battles of Saintes and Mauron 1351 and 1352*. New York: Guildford, 1918.

Butler, Pierce. *Women of Medieval France*. Philadelphia: Rittenhouse, 1908.

Froissart, Jean. *Chronicles*. Translated by Geoffrey Brereton. Reprint ed. New York: Penguin Classics, 1978.

Sewell, Elizabeth Missing. *Popular History of France: From the Earliest Period to the Death of Louis XIV*. London: Longmans, Green, 1876.

Taylor, Craig. "The Salic Law, French Queenship, and the Defense of Women in the Late Middle Ages." *French Historical Studies* 29, no. 4 (2006): 543–64.

4. A Cinderella Story Among the Corsairs

Abulafia, David. *The Great Sea: The Human History of the Mediterranean*. Oxford: Oxford University Press, 2011.

Freely, John. *Inside the Seraglio: Private Lives of the Sultans in Istanbul*. New York: Viking, 1999.

Grant, R. G., ed. *1001 Battles That Changed the Course of World History*. New York: Universe, 2011.

Konstam, Angus. *Piracy: The Complete History*. Oxford: General Military, 2008.

Mernissi, Fatima. *Forgotten Queens of Islam*. Minneapolis: University of Minnesota Press, 1993.

Peirce, Leslie. *The Imperial Harem: Women and Sovereignty in the Ottoman Empire*. Oxford: Oxford University Press, 1993.

Sancar, Asli. *Ottoman Women: Myth and Reality*. Clifton, NJ: Tughra Books, 2007.

Wilson, Peter Lamborn. *Pirate Utopias: Moorish Corsairs and European Renegadoes*. 2nd ed. Brooklyn: Autonomedia, 2003.

5. The Virgin Queen and Her Pirates

Chambers, Anne. *Granuaile: Grace O'Malley, Ireland's Pirate Queen*. Rev. ed. Dublin: Gill & MacMillan, 2009.

Fuller, J. F. C. *A Military History of the Western World: From the Defeat of the Spanish Armada to the Battle of Waterloo*. Boston: Da Capo, 1987.

Neale, J. E. *Queen Elizabeth I*. 2nd ed. London: J. Cape, 1934.

Ronald, Susan. *The Pirate Queen: Queen Elizabeth I, Her Pirate Adventurers, and the Dawn of an Empire*. American ed. New York: Harper, 2007.

Sjoholm, Barbara. *The Pirate Queen: In Search of Grace O'Malley and Other Legendary Women of the Sea*. Berkeley: Seal Press, 2004.

Tincey, John. *The Armada Campaign 1588*. Rev. ed. Oxford: Osprey, 1988.

6. The Golden Age

Breverton, Terry. *Admiral Sir Henry Morgan, King of the Buccaneers*. Gretna, LA: Pelican, 2005.

Exquemelin, Alexander. *The Buccaneers of America*. New York: Dover, 2000.

Kemp, Peter K., and Christopher Lloyd. *Brethren of the Coast: Buccaneers of the South Seas*. New York: St. Martin's, 1960.

Latimer, Jon. *Buccaneers of the Caribbean: How Piracy Forged an Empire*. Cambridge, MA: Harvard University Press, 2009.

Little, Benerson. *The Buccaneer's Realm: Pirate Life on the Spanish Main, 1674–1688*. Washington, DC: Potomac Books, 2007.

Rediker, Marcus. "Under the Banner of King Death: The Social World of Anglo-American Pirates, 1716 to 1726." *William and Mary Quarterly* 38 (1981): 203–27.

Sherry, Frank. *Raiders and Rebels: The Golden Age of Piracy*. Reprint ed. New York: Harper Perennial, 2008.

Snyder, Amanda J. "Pirates, Exiles, and Empire: English Seamen, Atlantic Expansion, and Jamaican Settlement, 1558–1658." PhD diss., Florida International University, 2013. ProQuest (UMI 3567348).

Sullivan, Timothy L. "The Devil's Brethren: Origins and Nature of Pirate Counterculture, 1600–1730." PhD diss., University of Texas at Arlington, 2003. ProQuest (UMI 3092489).

Talty, Stephan. *Empire of Blue Water: Captain Morgan's Great Pirate Army, the Epic Battle for the Americas, and the Catastrophe That Ended the Outlaws' Bloody Reign.* New York: Three Rivers, 2008.

7. His Majesty's Royal Pirates

Cordingly, David. *Seafaring Women: Adventures of Pirate Queens, Female Stowaways, and Sailors' Wives.* Reprint ed. New York: Random House, 2001.

Herman, Arthur. *To Rule the Waves: How the British Navy Shaped the Modern World.* New York: Harper Perennial, 2005.

Pepys, Samuel. *Memoires of the Royal Navy, 1679–1688.* Melbourne: Leopold Classic Library, 2015.

Rediker, Marcus. "When Women Pirates Sailed the Seas." *Wilson Quarterly* 17, no. 4 (1993): 102.

Simpson, Alfred W. B. "Cannibals at Common Law." *University of Chicago Law School Record* 27, no. 5 (Fall 1981): 3–10.

Swinburne, Henry Lawrence. *The Royal Navy.* Whitefish, MT: Kessinger, 2010.

Turley, Hans. *Rum, Sodomy, and the Lash: Piracy, Sexuality, and Masculine Identity.* New York: New York University Press, 1999.

8. "If He Had Fought Like a Man, He Need Not Have Been Hang'd Like a Dog"

Lives and Daring Deeds of the Most Celebrated Pirates and Buccaneers of All Countries. Philadelphia: George G. Evans, 1800.

Konstam, Angus, and David Rickman. *Pirate: The Golden Age.* Oxford: Osprey, 2011.

Kuhn, Gabriel. *Life Under the Jolly Roger: Reflections on Golden Age Piracy.* Oakland, CA: PM Press, 2010.

Pennell, C. R., ed. *Bandits at Sea: A Pirates Reader.* New York: New York University Press, 2001.

Pyle, Howard. *Book of Pyrates.* New York: Harper, 1949.

Rediker, Marcus. *Villains of All Nations: Atlantic Pirates in the Golden Age.* Boston: Beacon, 2005.

Sullivan, Timothy L. "The Devil's Brethren: Origins and Nature of Pirate Counterculture, 1600–1730." PhD diss., University of Texas at Arlington, 2003. ProQuest (UMI 3092489).

Woodard, Colin. *Republic of Pirates: Being the True and Surprising Story of the Caribbean Pirates and the Man Who Brought Them Down.* New York: Mariner Books, 2008.

9. Pirates of the New World

Appleby, John. *Women and English Piracy, 1540–1720: Partners and Victims of Crime.* Reprint ed. Woodbridge, UK: Boydell, 2015.

Ballagh, J. C. *White Servitude in the Colony of Virginia: A Study of the System of Indentured Labor in the American Colonies.* Baltimore: Johns Hopkins Press, 1895.

Ellms, Charles. *The Pirates Own Book.* Carlisle, MA: Applewood Books, 2008.

Jameson, W. C. *Buried Treasures of the Atlantic Coast.* Atlanta: August House, 2006.

Konstam, Angus. *Blackbeard: America's Most Notorious Pirate.* Hoboken, NJ: Wiley, 2007.

Mays, Dorothy A. *Women in Early America: Struggle, Survival, and Freedom in a New World.* Santa Barbara: ABC-CLIO, 2004.

Patton, Robert H. *Patriot Pirates: The Privateer War for Freedom and Fortune in the American Revolution.* Reprint ed. New York: Vintage, 2009.

10. Women on the Edge

Byrne, J. C. *Twelve Years' Wanderings in the British Colonies, from 1835 to 1847.* Vol. 2. London: Richard Bentley, 1848.

Eagle, John A. *The Canadian Pacific Railway and the Development of Western Canada, 1896–1915.* Kingston, ON: McGill-Queen's University Press, 1989.

Greenwood, F. Murray. *Uncertain Justice: Canadian Women and Capital Punishment, 1754–1953.* Toronto: Dundurn, 2000.

Rees, Siân. *The Floating Brothel: The Extraordinary True Story of an Eighteenth-Century Ship and Its Cargo of Female Convicts.* New York: Hachette, 2002.

Smith, Barbara. *Hoaxes and Hexes: Daring Deceptions and Mysterious Curses.* Victoria, BC: Heritage House, 2011.

Therry, Roger. *Reminiscences of Thirty Years' Residence in New South Wales and Victoria.* London: Sampson and Low, 1863.

11. The Most Successful Pirate of All Time

Elliott, Mark C. *Emperor Qianlong: Son of Heaven, Man of the World.* London: Pearson, 2009.

Hanes, W. Travis, III, and Frank Sanello. *The Opium Wars: The Addiction of One Empire and the Corruption of Another.* Naperville, IL: Sourcebooks, 2004.

Merwin, Samuel. *Drugging a Nation: The Story of China and the Opium Curse.* Whitefish, MT: Kessinger, 2010.

Murray, Dian H. *Pirates of the South China Coast 1790–1810.* Stanford: Stanford University Press, 1987.

Rowe, William T. *China's Last Empire: The Great Qing.* Reprint ed. Cambridge, MA: Harvard University Press, 2010.

Van Dyke, Paul. *The Canton Trade: Life and Enterprise on the China Coast, 1700–1845.* Hong Kong: Hong Kong University Press, 2007.

12. Veterans of the American Wars

Asbury, Herbert. *Gangs of New York: An Informal History of the Underworld*. Reprint ed. New York: Vintage, 2008.

Bernstein, Iver. "July 13–16, 1863: The New York City Draft Riots." *Civil War Times* 42, no. 3 (August 2003), 34–35.

Daniels, Roger. *Coming to America: A History of Immigration and Ethnicity in American Life*. 2nd ed. New York: Harper Perennial, 2002.

Giesberg, Judith. *Army at Home: Women and the Civil War on the Northern Home Front*. Chapel Hill: University of North Carolina Press, 2009.

Greenberg, Amy. *Manifest Destiny and American Territorial Expansion: A Brief History with Documents*. New York: Bedford/St. Martin's, 2011.

Moran, William. *The Belles of New England: The Women of the Textile Mills of New England and the Families Whose Wealth They Wove*. Reprint ed. New York: St. Martin's Griffin, 2004.

Peavy, Linda, and Ursula Smith. *Pioneer Women: The Lives of Women on the Frontier*. Norman: University of Oklahoma Press, 1998.

Rutkowski, Alice. "Gender, Genre, Race, and Nation: The 1863 New York City Draft Riots." *Studies in the Literary Imagination* 40, no. 2 (Fall 2007): 111–32.

Yenne, Bill. *Indian Wars: The Campaign for the American West*. Yardley, PA: Westholme, 2008.

13. Evil Incarnate and the Dragon Lady

Chang, Jung. *Empress Dowager Cixi: The Concubine Who Launched Modern China*. Reprint ed. New York: Anchor, 2014.

———. *Wild Swans: Three Daughters of China*. Reprint ed. New York: Touchstone, 2003.

Chang, Pang-Mei. *Bound Feet and Western Dress: A Memoir*. Reprint ed. New York: Anchor, 1997.

Hui, Wang. *China's Twentieth Century: Revolution, Retreat, and the Road to Equality*. Brooklyn: Verso, 2016.

Keefe, Patrick Radden. *The Snakehead: An Epic Tale of the Chinatown Underworld and the American Dream*. New York: Anchor, 2010.

Lilius, Aleko. *I Sailed with Chinese Pirates*. Reprint ed. Hong Kong: Earnshaw Books, 2009.

Meisner, Maurice. *Mao Zedong: A Political and Intellectual Portrait*. Malden, MA: Polity, 2006.

Wasserstrom, Jeffrey N. *China in the 21st Century: What Everyone Needs to Know*. Oxford: Oxford University Press, 2010.

14. The Pirates of the Silver Screen

Cook, Bernie, ed. *Thelma & Louise Live!: The Cultural Afterlife of an American Film*. Austin: University of Texas Press, 2007.

Haskell, Molly. *From Reverence to Rape: The Treatment of Women in the Movies*. 2nd ed. Chicago: University of Chicago Press, 1987.

Kaplan, E. Ann. *Women & Film: Both Sides of the Camera*. Rev. ed. New York: Routledge, 1990.

Parrish, James Robert. *Fiasco: A History of Hollywood's Iconic Flops*. Hoboken, NJ: Wiley, 2007.

Petersen, Anne Helen. *Scandals of Classic Hollywood: Sex, Deviance, and Drama from the Golden Age of American Cinema*. New York: Plume, 2014.

Steinhoff, Heike. *Queer Buccaneers: (De)Constructing Boundaries in the Pirates of the Caribbean Film Series*. London: LIT Verlag, 2011.

Thornham, Sue. *Feminist Film Theory: A Reader*. New York: New York University Press, 1999.

Index